Coping with Work Stress

Coping with Work Stress

A Review and Critique

Philip J. Dewe, Michael P. O'Driscoll and
Cary L. Cooper

WILEY-BLACKWELL

A John Wiley & Sons, Ltd., Publication

Wiley-Blackwell is an imprint of John Wiley & Sons, formed by the merger of
Wiley's global Scientific, Technical, and Medical business with Blackwell Publishing.

Registered Office
John Wiley & Sons Ltd, The Atrium, Southern Gate, Chichester, West Sussex,
PO19 8SQ, UK

Editorial Offices
The Atrium, Southern Gate, Chichester, West Sussex, PO19 8SQ, UK
9600 Garsington Road, Oxford, OX4 2DQ, UK

350 Main Street, Malden, MA 02148-5020, USA

For details of our global editorial offices, for customer services, and for information
about how to apply for permission to reuse the copyright material in this book please
see our website at www.wiley.com/wiley-blackwell.

The right of Philip J. Dewe, Michael P. O'Driscoll and Cary L. Cooper to be
identified as the authors of this work has been asserted in accordance with the UK
Copyright, Designs and Patents Act 1988.

Library of Congress Cataloging-in-Publication Data

Dewe, Philip J.
    Coping with work stress : a review and critique / Philip J. Dewe,
Michael P. O'Driscoll, and Cary L. Cooper.
        p. cm.
    Includes bibliographical references and index.
    ISBN 978-0-470-99766-6 (cloth) – ISBN 978-0-470-99767-3 (pbk.)   1. Job stress.
2. Stress management.   I. O'Driscoll, Michael P.   II. Cooper, Cary L.   III. Title.
    HF5548.85.D49 2010
    158.7′2–dc22

                                                                    2010017951

A catalogue record for this book is available from the British Library.

Set in 10.5 on 13 pt Minion by Toppan Best-set Premedia Limited
Printed and Bound in Singapore by Ho Printing Singapore Pte Ltd.

01   2010

Contents

1

Work Stress and Coping: Setting the Scene

This book is about coping. More particularly, it is about coping with work stress. For over 50 years, researchers have been interested in coping. Over that time the 'dramatic proliferation' of research (Folkman & Moskowitz 2004), while, at times, producing debate and disappointment about progress, has maintained such a momentum that it is now probably one of the most extensively explored subjects in contemporary psychology (Somerfield & McCrae 2000). This sustained interest could be explained in terms of coping's relevance to people (Aldwin 2000) and to society more generally (Snyder 1999), or because understanding how people cope is in itself intrinsically appealing. However, it is more likely to reflect the fact that the better we understand coping, the better we understand stress and how to manage it. Its allure is not just as an important explanatory variable (Folkman & Moskowitz 2000) but because it is fundamental to our understanding of the stress process.

Coping, as Zeidner and Saklofske (1996) point out, is more than simple adjustment. Its meaning extends beyond issues of basic survival to express the very essence of individual growth and development, allowing us to thrive in an ever-changing world. It is at the very heart of the human change process (Snyder 1999) and inextricably linked to the quality of our lives. Nevertheless, despite the fundamental importance of coping, the 'boundless enthusiasm' for coping research (Somerfield & McCrae 2000) and the fact that coping as a topic has been explored by a substantial number of researchers from an array of fields (Snyder 1999), coping research is not without its controversies, disappointments and questioning

Coping with Work Stress: A Review and Critique, Philip J. Dewe, Michael P. O'Driscoll and Cary L. Cooper, © 2010 John Wiley & Sons Ltd.

of what progress has been made (Dewe & Cooper 2007) and where research may have fallen short of expectations (Burke 2002). However, even researchers who have been critical of coping research (such as Coyne 1997) have suggested ways to move forward. The aim of this book is to critically review the issues surrounding work stress and coping research, explore what may be needed to sustain coping research over the next decade and to identify possible strategic pathways that not only require a change from, and challenge, traditional conventions, procedures and methods but also capture the resourcefulness and creativity of those working in the field.

This chapter provides the context for the chapters that follow. It begins by briefly reviewing traditional approaches to defining stress and explores whether more contemporary definitions of stress provide the field with an 'organizing concept' for the future. Liddle describes an organizing concept as one with 'sufficient logic and emotional resonance to yield systematic theoretical and research enquiry that will make a lasting solution' (1994, p. 167). The chapter then outlines the costs to the individual, organizations and society of stress, looking particularly at stress-related absenteeism, turnover and presenteeism before exploring more general issues of mental health at work. The chapter ends with a review of the causes of work stress, extending the analysis to explore the changing nature of work. These changes and the challenges and tensions they create between the way we work, the way we want to work and the way we want to live our lives provide an opportunity to explore new and emerging causes of work stress and a context for better understanding coping. An understanding of coping processes will be of substantial benefit in the development of effective approaches for managing life's challenges, and helping people to enhance their lives generally (Snyder 1999).

The Term 'Stress'

Towards the end of the 1950s, stress was recognized as a legitimate topic for academic research (Newton 1995). Even then, doubts were being expressed as to whether the term, indeed the entire subject, was just another fad. At that time, the paucity of scientific evidence to validate it suggested it did not merit the amount of enthusiasm it was attracting (Haward 1960). The term 'stress' has of course survived and, as Jones and Bright (2001) suggest, taken such a hold on our society that it is likely to be with us for a long time yet. Concerns still linger, however, but more around stress as a label rather than stress 'the concept' and more around the inconsistencies and looseness with which the term has been used and the multitude of meanings the term has come to assume. So giving careful consideration to how stress is defined is important for a number of reasons, not the least of which concerns the obligations we have to those whose working lives we study. Failure to capture the essence of the stress experience will simply trivialize encounters that have an adverse impact on people's psychological well-being (Brief & George 1991).

Traditionally, stress has been defined as a stimulus, response or interaction between the two. These definitions now have a historical as well as an empirical value, as they embody a sense of time, of why certain ideas prevailed and provide an understanding of why different research approaches have been adopted, why particular research questions have been asked, the knowledge that has accumulated, the debates that have emerged around the findings and questions about the future directions the study of work stress may take. A considerable body of data has emerged when these definitions have been used to frame research. However, there still remains, when these definitions are reviewed, a sense that while structurally we now have a better understanding of the nature and characteristics of the different components in the stress process and how they interact, such definitions have not been helpful in facilitating an understanding of the stress process itself (Cooper, Dewe & O'Driscoll 2001; Dewe 2001). The significance of these traditional approaches to defining stress must now be evaluated, less in terms of the information and knowledge they have provided and more in terms of whether, considering our present state of knowledge, they have the power to take forward and support a theory of stress (Lazarus 1990).

In the future, as Kaplan (1996) suggests, if researchers pay greater attention to the processes accompanying stress and the sequence of events which culminate in stressful experiences, rather than only exploring simple relationships between stressors and strains, a better understanding of the mechanisms underlying stressful encounters will be achieved. This suggestion lies at the heart of the transactional framework (Lazarus 2000), which explores stress in relational terms, where the emphasis is on the nature of the relationship, those processes that link the individual to the environment and on describing the manner in which the transaction occurs (Aldwin 2000). So, the authority of the transactional approach lies in the fact that it draws attention to, and has at its heart, those processes that bind the person and the environment, or as Lazarus describes 'the *relational meaning* that an individual constructs from the person–environment relationship' (2000, p. 665). These 'relational meanings' are captured through the process of appraisal. Stress therefore arises from the appraisal that particular environmental demands are about to tax individual resources, thus threatening well-being (Holroyd & Lazarus 1982).

Lazarus (1990) identifies two types of appraisal. The first he describes as 'primary appraisal'. Primary appraisals are where the individual evaluates and gives personal meaning to events and considers the significance of 'what is at stake' in terms of harm, threat or challenge. The individual constructs these meanings from the events themselves (Lazarus 2001). In essence, it is the recognition that the events involve something of significance to the individual. It is, as Parker and De Cotiis (1983) suggest, a level of appreciation that in the experience of the individual there is some impact on normal functioning. However, primary appraisal is not by itself sufficient to decide the significance of an event. 'Secondary appraisal' further refines the meaning surrounding the event and addresses the question 'What can I do about it?'. It is where the individual evaluates the availability of coping resources to deal with the appraisal of harm, threat or challenge (Lazarus 2001).

Coping is central to this appraisal and is utilized to manage and deal with demanding events (Lazarus 1990). The distinction between primary and secondary appraisal is more one of content than of timing (Lazarus 1999), as each is part of a dynamic process where the two are engaged in a complex interchange. These two appraisal processes shape and give meaning to environmental events. Because they shift the focus to exploring and investigating what people actually think and do in a stressful encounter, they represent a process-oriented approach that captures 'the changing person–environment relationship' and offers a way of understanding the 'stress of the stress process' (Lazarus 1990, p. 4). Failing to explore the explanatory power of these appraisal processes and those relational meanings that bind the stress process together (Dewe 2001) ignores the importance of developing a theoretical framework which encapsulates critical dimensions of the stress process.

It is clear that *conceptually* stress should now be thought of in transactional terms, with the appraisal process providing a causal pathway between the individual and the environment that is absent from more traditional definitions of stress. Yet despite these advances in conceptualizing and defining stress and the 'rigor and intellectual precision' (Harris 1991, p. 28) that accompanies the transactional approach, we are still left with the troublesome *word* 'stress' and what it means. Much has been written on what has been described as the 'discourse of stress' (Newton 1995; Wainwright & Calnan 2002) and, while the word has become part of our everyday language, it is important to consider from time to time whether the way in which we currently represent stress actually reflects what it is that individuals are experiencing (Newton 1995). We approach this 'representation' issue in two ways: first by looking at the work on lay representations of stress and whether lay ideas about stress parallel in some way those in the academic literature and, secondly, by suggesting that stress is not simply an emotional reaction, but rather that emotion is at the heart of the stress experience (Lazarus & Cohen-Charash 2001). Emotions experienced in the work setting better reveal the dynamics of the individual's transaction with organizational life (Lazarus & Cohen-Charash 2001) and so it is emotions rather than stress that should become the common language of the researcher.

Lay theories refer to those common-sense ways that people describe concepts like stress (Furnham 1988). The importance of understanding these lay ideas lies in the 'profound impact' that such ideas can have on how individuals interpret what goes on at work, how they may react and the health consequences that may follow (Kinman & Jones 2005). It has been possible from this research to identify parallels between lay accounts of stress and those defined in the literature. However, the overriding sense from this work is that there is little in the way of a consensus about how work stress should be interpreted, with multiple definitions of the concept available (Kinman & Jones 2005). It would appear that the lack of consistency in lay representations of stress in many ways mirrors the lack of consistency among stress researchers themselves. Nevertheless, as Kinman and Jones concede, this makes it even more important to continue to explore lay meanings using a range of methods simply because the term is generally used without reference to the meanings it may have for individuals.

When it comes to thinking in terms of emotions, it is as if two research literatures have developed, 'one centred on stress the other on emotion which, given their interdependence, is illogical and counterproductive' (Lazarus & Cohen-Charash 2001, p. 52). Stress always implies emotion and should therefore be viewed as a key element of emotional states (Lazarus & Cohen-Charash 2001). Understanding discrete emotions will yield a better representation of people's efforts to adapt to their life circumstances than simply examining levels of reported stress. It is clear that the more we focus our research, the less reliant we have to be on the concept of stress

(Kasl 1983). Two points emerge from this: the need to continue to ask whether our representations of stress actually reflect what individuals are experiencing; and whether it is now time to represent stress through discrete emotions as these emotions provide valuable information on the outcomes of people's efforts to adapt to their environment.

These points are important not just because of the difficulties surrounding the word 'stress' but also because they require researchers to review whether the methodologies we use to research stress have become so divorced from the phenomena they are purporting to measure that we must now question the structured reality imposed by such approaches (Dewe 2000). Researchers need now to consider just what is being measured when we measure stress, whose reality is it, where are current methodologies taking us and what can alternative methodologies provide (Van Maanen 1979)? The challenge, as Newton (1995) suggests, is to move towards a language of stress that captures those issues that reflect and shape individual stressful experiences – themes that we will, without doubt, return to later in this book.

The Costs of Stress

When raising the question of 'why study stress', Bartlett (1998) argues not only that stress represents a fundamentally important element of health psychology but also that the concept itself brings together knowledge about overall human functioning. In this integrated knowledge stress, health, work and well-being have become inexplicably linked. The stress paradigm is now the most frequently used framework for understanding employee health and well-being (Tetrick 2002), and it is through this lens that attempts have been made to understand the 'costs of stress' to employees, employers and society. Government's policies too recognize as 'important in its own right' the quality of the work experience and the need to make work 'fulfilling' (Brown *et al.* 2006). The recent Black (2008) report entitled *Working for a healthier tomorrow* states that there is now a compelling case 'to act decisively in order to improve the health and well-being of the working age population [with] employers and employees recognising not only the importance of preventing ill-health but also the key role the workplace can play in promoting health and well-being' (p. 10).

Stress at work is widely recognized as a global challenge. Data from a number of national surveys capture the impact of work on health and well-being. One theme to emerge from the different surveys is the impact on health and well-being of working long hours. The Chartered Institute of Personnel and Development's 2003 *Living to work?* survey found that 25% of employees surveyed reported some sort of negative health impact from working long hours. Long hours were reported by 40% of the sample as having a negative impact on their domestic relationships, with most reporting that they had a negative effect on their job performance as well. Results from the Work Foundation's survey entitled *The joy of work?* (Isles 2005) identifies three main reasons why those sampled worked long hours. They were 'to speed up getting promoted' (60%), 'because they were scared of losing their job' (39%) and 'because of the volume of work' (25%).

This culture of long hours is reported to result in more stress at work, growing difficulties in combining work with family and social life and a sense that achieving some sort of work–life balance is increasingly improbable (Crompton & Lyonette 2007). Data from the 2004 *British Social Attitude* survey (Bell & Bryson 2005) express the impact of working long hours when 54% of those surveyed reported that they come home from work 'too tired' to do everything they need to do. These findings led the Equal Opportunities Commission (2007) to comment that 'the way we work no longer fits the changing world we live in; as we look to the future it looks increasingly unsustainable' (p. 13).

When it comes to work stress, the data are clear and worrying. Data from the Health and Safety Executive (2007a) indicate that 420,000 employees in Britain believed they were experiencing stress, depression or anxiety at levels that were making them ill. During 2006, stress, depression and anxiety accounted for 195,000 new cases. The prevalence rate of stress, depression and anxiety by then was around double the level of the 1990s. The *Psychosocial Working Conditions* (Health and Safety Executive 2005) surveys indicate that around 1 in 6 of all working individuals thought their job was very or extremely stressful. In addition, 63,000 employees (Health and Safety Executive 2006) reported work-related heart disease, ascribing their illness to work stress. From these data, the Health and Safety Executive (2007b) concluded that the most widespread workplace hazard is stress at work. Further data analysis by the Health and Safety Executive (2007a) identified a number of occupational groupings (teaching and research, protective services, health and social welfare, customer services, corporate managers, business and public services) where work-related illness was significantly higher than the overall rate. Economic analysis of future employment patterns by Oxford Economics suggests that 'we may expect to see a gradual rise in reports of stress, depression and anxiety over the coming years, as employment shifts towards professional and service occupations where the prevalence of stress, depression and anxiety is reportedly higher' (2007, p. 15).

Measuring stress by the extent to which employees worry about work outside of working hours, the *Workplace Employment Relations Survey* (WERS) 2004 data showed an increase over the period 1998 to 2004 of 2.5% or around 675,000 employees, with 27% of all employees in 2004 agreeing or strongly agreeing that they worried a lot about work outside of office hours (Brown *et al.* 2006). The WERS data also showed that over the period 1998 to 2004 the percentage of employees who agreed or strongly agreed that 'their job required them to work hard' and 'they never have enough time to get work done' remained high at 76% and 40% of those surveyed (Brown *et al.* 2006). These figures are, of course, of concern to government agencies. The impact of work-related stress can be felt in all corners of society. The extent of the problem can be judged by the fact that if the targets set by government to 'inspire action' to reduce the incidence and effects of work-related stress are met, then by 2010 the actions taken and the strategies put in place could save society between £8.6 and £21.8 billion (Health & Safety Commission 2000).

Sickness Absence

The stark reality of the costs of work stress become even clearer when the emphasis shifts to exploring issues like sickness absence, turnover and presenteeism (see Cooper & Dewe 2008). We begin by exploring these three issues and then conclude this section on the costs of work stress by exploring mental health at work more generally. We turn first to sickness absence. The principal data source for sickness absence is the annual survey of self-reported work-related illness (SWI) produced by the Health and Safety Executive (2007c). These data are comprehensive and suggest an increasing trend in SWI. The figures for 2006/07 show that for that year 29.96 million working days were lost because of work-related illness. A closer examination shows that work-related illnesses described in terms of stress, depression or anxiety accounted for 13.76 million days lost or 46% of all reported illnesses, making this the single largest cause of all absences attributable to work-related illness. Set against the previous year (10.54 million), the number of days lost in terms of work-related stress, depression or anxiety in 2006/07 grew by 3.22 million days, or 30.6%. Viewed over the last five years, work-related stress, depression or anxiety remains for each year the single most reported complaint (Cooper & Dewe 2008).

Employers have become increasingly concerned about levels of sickness absence among employees (Bevan 2003). Data reviewed by the Sainsbury Centre for Mental Health (2007a) suggest that different sources of information provide comparable data on sickness absence, and that the average rate of employee absence due to sickness is around seven days per year. The Sainsbury Centre for Mental Health's report suggests that the proportion of sickness absence that can be attributable directly to mental health problems is approximately 40%, or 2.8 days per year. Put another way, for the United Kingdom's working population this means around 175 million working days are lost each year because of sickness absence, with around 70 million days lost (40%) to mental health problems generally (see Sainsbury Centre for Mental Health 2007a; Cooper & Dewe 2008). If, as indicated earlier, the Health and Safety Executive's 2006/07 sickness absence figures suggest the days lost due to work-related causes (stress, depression or anxiety) are 13.7 million, then work-related causes represent around 20% of those 70 million days lost as a result of mental health problems.

What then is the cost if 13.7 million days are lost each year to work-related sickness absence? The different data sources on cost come, of course, with their own strengths and weaknesses, and although 'no single source can therefore be considered wholly reliable' (Sainsbury Centre for Mental Health 2007a, p. 8) each provides a basis for considering the cost of sickness absence. The Chartered Institute of Personnel and Development's report entitled *Absence management* calculates a figure of £659 per employee per year but adds the proviso that 'less than half [45%] of organizations [in their sample] actually monitor the cost of absence' (2007a, p.15). The CBI/AXA (Confederation of British Industry 2007) in their *Attending to absence* report identify a direct cost of £537 per employee per year for 2006, but in terms of indirect costs add that 'very few respondents were able to provide an estimate, but those who did report it added £270 per employee per year' (2007, p. 14).

Notwithstanding that these two reports indicate that absence costs showed noticeable variation across sectors, both reports agree that efforts to monitor and reduce the costs of absence will yield considerable benefits for employers (Confederation of British Industry 2007). The worry remains, however, that many organizations still do not have the systems in place to assess and monitor their absence problems (Bevan 2003). The costs calculated in the Chartered Institute of Personnel and Development and the CBI/AXA reports are based on all causes of sickness absence. Taking the figure of 40% as reflecting the proportion of sickness absence that can be attributable to mental health generally, this alone would represent an annual cost of £8.1 billion. As 20% of sickness absence can be attributable to work causes (stress, depression or anxiety), the cost to employees for work-related causes would be around £1.6 billion a year.

Labour Turnover

While the social, psychological and economic impact of labour turnover seems apparent to all commentators, a commonly-agreed model of reasons for leaving jobs has not been developed (Morrell, Loan-Clarke & Wilkinson 2001). Measuring the costs of labour turnover is therefore far from straightforward, with 'the great majority of UK employers not [well] informed about the overall costs of staff turnover' (Sainsbury Centre for Mental Health 2007a, p. 16). Perhaps a less contentious measurement is the calculation of the rate of turnover. The Chartered Institute of Personnel and Development (2007b) reports a median employee turnover rate of 18.1% for 2006. The CBI/AXA's (2007) survey reports for the same year an average turnover rate of 14.7%. There was considerable variation in turnover rates between different sectors, although with some consistency across the two surveys as to those sectors where high rates were reported. These figures describe a 'raw quit rate' because no allowance is made for the characteristics of the workforce or for the type of turnover. Neverthe-less, the way in which *all* turnover is managed remains an important organizational issue, particularly when set against the finding that 71% of the Chartered Institute of Personnel and Development respondents reported that the effects of employee departure on business performance range from minor to serious (Chartered Institute of Personnel and Development 2007b).

The Chartered Institute of Personnel and Development's (2007b) survey explored the costs associated with employee turnover. While 39% of those surveyed reported an increase in turnover and 52% said they would want to reduce turnover, only 10% reported actually calculating a range of costs associated with turnover, with 66% giving as a reason for not calculating the cost of labour turnover that the organization does not require such information. Other reasons for not calculating turnover costs included 'too time consuming', 'too complicated' and 'too costly' (Chartered Institute of Personnel and Development 2007b). For those who do calculate a broad range of costs associated with turnover, the Chartered Institute of Personnel and Development (2007b) places the estimated overall cost of turnover per employee at £7750. While this cost covered, for example, training and induction costs, the more difficult turnover cost to calculate is the time needed for a replacement employee to reach the productivity level of the previously employed employee (Cooper & Dewe 2008). In all probability, the Chartered Institute of Personnel and Development's figure represents a fairly conservative estimate of what the costs of turnover may be (see also the Sainsbury Centre for Mental Health 2007a).

Respondents in the Chartered Institute of Personnel and Development's (2007b) survey were also asked to list the key reasons for employee turnover. While respondents could give multiple responses, 14% cited 'stress of job/role' and 13% cited 'ill-health other than stress' as the key reasons for employee turnover, while potential stress-related problems such as 'level of working hours' and 'level of workload' were cited by 12% and 11% respectively as further reasons for turnover. The proportion of turnover attributable to stress is 'almost certainly lower' than the percentages quoted above, for no other reason, as the Sainsbury Centre for Mental Health (2007a) point outs, than there is a range of other more commonly mentioned causes of turnover. Refining its arguments still further, the Sainsbury Centre for Mental Health suggests a 'reasonable estimate might be that, at most mental health problems including stress account for five percent of total stress turnover' (2007a, p. 16). On this estimate, assuming a conservative turnover rate of 14% of which 5% is attributable to stress and mental health, the overall annual cost of employee turnover attributable to stress and mental health could be in the region of around £1.35 billion.

Presenteeism

Up until now, we have been exploring how work impacts on employee health and well-being. Presenteeism, on the other hand, is defined in terms of lost productivity that occurs when employees come to work ill and perform below par because of that illness. Hemp (2004) argues that presenteeism can be more costly for productivity than absenteeism, although its direct impact is not always immediately apparent. It is clear when an employee doesn't come into work, but it is plainly more complicated to tell when and in what way performance is hindered by employees coming to work ill. 'When people don't feel good,' Hemp adds, 'they simply don't do their best work' (p. 55). As the interest in the relationship between employee health and productivity has developed so too has the need to develop ways to assess the productivity losses due to ill health (Lofland, Pizzi & Frick 2004).

While researchers acknowledge there is still more development work to be done, they make clear that there is merit in 'describing what is known so far', not just to identify 'needs for future investigations' but also to determine 'when and where' to use such measures (Goetzel *et al.* 2004, p. 411), what guidance to provide employers as to how to choose an appropriate measure (Ozminkowski *et al.* 2004) and that evidence exists supporting the validity of the measures and that 'soundly based comparisons can be made' across a 'range of jobs' (Sainsbury Centre for Mental Health 2007a, p. 11). The common feature of these instruments is that they are designed to measure the scale and cost of presenteeism by assessing the notion of workplace productivity losses as affected by health or the effects of a particular health condition (Cooper & Dewe 2008). Depending on how these data are expressed, the findings that emerge point to the sheer scale of the problem. Most of the presenteeism research comes from the United States, Canada and Australia, with little published UK data to draw on.

As an example of the nature of the problem, the Chartered Management Institute's (2007) research on managers' health shows, for example, that while 30% of managers sampled reported experiencing stress at work only 9% with these symptoms took any time off. Similarly, for common illnesses like colds and headaches 55% and 46% reported experiencing such symptoms but only 17% and 3% reported taking time off. A range of health-related conditions that affect the ability to work and are costly to employers has been explored, of which depression is a major contributor (Stewart *et al.* 2003). A study by Medibank (2007), for example, reports that depression accounted for around one-fifth of the overall productivity loss through presenteeism, while Goetzel and his colleagues (2004) note that, among the 10 conditions they measured, depression-sadness-mental illness reported one of the largest presenteeism losses. Stewart concludes that 'a majority of the lost productive time costs that employers face from employee depression is invisible and explained by reduced performance while at work' (2003, p. 3135).

These data need to be treated cautiously, as measuring productivity is still quite difficult particularly when set against the sensitivities around the productivity requirements of different industries and the measurement strategies adopted by the different instruments. However, from the various studies there would appear to be general agreement that lost productive time from health-related presenteeism is costly for employers and may have a greater negative impact than absenteeism on employee performance (Sainsbury Centre for Mental Health 2007a). Reworking data from US research, the Sainsbury Centre for Mental Health (2007a) arrived at a figure for the UK that implies that presenteeism may be up to twice as important as absenteeism in cost-effectiveness terms. Whatever the ratio, two points are clear: (a) health-related presenteeism has, relative to absence, the larger effect and (b) mental ill-health may manifest itself more frequently in presenteeism than absenteeism (Sainsbury Centre for Mental Health 2007a).

Work and Mental Health Generally

For many the workplace can be a source of stress, depression and anxiety, and it is the relationship between work and stress that has captured the attention of many researchers. However, the scale of mental health problems at work cannot be understood or measured through work-related causes alone. Common mental health problems stem from an array of causes, many unrelated to work, and for the most part those with such problems are as likely to be working as anyone else is. Mental health problems 'are almost as common in the workplace as they are anywhere else' (Sainsbury Centre for Mental Health 2007a, p. 6) so clearly the impact of mental ill-health at work is far greater than generally acknowledged and extends beyond just work-related causes. From the Office of National Statistics (Singleton *et al.* 2001) the Sainsbury Centre for Mental Health pointed to data that showed that 22.3% of all people in paid employment have some kind of mental health problem (15.4% if alcohol and drug dependency are excluded). 'In other words,' the Sainsbury Centre concludes, 'employers should expect to find on average that nearly 1 in 6 of their workforce is affected by depression, anxiety or other mental health conditions ... or around 1 in 5 if alcohol and drug dependency are included' (2007a, p. 6).

The concern is that these levels of mental ill-health in the workplace are just not recognized by employers. Research tends to confirm this concern. Work by the Shaw Trust suggests that while respondents were able to identify stress and depression when asked 'What specific disorders do you think of when you hear the term "mental ill-health in the work-place"?', over a third couldn't give an answer to this question. Similarly, when asked 'What percentage of employees do you think will have a mental health problem at some point during their working life?', 6% of respondents didn't feel they could even hazard a guess, 45% said none and a further 26% indicated 5% or less, leaving, of the remaining respond-ents, only around 17% who were able 'to estimate the magnitude of the impact of mental health to any accurate degree' (Shaw Trust 2006a, p. 16). The Shaw Trust (2006b, p. 1) concludes that 'employers seriously underestimate the extent to which employees and fellow managers are experiencing stress, anxiety, depression and other forms of mental ill-health', along with the damaging impact that mental ill-health may be having on their business.

In terms of policy awareness and understanding the Shaw Trust's (2006b) research found that 80% of its sample of 550 senior managers did not, to their knowledge, have a formal policy on stress and mental health in the workplace and of those who did only 14% said it was effective and only 16% felt it was well understood. Few employers have had experience in dealing with or recruiting applicants with mental health problems (Char-tered Institute of Personnel and Development 2008; Shaw Trust 2006a). Perhaps because of this inexperience and because employers 'want to do the right thing' and recognize that they need more support to deal with mental health problems in the workplace (Shaw Trust 2006a), employers reveal a sense of discomfort and hesitancy when confronted with issues around mental illness and mental ill-health in the workplace. There is clearly a need for more education and a continuing need to raise awareness. The Shaw Trust (2006a) concludes that government and industry need to collaborate in the development of support and structures to address mental health problems at work.

Because, as Rolfe, Foreman and Tylee (2006) suggest, the relationship between stress and mental health is not well understood and because employers are, perhaps, somewhat concerned to draw a distinction between the two, stress is seen as more of a key issue and mental health less so. Perhaps employers are more comfortable with the term 'well-being'. Drawing on the themes that emerge from its 2007 surveys, the Chartered Institute of Personnel and Development in its *Barometer of HR trends and prospects* (2008) indicates that 44% of organizations had a well-being strategy or similar initiative and that 42% of respondents also planned to increase spending on well-being measures in 2008. Nevertheless, despite identifying a number of commonly provided well-being measures, 40% of respondents to the 2008 survey reported that their organization's communication strategy was poor and only 11% believed that employees fully appreciated what was spent on well-being benefits.

There is no doubt that workplaces can do much to enhance individual workers' health and well-being (Black 2008), and that good health is good business. After reviewing evidence on this issue, Waddell and Burton (2006) confirm that there is 'a strong evidence base showing that work is generally good for physical and mental health and well-being' (p. 38). The review by Rolfe, Foreman and Tylee (2006) makes it clear that, in terms of stress and mental health, the role of the manager is crucial in responding to and managing stressful events. In dealing with mental issues at work, the Sainsbury Centre for Mental Health (2007b) went a step further and made the point that changing how mental health is managed must now be the responsibility not just of managers but also of all health professionals. The Centre suggested that by working together, and sharing expertise and training, all concerned professionals would benefit in terms of better understanding the relationship between work and health.

The Changing Work Context and Work Stressors

Snyder (1999) argues that coping with the demands of work will influence the goals which workers set themselves. There is no doubt that over the last four decades there has been profound change across all aspects of society. There is now general agreement (see Dewe & Kompier 2008) that the landscape of work and society generally will be influenced by three prevailing forces. The first – internationalization and global competition – includes the growing importance of the economies of China and India, the continued accelerated flow of capital, a more mobile labour market, the reduction of trade barriers and an increase in the use of 'resource-based strategies' that emphasize the importance of competing through people. The second – technological innovation and the increased utilization of ICT – will see technological advances influencing the rate of knowledge transfer, how capital and labour markets are organized and where they are located, the growth of, and demand for, 'knowledge intensive' skills leading to a higher skilled workforce with more flexibility in terms of how work is organized and how organizations are structured and an economy where intangible characteristics such as human intelligence, creativity and even personal warmth take on increasing value (Coyle & Quah 2002).

The third force – demographic shifts in the workforce – will see the ageing of the workforce, which may be the most significant demographic change over the next 15–20 years (Madouros 2006). These demographic shifts are coupled with workforce generational differences in aspirations and values, including the importance of the role of women in the work-force, with significant change coming from identifying those aspects of the gender gap and using them as drivers for economic change, and an increas-ing trend towards a more culturally diverse workforce, influenced by pat-terns of immigration. All these forces will influence, and be influenced by, issues surrounding climate change, the demands for eco-friendly manage-ment techniques, ethical leadership that fosters sustainability, fair trade innovations and work patterns and structures that reflect high-efficiency/ low-carbon initiatives.

It is not difficult to trace the impact that these forces are having and will continue to have on working arrangements and the structure of organiza-tions. The 'vertical disaggregation' of organizations resulting in the out-sourcing of non-core functions, flatter structures and the redefinition of working relationships has ushered in increasingly familiar management techniques that focus on performance-related issues, smart working, just-in-time deadlines, cost-effectiveness strategies and lean organizational practices. These changes also mean that working relationships become more demanding as organizations attempt to maximize the use of their 'human capital' through competency-based initiatives, resource-based strategies, multi-skilled role requirements, team working, talent manage-ment, continuous improvement and a compulsive drive towards the use of new technology and continuous technological development. As a result of these changes, work is becoming more intense, taking on more of an emotional quality and producing more complex working patterns and interpersonal relationships. Longer working hours have become the norm; combining work with family and social life is becoming increasingly dif-ficult, adding to the social cost of work, and work practices are now clearly at odds with the way people want to live (Equal Opportunities Commission 2007).

'Work–life balance considerations clearly matter a great deal to a signifi-cant proportion of employees' (Bell & Bryson 2005, p. 51), increasing the demand for flexible working arrangements. Yet despite this demand and the development of common flexible working practices, changes to working arrangements are not happening fast enough, or in the right way, to deliver what people and organizations want (Equal Opportunities Commission 2007). All these issues clearly have an impact on the health and well-being of employees. Employees want more control over their working lives and in terms of their satisfaction and development want jobs to be interesting and meaningful, that allow them to express their talents, utilize their skills and provide opportunities for achievement and scope for development.

How employees experience work and the satisfaction they derive from it is a key indicator of well-being. Policy strategies that recognize the quality of the work experience represent significant steps in meeting the aim of making employment a more fulfilling experience (Brown *et al.* 2006). Yet the changes to work and organizations and the complexity of working arrangements continue to tax the well-being and resources of employees. It is as important to monitor those work events that have the potential to cause stress as it is to provide employees with the resources to cope and flourish. Changes to work and working life inevitably bring new potential sources of stress and alter the nature of those traditionally identified. It is to these events that we now turn our attention.

Work Stressors: Some Issues

In their seminal work on work stress, employee well-being and health, Beehr and Newman (1978) make the point that as most people spend more than half their waking lives at work it is highly likely that work issues will significantly influence how they feel. There is, in work stress research, a long and rich history of identifying those work factors that have the potential to cause stress. The identification by Kahn and his colleagues (1964) of role conflict and role ambiguity quickly followed by role overload introduced researchers to the 'costly ideology of bureaucratic conformity', 'identity destroying' and 'emotional turmoil' (Cooper & Dewe 2004; Kahn *et al.* 1964, p. 6) caused by work and ushered in the first set of work stressors that continue, even today, to capture the attention of many researchers. Since the original work by Kahn and his colleagues, the types of work stressors have continued to expand, prompted by significant economic, social and political change, to include, in addition to the role requirements of the job, demands intrinsic to the job, career development issues, relationships at work and organizational structure and culture issues (Beehr & Newman 1978; Cooper & Marshall 1976) followed by work–life conflicts,

mergers and acquisitions, organizational change and transition, retrench-
ment, redundancies and outsourcing (Sulsky & Smith 2005).

The importance of this brief historical review is to draw attention to the
fact that while instruments for measuring many of these work stressors
have long been available and continue to be used this should not mean we
ignore our responsibility to better our understanding of the evolving nature
of these stressors. The considerable economic and social change that has
occurred since many stressor measures were first developed has meant that
these measures may now be prone to an 'inherent bias', where we overem-
phasize the importance of some stressor events, ignore others and fail to
consider the significance of such stressors to the individual (Brief & Atieh
1987; Glowinkowski & Cooper 1985). When it comes to measuring work
stressors, the question must become one of relevance, where the measures
being used capture those stressors and those events that reflect the individual's experience. The value of continually developing our understanding of different stressors must be seen, at any one time, to lie more in their
ability to describe particular experiences rather than to define them.
Accepting uncritically the a priori labelling of a stressor as always reflecting
the same events, or expressing the same meaning or events always falling
within a particularly category, is to ignore the evolving nature of stressors
and the influence of social, economic and organizational change.

Organizations, whatever their size, and work relationships, however
structured, are not immune from economic and social turmoil, government initiatives and regulations, management styles and practices and
employee expectations and needs. These factors help shape work stressors
and point towards the types of work stressors that may be encountered in
the future. These factors have something of a dual role in that at one time
they may influence the nature of work stressors and at another become
work stressors themselves, so that change and stressors are interrelated with
each helping to shape the other. From the many issues that may emerge
from this economic, social and political change three capture the way work
is transforming and signal what may yet be experienced in terms of work
stressors. These three issues are job insecurity, the increasing emotional
qualities of work and work–life balance where 'the way we work no longer
fits the changing world we live in' (Equal Opportunities Commission
2007, p. 7).

When the banking crisis of 2008 hit – 'possibly the largest financial crisis
of its kind in human history' (Hayman 2008, p. 1) – job losses were predicted, for the United Kingdom alone, to be 60,000 per month during the

consequent downturn. Feelings of job insecurity heightened by memories of past recessions and fuelled by an incredible sensitivity to the vagaries of market and economic trends are again a reality but this time a reality across all sectors of the economy. Fears of job insecurity spread throughout the 1990s, resulting in a deterioration in physical and mental health (Burchell *et al.* 1999). Job insecurity also comes with feelings of work intensification. The demands on employees in terms of efficiencies and greater productivity are associated with changes in the way work is allocated, organized, controlled, performed and rewarded, thereby intensifying the work experience. Considerable numbers of employees indicate that they work longer than their basic working hours, feel that speed of work and the effort they put into their jobs have increased and believe that their current staffing levels are inadequate or very inadequate (see Burchell *et al.* 1999, pp. 2–3). With employees feeling they are working harder with fewer resources in increasingly competitive and uncertain markets where performance is controlled through financial incentives, despite the benefits that flow from performance-related techniques the work environment is becoming increasingly stressful for many workers (Equal Opportunities Commission 2007).

Because the service sector currently represents around 81% of the total workforce and because of the widening spread of job insecurity fears, the continuing uncertainties in the global economy, increasing competitive pressures, slowdowns in the rate of economic growth and concerns around domestic inflation, the impact on the health and well-being of workers in this sector simply because of the numbers employed is potentially enormous. Job insecurity fears coupled with work intensification – concerns about resources, loss of valued aspects of the job, increased responsibilities and fewer opportunities for development (Burchell *et al.* 1999) – must increase the likelihood of stress. What distinguishes this sector from other sectors of the workforce is that it is made up of many occupations where the job roles require such an intensity of 'client' interaction that work assumes much more of an emotional quality. Researchers are familiar with the effects of emotional labour and job-related burnout. For many service workers their work leaves them feeling emotionally exhausted with a need at times to distance themselves from what is going on around them. These feelings may also help to explain why, in recent surveys, the majority of respondents described themselves as disengaged or only moderately engaged (Towers Perrin 2006). There is, as the report points out, a considerable difference between being willing and being engaged. While terms like 'emotional capital' and 'emotional competencies' have now joined the management lexicon, they nevertheless 'shed light on a once hidden aspect of service work' and there is no ignoring the fact that 'many organizations today see the ability of their frontline staff to manage their feelings as well as those of the customer as key to competitive success' (Payne 2006, p. 5).

The demand for change in the organization and structure of work – stemming from global competition and technological change, the transformation of the labour market with more women in paid employment, a changing age structure with a need to sustain the employability of older workers and the importance of caring responsibilities – has led to policies which promote mechanisms for employees to more effectively combine their paid work with other aspects of their lives (Bell & Bryson 2005). It is clear that many employees have difficulty balancing work and home life, illustrated by on the one hand coming home too tired and running out of time to complete jobs at home, while on the other finding it difficult to concentrate at work because of family responsibilities (Bell & Bryson 2005). The overwhelming desire to have more time for family, friends and leisure, coupled with meeting the demands of work, has heightened the difficulties associated with combining paid employment with family and social life (Crompton & Lyonette 2007). The way we work, argues the Equal Opportunities Commission, 'is not responding fast enough to the challenges presented by changes in the world around us' (2007, p. 16), making this another factor that will help shape work stressors.

Changing Work Stressors

Against this backdrop of social, economic and political change, we identify a number of work stressors that provide a context for better understanding the changing nature of work and changing work stressors. It is within this context that coping takes place. It is clear that many of the work stressors traditionally identified will continue to have an impact on employee health and well-being. What is important is to accept that the characteristics and boundaries of these stressors continue to change and evolve and that in capturing this change we are better equipped to understand the work environment and the issues facing those who have to cope with it. The most frequently measured work stressors are without doubt overload, conflict and ambiguity. Researchers have for some time distinguished between quantitative and qualitative overload, but it is clear that we are witnessing a change in the nature of these stressors. Quantitative overload will continue to reflect the amount of work and its time dimension, but these elements may, through the intensification of work, include efficiency and quality-performance issues, responsibility but without the necessary control or the appropriate resources, continually working to targets and the urgency of maximizing workloads set against job insecurity and uncertain economic times.

The qualitative dimensions of overload that reflect the more 'cognitive' aspects of the job will see greater demands in terms of skill requirements, continual learning, working with complexity of procedures, policies and technology and the continual requirements for career and professional development and 'upskilling'. It could be that qualitative overload may include elements of what has been described as 'techno-stress' (O'Driscoll & O'Driscoll 2008), including concerns about being able to learn and use new technological techniques, problems owing to limitations or expectations about what different technological platforms can do and the eroding of social relationships at work as a result of how different applications change the way we work and the way we interrelate with colleagues. It is also clear that the boundaries between different role stressors will become blurred as conflicts and ambiguities begin to reflect lack of opportunities in terms of growth and development, feelings of career stagnation coupled with the wearing away of those aspects of the job that give value, meaningfulness, social worth and satisfaction. Conflicts may also emerge in terms of personal goals, ethics, values and job demands and the need to perform under conditions of uncertainty that extend beyond role requirements to tenure and survival.

We are already witnessing a greater array of complex human resource rules and regulations. Not only is there a greater urgency to engage in resource-based strategies where economic advantage is best achieved by competing through people, but relationships within the organization are becoming more complex. This contributes to increasingly reported incidents and growing concerns around harassing, bullying, fear and violent behaviours at work. Behaviours like bullying are complex and sometimes cross a fine line between appropriate forms of management and inappropriate interpersonal styles (Chartered Institute of Personnel and Development 2005). Bullies are often unaware of their actions on others, but the cost of bullying in the United Kingdom is estimated to reach beyond £2 million, taking up around 450 days of management time a year, creating profound distress for victims that extends beyond the effects of more common workplace stressors (Chartered Institute of Personnel and Development 2005).

Workplace violence is also on the increase and becoming widespread across all sectors of the workforce. As over 80% of the workforce work in occupations where 'client contact' is central to the job, for some occupations forms of violence have reached epidemic proportions. Retail industry research reports that every minute of the working day a shop worker is verbally abused, threatened with violence or physically attacked (Union of Shop, Distributive and Allied Workers 2007). The *Workplace Health and Safety Survey* indicates that over a third of those who have experienced threats, abuse or attacks thought the risk of such behaviours would increase (Hodgson *et al.* 2006). The Health and Safety Executive's *Violence at work* report (2007a), using estimates from the British Crime Survey, indicates that for 2004/05 there were around 339,000 threats of violence and 317,000 physical assaults by members of the public on workers. The costs of workplace violence and other threatening behaviours like harassment and bullying 'can cause unimaginable levels of occupational stress', leaving the question of just 'how you begin to estimate the true human cost' (UNISON 2005, p.7) hanging.

Organizational restructuring, process re-engineering, the drive for efficiency and performance and the importance given to 'people management' strategies have led to issues concerning the levels of control employees have over their work, their flexibility to manage their work arrangements, the challenges they get from work and the spillover from work to home life. The stressors that emerge express the tensions in terms of how people want to work, how they have to work and the satisfactions they get from work. These tensions are heightened when set against the changing nature of the workforce, the competing demands of home and work, the flattening of organizational hierarchies, the blurring of demarcation lines between jobs, the intensification of work and the loss of valued job features like control and flexibility (Burchell *et al.* 1999). The sustainability of contemporary work practices and the competition between job demands and worker expectations have worrying implications for employees, their families and management alike, and cause considerable stress.

The stressors discussed above are not meant to be a definitive list but are mentioned to illustrate how they change and evolve over time. Stressors emerge from the complexities of the social, economic and working environment. They interact with each other and the existence of one stressor will, more than likely, lead to a vulnerability to others. It is clear from those discussed that they will spill over into other aspects of work and life and will themselves be influenced and changed by these and other events. Inevitably, stressors should be viewed as moulded by the past, expressing the present yet tempered by the future. They are discussed here to provide a context for understanding coping research, the way our knowledge of coping has developed and why it has, at times, taken different directions and focused on different issues. Understanding coping is not just about stressors; it is also about how we define stress, how we capture that experience in our research, what measures we use, whose reality those measures express, how researchers interpret their results and how this knowledge contributes to theory, practice and those whose working lives we study. Coping research needs to be understood within this complex and changing context, a complexity that determines not only how people cope but also how effective their coping is and what this means for their health and wellbeing. It is this complexity and these changes that also influence how researchers go, and have gone, about investigating the coping process and it is to these issues that we now turn our attention.

2

Coping: The Measurement Debate

The past 40 years have seen 'a dramatic proliferation' of coping research across a range of disciplines (Folkman & Moskowitz 2004, p. 745). This 'boundless enthusiasm for coping research particularly since the 1980s' makes 'coping arguably the most widely studied topic in all of contemporary psychology' (Somerfield & McCrae 2000, p. 620). Yet despite this volume of research and the tremendous energy and attention given to the coping process (Burke 2002), there is a sense that much of this research has not produced substantive results (Coyne & Racioppo 2000) and that in many ways our expectations may have been set too high (Burke 2002). While researchers may now have to temper their views as to what has and can be achieved, there is still a sense that despite some difficult methodological issues the field encompasses an increasing number of creative, capable and vigorous researchers who are committed to investigating the structure of coping (Lazarus 2000). Even the most strident critics of the well-established conventions dominating existing research point to ways forward, offer new directions, argue for a realism in terms of what can be achieved and propose a new focus for coping research that requires a change from, and challenge to, the convenience and comfort of established methods and practices (Coyne 1997; Somerfield 1997a).

In order to capture the issues facing coping researchers, this chapter focuses on what is at the heart of the coping debate: the measurement of coping itself. The chapter opens with a brief historical review of coping and the issues surrounding how it has been defined. It then focuses on the measurement of coping, taking as a starting point the utility of coping

Coping with Work Stress: A Review and Critique, Philip J. Dewe, Michael P. O'Driscoll and Cary L. Cooper, © 2010 John Wiley & Sons Ltd.

questionnaires and the debate that surrounds their use. Although many of the measurement issues have been the subject of numerous reviews, they are still significant enough to be re-examined (Dewe 2001) in order to stimulate new ways of looking at old problems. Measurement issues lead naturally into the classification of strategies and the robustness of such classifications when coping strategies are considered within the context of the coping process. From here the chapter moves to discussing alternative approaches to measurement, not in the sense of one methodology replacing another but as an exploration of what alternative methods can provide and how new approaches are an important and necessary element in developing our understanding of coping (Lazarus 2000). The chapter concludes by reviewing the different measurement issues in terms of theory, research and practice, and sets the context for the chapter that follows, where new and promising developments in coping research are identified and reviewed (Folkman & Moskowitz 2004).

A History and Some Definitional Issues Surrounding Coping

While the research interest in coping took some time to develop, the idea of coping has been around for some time (Lazarus 1999). When the history of coping is discussed, reviewers have identified three approaches that best express developments in our understanding of coping (Schaufeli 2002). The first approach grew out of the psychodynamic tradition that spanned the late nineteenth and early to middle twentieth centuries. This approach viewed coping primarily in terms of a defence mechanism, where individuals used various techniques to adjust the meaning of the stressful event so as to be able to manage any distress it caused. As work on identifying different defence mechanisms developed, researchers began to think of them as reflecting some form of hierarchy that distinguished maladaptive or immature defences from adaptive or mature defences (Parker & Endler 1996). The use of mature defences should promote better health and well-being than might the use of immature defences, which are presumed to be associated with pathology. The work on defence mechanisms also led to the idea that individuals may have a preference for certain strategies when managing stressful encounters and that particular defence modes may be associated with specific outcomes (Parker & Endler 1996).

From this work it wasn't long before researchers began to equate personality with coping, focusing on the trait-like properties of coping. This perspective suggests that there is a common base between personality and coping (Connor-Smith & Flachsbart 2007), with the result that a substantial part of the history of coping cannot be divorced from the study of individual differences (Suls, David & Harvey 1996). This second approach to understanding coping is best considered from the standpoint that 'personality and coping are overlapping constructs, but hardly synonymous' (Suls & David 1996, p. 994). The point of maximum overlap occurs when a characteristic pattern of behaviour (personality) generally defines the strategy used to cope with a stressful encounter, supporting the contention that aspects of personality are associated with certain preferred styles of coping (Suls & David 1996). Not without its critics (e.g. Lazarus 1999), investigation of personality traits or dispositions which may influence coping strategies remains an integral part of coping research.

Capturing the complexity of the personality/coping relationship has led researchers to explore a number of new directions including, for example, how competent individuals are in executing the coping strategies they use (Suls & David 1996), whether it is possible to differentiate between 'strong' and 'weak' situations, where some situations may make it easier than others for personality traits to be expressed (Suls & David 1996), whether earlier stressful experiences and stressors themselves influence personality (Suls & David 1996), how personality may shape positive meanings and benefit finding in stressful encounters (Affleck & Tennen 1996) and how personality enhances the accumulation of 'personal coping resources' (Schaufeli 2002). The important aspect of this work is the acknowledgement of both situational and individual determinants of coping (Suls, David & Harvey 1996). Nevertheless, as many of these commentators agree, in order to better understand the personality/coping relationship, serious methodological issues remain, not least of which is how coping should be measured.

Research on coping as a distinct field of psychological inquiry (Folkman & Moskowitz 2004) began in earnest in the early 1970s, motivated by the early work of Lazarus (1966). This work set a new course and shifted the focus of coping research beyond defence 'to include a wider range of cognitive and behavioural responses that ordinary people use to manage distress' (Folkman & Moskowitz 2004, p. 746). This third approach positioned the coping *process* as central to an understanding of coping, which is viewed in transactional terms. 'Transaction' implies process, where stress is neither in the environment nor in the individual but in the transaction between them, the constantly changing and continual interplay between the two (Lazarus 1990). The authority of Lazarus's approach lies in the fact that to understand the nature of a stressful transaction requires researchers to explore cognitive processes that link the individual to the environment (Dewe & Cooper 2007). At the heart of Lazarus's theory is the concept of cognitive appraisal; once an encounter has been appraised as stressful, coping strategies (behaviours) are initiated to deal with the disturbed person–environment transaction (Lazarus 1990).

Lazarus identified two types of appraisal. The coping process is initiated by what is described as 'primary appraisal', which occurs when the individual evaluates and gives meaning to an encounter (Lazarus 2001). This entails recognition that something of significance is at stake and the encounter is appraised in terms of harm, threat, loss or challenge to the individual. 'Secondary appraisal' focuses on what can be done. It is an evaluation of coping options and is at the heart of and underpins the cognitive nature of coping (Lazarus 1999). Owing to the dynamics of the stress process, it is often difficult to distinguish between these two types of appraisal (Lazarus 1999). Both occur as part of a complex process and, while they are described as primary and secondary, these terms are, as Lazarus (1999) suggests, not meant to indicate that one is any less important than the other but that both are required to shape responses to a particular encounter. Each is dependent on the other, and they should be regarded as part of the same process. Any difference between the two types of appraisal should be viewed in terms of content rather than timing.

The transactional approach, with the concept of appraisal as its central plank, has been readily accepted as an important focus in the general stress literature, but this has not been the case when it comes to work stress research (Jones & Bright 2001). Schaubroeck (1999) suggests that there are compelling reasons why work stress researchers have not given appraisal the attention it deserves. These motives seem generally to stem from two concerns. The first is that focusing on individuals' personal appraisals and meanings necessarily limits what can be generalized to most employees and the relevance of this type of information for management (Harris 1991; Schaubroeck 1999). The second relates to the limitations imposed by the intra-individual focus but this time centres around the argument that only by objectively measuring stressors will researchers be able to meet their social responsibilities to identify working conditions that 'adversely affect the well-being of *most* workers' (Brief & George 1991, p. 6). Nevertheless, despite these arguments, the essential point still remains that to some extent sources of stress are always personal and idiosyncratic, as are the coping strategies that people use to cope with them (Lazarus 1991). To ignore the role and importance of appraisals is to ignore what are, potentially, the most significant explanatory variables in understanding the coping process. Work stress and coping researchers acknowledge the importance of the transactional model and note not only that it is ideally positioned to offer a more dynamic view of work stress (Harris 1999) but also that examining appraisals is essential if we are to better understand the richness of the stress process (Perrewé & Zellars 1999). Most researchers agree that these arguments can only be decided empirically and that it is through this route that the debate should now be expressed.

Defining Coping and Definitional Issues

Although the construct of coping is clearly embedded in the transactional stress process, this has not meant that how we define it is free from debate. Despite, or perhaps because of, the level of research directed towards understanding coping as a construct, it has emerged as increasingly more complex (Snyder 2001) and studying it is not without its difficulties (Aldwin 2000). Discussing and debating the definition of coping reflects a maturing discipline where issues can be raised, change can be provoked, boundaries can be refined and tested and researchers can become more responsive to what needs to be explored, how it needs to be measured and how it contributes to those whose working lives we study (Dewe 2001; Dewe & Cooper 2007).

The *Collins Dictionary & Thesaurus* (1993, p. 216) defines 'to cope' as 'to contend against; to deal successfully with; manage'. This definition carries an expectation that coping will be successful or managed and reflects the 'value-laden' nature of the word (Beehr & McGrath 1996, p. 66), and illustrates how coping is frequently defined in ways that may not be evident from the coping strategy itself. While defining something as coping requires some interpretation of what the person was trying to do, and while concepts like adaptation and adjustment are part and parcel of our understanding of coping (Zeidner & Saklofske 1996), researchers agree that the concern is more about context, where definitions capture coping in terms of what is being done, for whom and under what circumstances, rather than on prejudging its effect. Interpretation is difficult at the best of times and is dependent on whose judgement is being sought. Differences emerge when coping is considered from the point of view of the person doing the coping (the insider approach) rather than when other people (the outsider approach) are doing the interpreting or judging (Snyder 1999). Interpreting how different coping strategies are actually used cannot be divorced from issues of measurement and research design (Dewe & Cooper 2007), hence coping measures inevitably reflect certain assumptions which make their meanings more complex than just being objective indicators (Beehr & McGrath 1996), and that people are not 'passive responders' to environmental conditions (Aldwin 2000).

The most frequently quoted but not always generally agreed definition is the process view proposed by Lazarus, who defines coping as 'the constantly changing cognitive and behavioural efforts a person makes to manage specific external and/or internal demands that are appraised as taxing or exceeding the resources of the person' (1999, p. 110). Defined in this way, coping is seen as a process and must be understood within the transactional terms of context and appraisal (Lazarus 2001). It offers through its transactional lens the significance of the appraisal process and in doing so provides a framework for understanding how the stress process may unfold. Lazarus' definition stated somewhat simply emphasizes the 'effort to manage' (1999, p. 111) and draws attention to the idea that coping involves strategies that may or may not be effective since they will be directed as much towards managing encounters as towards avoiding or lessening them. There is a need to describe in detail what the person is thinking or doing. In addition there are at least two major functions of coping – problem-focused and emotion-focused – and a full understanding of coping requires both functions be considered (Lazarus 1999, 2001).

For Lazarus, coping thoughts and actions are defined contextually, set within an encounter that is demanding, and appraised as taxing or exceeding the resources of the person. This approach is not without its critics. At the heart of this criticism is the view that what Lazarus defines as coping is limiting (Snyder 2001) and excessively restricting (Coyne & Gottlieb 1996). For many commentators, Lazarus' approach limits coping to intentional strategies initiated in the context of a stressful encounter (Coyne & Gottlieb 1996). One issue concerns the distinction between coping and adaptation. The latter is a broad term involving a range of behaviours that include, under the general rubric of everyday skills for getting along (Aldwin 2000), habitual, automatic or routine behaviours (Costa, Somerfield & McCrae 1996; Coyne & Gottlieb 1996) and management skills (Aldwin 2000).

If the distinction between coping and adaptation blurs as one fades into the other (Costa, Somerfield & McCrae 1996), why is it, ask Coyne and Gottlieb (1996), that behaviours like habits and routines are not included in any definition of coping. A possible answer lies in the distinction first mooted by Lazarus and Folkman (1984) between intentional and unintentional acts and that, while this distinction is not sacrosanct, habits and routines fall short in terms of this distinction and are more properly seen as aligned with adaptation (Suls & David 1996). Coping has come to be accepted by many as a particular type of adaptation (Costa, Somerfield & McCrae 1996) elicited in response to taxing encounters; habits, routines and automated behaviours are not seen as sitting easily with the idea that coping be extended to include these behaviours (Dewe & Cooper 2007).

These arguments cannot, of course, be separated from issues of measurement when deciding whether something is a habitual or automatic response or a more intentional, deliberate act. The current measurement practice of using checklists does not enable us to make this distinction (Coyne & Gottlieb 1996), and without such data the level of constancy in coping strategies remains unclear (Suls & David 1996). The debate continues both conceptually, with the exclusion of habitual and routine behaviours being seen as a significant omission (Coyne & Gottlieb 1996), and operationally, where perhaps all the different forms of coping will require their own particular methodology if we are to advance our understanding beyond what currently amounts to somewhat broad generalizations (Costa, Somerfield & McCrae 1996).

It is not just a question of coping versus adaptation that has caught the attention of reviewers when it comes to considering how coping should be defined. Reviewers have also drawn attention to the ambiguity that surrounds the term 'effort' when it comes to defining coping, and query not just who defines what is meant by effort, but where the threshold lies and how this will fit with 'the minimalist perspective' where doing very little 'is the most productive level of effort' (Snyder 2001, p. 4). Reviewers have also pointed to the idea of anticipatory coping, which occurs before the onset of a stressful encounter, and argue that by excluding these types of actions when defining coping we somewhat misrepresent the nature of the stress and coping process (Coyne & Gottlieb 1996).

None of these issues that surround the definition of coping is mutually exclusive and all relate to the issue of consciousness and coping. Ambiguity surrounds the term 'consciousness'. This leads to the difficulty of who is making the judgement about what is consciousness. To avoid, argues Snyder (2001, p. 5), 'all or nothing' arguments the best approach is simply to attempt to answer the question of whether coping always has to be a conscious process. What appears to emerge when reviewers tackle this question is the issue of whether an action or behaviour can still be defined as coping if by repeatedly using it we become unaware of doing so. The debate and the evidence support both views: that some coping flowing from experience precedes any significant cognitive activity (Coyne & Gottlieb 1996) and that it is likely for the most part that coping responses embody a sense of awareness (Snyder 1999). The challenge lies as much in determining what constitutes a level of awareness as it does in considering just how such coping actions would be measured.

The debate surrounding how coping should be defined continues. The debate can best be expressed and summarized in terms of three related themes. The first theme focuses on the complexity of the coping process and the difficulties involved in studying it (Aldwin 2000), and argues that in many ways our goals were undoubtedly set too high (Burke 2002), that researchers need to be a little more 'modest' in their goals and carefully think through the possible ways coping research can contribute. Individuals spend many years developing their coping behaviours (Somerfield & McCrae 2000) so the complexity of the coping process should not be reduced to a few interdependent causal variables (Lazarus 1997). The second theme concerns whether coping should be defined broadly to encompass a wider range of adaptational behaviours or less so where the hallmark of any definition emphasizes effort, purpose and context. It is this theme that leads into the third, and perhaps most powerful, theme, where the focus is on measurement, and the argument that current methodologies have become 'too narrowly method-bound', with the consequence that coping is simply defined via the analysis that emerges from the uncritical use of coping checklists (Coyne & Gottlieb 1996, p. 961).

At the heart of this third theme is the belief that in order to resolve many of the issues surrounding what is and what isn't coping requires researchers to accept that changes to current measurement practices will need to be made and questions asked about where current methodologies are taking us and what alternative methodologies can provide. How best to measure coping still needs to be resolved, but what also needs to be confronted if we are going to advance our understanding of coping is the discrepancy between what is considered conceptually relevant and what it is our measures are yielding (Suls, David & Harvey 1996). Researchers are urged to make a clean start, to break away from the convenience of established measurement practices, to contemplate what they should be asking respondents and to consider what may now need to be done that has a more focused relevance for research and practice (Coyne 1997). If, as a starting point, coping is defined in transactional terms, as involving effort and intentional choice set within the context of a stressful encounter, these qualifiers provide a framework for research and investigation. Nevertheless, researchers have a responsibility to acquaint themselves with the debate surrounding current measurement practices and to be more responsive to those issues that need investigating and, more importantly, the techniques needed to investigate them (Dewe & Cooper 2007).

The Measurement of Coping

It is clear from the debate on how coping should be defined that while everyone agrees that coping is an important explanatory variable there is no clear consensus on how it should be measured (Aldwin 2000). The disagreement reaches its greatest intensity when self-report coping questionnaires or checklists are the focus of attention. These approaches offer an initial means of conveniently and economically collecting data and are 'helpful in that they allow multidimensional descriptions of situational-specific coping thoughts and behaviours that people can self-report' (Folkman & Moskowitz 2004, p. 748). However, even those sympathetic to their use recognize their shortcomings and design faults. The genuine concern that the repeated use of checklists has seen the field weighed down by tedious and somewhat self-evident findings, with their continued use implying a level of acceptable reliability, suggests that perhaps checklists should have been regarded as 'first steps' and not, as what seems to have happened, as the generally accepted method or the only possible mechanism for assessing coping strategies (Coyne 1997).

These arguments need, of course, to recognize that it is only over time, as our knowledge develops and we accumulate the findings to critically review our progress, that we can begin to make such judgements. The view that 'fixing and cleaning up' checklists with 'seemingly helpful bits of advice' (Coyne 1997, p. 154) should be abandoned in favour of more radical measurement solutions must be set against the view that the utility of checklists is only as good as our motivation to continue to improve their reliability and validity (Folkman 1992). Researchers need to become more sensitive to when it is appropriate to use such instruments (Lazarus 1995) and that we should not be defeated by the difficulties associated with checklists (Lazarus 1999). There is a third approach (Dewe 2001), which seems to have the agreement of all researchers irrespective of their views on checklists, and that is if we are to capture the richness and complexity of the coping process there is now a need to give more attention to the explanatory potential of alternative methods.

Giving more attention to alternative methods has long been an undercurrent in coping research. However, by emphasizing analysis over synthesis, researchers have failed to recognize that both are essential for understanding coping, that one should not be seen as a substitute for the other, but rather both complement each other (Lazarus 2000) in advancing our understanding of coping. Distinguishing between analysis and synthesis points to the subtle difference between analysing component parts of the coping process and confusing that with treating those parts as if they were the whole (Lazarus 2000). Although each complements the other, their research objectives are, as Lazarus (2000) suggests, significantly distinct enough to demand different ways of thinking about research procedures. There is a clear role in coping research for a research style that gives qualitative meaning to what is happening in any demanding encounter, a style in which the person is considered in a more holistic way. This requires methods that provide an in-depth investigation of what it is the person is experiencing (Lazarus 1990). What lies behind these views has been a lingering concern that, despite the huge number of studies, little progress has been made in advancing our understanding of the role of coping in stressful encounters (Coyne & Gottlieb 1996), and the realization that changes must be made if our understanding of coping is to progress. It is clear that coping researchers need now confront the methodological problems and limitations that accompany the use of checklists (Suls & David 1996). Ignoring the above concerns will restrict further understanding of the underlying role of coping in the overall transactional process (Lazarus 1997).

Coping Checklists

It is clear from the debate that surrounds coping checklists that when exploring the theoretical basis that underwrites checklist design and how that basis influences our understanding of coping (Stone, Helder & Schneider 1988), and how therefore their reliability and validity can be improved (Folkman 1992), this exploration should not lead to a 'more of the same' attitude concerning methods (Snyder 1999), discourage the search for new and innovative ways to research coping (Coyne & Racioppo 2000) but should run parallel with strategies that initiate and investigate new methods that capture the richness of the coping process (Dewe & Cooper 2007). The message that needs to be taken to heart is that 'the art' when it comes to measuring coping lies in adopting an approach that matches the research objectives set, recognizing that the best way forward may be to consider the use of a number of approaches (Folkman & Moskowitz 2004). When considering how best to refine coping checklists, it is important to recognize that this is as much an exercise in improving reliability, validity and predictability as it is in identifying where alternative measurement approaches may be better placed to capture the complexities of coping.

Many of these refinements have been discussed before (e.g. Aldwin 2000; Coyne 1997; Coyne & Gottlieb 1996; Coyne & Racioppo 2000; Dewe 2000, 2001; Dewe & Cooper 2007; Folkman & Moskowitz 2004; Lazarus 1990, 1997, 2000; Schwarzer & Schwarzer 1996; Somerfield 1997a; Somerfield & McCrae 2000; Stone & Kennedy-Moore 1992). We repeat them here simply to reinforce that it is only through continuing to improve our measures that we recognize the complexity of the issues we are researching, the need for additional data collection and analytical methods and the moral responsibility that we have to those whose working lives we study.

Different authors have taken different approaches to identifying the refinements that need to be considered when checklists are the measure of preference. Recognizing that there are many limitations associated with using coping checklists, Folkman and Moskowitz (2004, p. 749) suggest that researchers should, for example, give consideration to the potential conflict between overly long checklists and the need to adequately cover a range of coping strategies, ambiguities surrounding item meanings, the confounding of items with their outcomes, response keys that make interpretation difficult and the unreliability of recall prompted by variations in recall periods. Reviewing the work of others, Dewe and Cooper (2007, p. 167) suggest that 'when it comes to refining such measures researchers should give attention to the way instructions are worded, how checklist items are generated, how they are worded and the wording of scoring keys'. As a final example illustrating differences in approach, Coyne and Gottlieb (1996) point to the limitations when using off-the-shelf coping checklists and argue that these limitations will become even more apparent as our understanding of the issues faced by respondents when filling out checklist develops and when researchers attempt to interpret these data. The major limitation for respondents identified by these authors is that because checklist items are often 'thin descriptions of coping [that are] vaguely worded' (p. 976) they can create a range of ambiguities in the mind of the respondent and wide variations in how items are interpreted, making the interpretation of scale scores by researchers more contentious (Coyne & Gottlieb 1996).

It is worth, by drawing on the work of those cited in the preceding paragraphs, considering in a little more detail a number of the more frequently mentioned checklist refinements. By going into a little more detail, the hope is that this will make researchers more attuned to, and appreciative of, the issues facing respondents when completing a coping checklist (Coyne & Gottlieb 1996). This understanding should, at the very least, draw attention to the potential risks when attempting to meaningfully interpret findings and provide the motivation to initiate changes to the design of coping checklists that mitigate such risks. In order to be useful, coping checklists should be continually re-examined by researchers in order to improve their reliability and validity (Folkman 1992). In coping research there is a role for checklists and the data they provide, so the functional difficulties identified when using this form of self-reporting should not be allowed to defeat us (Lazarus 1999).

The first of the specific refinements that confronts researchers concerns the specificity of the instructions given. Instructing respondents to indicate in general terms how they cope in contrast to instructions that specifically instruct respondents to link coping strategies to a particular stressful encounter produces quite different data. The contrast here is whether general instructions are likely to produce styles of coping, with specific instructions producing specific coping behaviours. Failure to make this distinction raises questions about how findings are interpreted and described (Dewe 2001). No matter how the instructions are phrased, they are likely to assume that whatever encounter the respondent has in mind that encounter is perceived as being significant enough to require effortful coping (Coyne & Gottlieb 1996), raising further issues about how the instructions are being interpreted, what is actually being recalled (Folkman & Moskowitz 2004) and what this means in terms of at what stage respondents are in actually dealing with the encounter (Stone & Kennedy-Moore 1992).

This latter point also suggests that even when respondents are instructed to consider an encounter within a particular period, they have the freedom to choose the time within that period (Stone *et al.* 1991), will appraise the encounter in different ways (Dewe 2001) and shape their response depending on where they are in resolving the encounter (Stone & Kennedy-Moore 1992). The specificity of instructions, interpretations surrounding the period and the inherent assumptions as to the nature and significance of the encounter all point to the difficulties involved when coping instructions become too de-contextualized (Lazarus 1999). Coyne (1997) suggests that by reflecting on exactly what it is we are asking of respondents we may conclude that it is time to consider alternative but parallel approaches. One way forward would be to embed checklist instructions into a more narrative approach, where respondents would be asked to provide a narrative about the stressful encounter, including the nature of the encounter and what they actually thought and did as the encounter developed (Folkman & Moskowitz 2004). In this way checklist instructions would be returned to their theoretical roots where the emphasis would be on learning about what, in any encounter, respondents were thinking and doing. It is clear that if we are to advance the measurement and assessment of coping, this must be achieved by developing our capacity to better understand the context within which coping occurs (Folkman 1992).

Researchers have also been particularly critical of the way coping items have been worded (Dewe 2001), offering even more fertile ground for those interested in the utility and reliability of coping checklists. Two issues emerge from this criticism. The first concerns the way in which coping items are derived and the second the way they are worded. Returning to the view that coping checklists must reflect what respondents actually think and do (Holroyd & Lazarus 1982), generating coping items must reflect the reality of those whose working lives are being investigated. The merits of deductive versus inductive methods in relation to generating coping items have been regularly debated (Dewe & Cooper 2007; Schwarzer & Schwarzer 1996; Stone & Kennedy-Moore 1992). The generally accepted view emerging from this debate seems to focus less on the qualities of the different approaches, although a balance between the two is recommended, and more on the unsystematic way in which they have been used to generate items (Schwarzer & Schwarzer 1996).

It is clear that, however derived, coping items must reflect a sense of comprehensiveness (Stone & Kennedy-Moore 1992). At the same time comprehensiveness must be balanced against the potential onerous length of the checklist (Folkman & Moskowitz 2004; Stone & Neale 1984). Yet it is neither method nor comprehensiveness that now lies at the heart of the debate surrounding item derivation; it is the somewhat arbitrary procedures that researchers seemingly use to generate coping items (Dewe & Cooper 2007). It is as if, when generating coping items, researchers seem to give little attention to whether the items themselves have any particular significance or relevance, the context within which they are used is of no consequence and the assumptions made about how respondents cope is of no particular importance. If, as Coyne and Gottlieb (1996) suggest, researchers robustly insist they are, when administrating coping checklists, assessing what respondents are actually thinking and doing then method and comprehensiveness should once again be at the forefront of how coping items are selected rather than what can be gained from the convenience offered by arbitrarily deriving items.

It is not just how items are derived that has captured the attention of those concerned with the robustness of coping checklists. How items are worded has attracted the most persistent and trenchant criticism (Dewe 2001; Dewe & Cooper 2007). At one level the criticism is directed towards whether items are worded in ways that conform to the respondents' notion of coping (Coyne & Gottlieb 1996). At another level the criticism centres on whether their wording presumes they are being used in a way that conforms to the researcher's notion of how they should be used. At another level there is the issue of how general a coping item can be expressed before it loses its usefulness (Aldwin 2000), or before it shifts into the 'gray zone' that more likely reflects daily management skills (Coyne & Gottlieb 1996, p. 977), or because it can be applied to almost any situation the context-specific nature of coping is sacrificed (Coyne & Gottlieb 1996), or because it is so broadly applicable it makes it more likely to be endorsed (Coyne & Gottlieb 1996). In addition, items may be worded in such a way that they invite respondents to endorse them. That is, the assessment procedure may be laden with social desirability. For example, items that use words like 'try' or 'achieve' or 'gain' may be endorsed because respondents are concerned to show that they are capable and competent or that they are trying hard or doing things, because they see themselves as doing them or because they are things they should be doing or that others are doing and so should they (Coyne & Gottlieb 1996).

On the other hand, some items may be avoided because they are worded in ways that to endorse them would make respondents appear antisocial or engaging in strategies that run counter to the prevailing culture, or make them look as if they are coping ineffectively (Coyne & Gottlieb 1996). Finally, there are items that are worded in such a way that they may confound or confuse respondents: for example, where an item includes two different behaviours like 'tried to feel better (a goal) by going out for a walk (coping strategy)' or is more of a goal than coping like 'aimed to become a more tolerant person' or where emotions and coping merge like 'lost my temper' or perhaps confuse coping and appraisal like 'changed what the situation meant to me' (Coyne & Gottlieb 1996; Dewe & Cooper 2007; Schwarzer & Schwarzer 1996; Stanton *et al.* 1994).

Getting the wording right is important if we are to further our understanding of what it is that people think and do, but checklists leave unanswered questions about why respondents choose different coping strategies, the way they use them or why they may be being used in a particular combination or package. As part of the process of refinement, researchers would do well to consider those research questions best suited to checklists and those best answered by adopting alternative methodologies (Dewe 2001; Dewe & Cooper 2007).

Finally, there is the issue of the scoring key. It is clear that a variety of methods have been used including, for example, frequency, likelihood, extent and usefulness (e.g. Aldwin 2000; Dewe 2001; Dewe & Cooper 2007; Stone & Kennedy-Moore 1992). The appropriateness of the scoring key will, of course, depend on the research question being asked, but even then there are issues around how it is being interpreted (Stone & Kennedy-Moore 1992): whether that interpretation remains constant across different coping items and across different encounters (Zeidner & Saklofske 1996), whether a scoring key should be defined with respondents being instructed to follow that definition when checking each coping item (Stone *et al.* 1991), whether scoring keys, however stated or defined, can capture the complexity of intra-individual coping items (Stone & Kennedy-Moore 1992), similarly whether scoring keys can be properly understood or interpreted without being located within the context of the stressful encounter (Dewe 2001; Dewe & Cooper 2007), and how with any scoring key account is taken of issues such as effort and the duration of coping behaviour (Dewe 2001).

Like other refinements to coping checklists, researchers have to adopt a pragmatic approach, but this pragmatism should not be at the expense of carefully considering what it is that the response key should be measuring and how this can best be achieved (Stone & Kennedy-Moore 1992). The issues raised in this section on refinements aim to improve our understanding of what people actually think and do in a stressful encounter by focusing on the design inconsistencies and ambiguities present in established coping checklists. Achieving this aim is in many ways a double-edged sword for pointing to these design issues and how they may be resolved raises questions as to whether checklists can, despite improved reliability and validity, ultimately capture the richness and complexity of the coping process. While no one wants coping research to crumple under a load of tedious and sometimes glaringly apparent conclusions that flow from the seemingly uncritical use of checklists (Coyne 1997) there remains, as Folkman (1992, p. 216) so neatly suggests, the irony that 'a practical easy-to-administer coping questionnaire may be the most difficult of coping assessment to develop'.

It is now over 20 years since reviewers first commented on the challenges confronting the use of coping checklists as an assessment tool. This section on refining checklists has outlined the debate by drawing on what is now a rich history of comments and criticisms, and followed a structure that is common to our earlier work (Cooper, Dewe & O'Driscoll 2001; Dewe 2000, 2001; Dewe & Cooper 2007). If researchers are serious about understanding how people cope, then facing up to and resolving the measurement challenges when using checklists must be coupled with recognizing that coping research should not be allowed to become method bound (Coyne 1997). If, to some (Coyne & Racioppo 2000), checklists simply deter researchers from seeking out or developing more creative, person-centred methods then there is, they argue, no way forward but to drastically overhaul coping research. Checklists will, of course, continue to play an important role in coping research. However, to portray coping research as over-reliant on checklists (Coyne & Racioppo 2000) must be set against the growing number of researchers who are not wedded to such instruments and whose work already represents examples of innovative and creative approaches that can serve as templates for those wishing to explore alternative ways of understanding coping (Dewe & Cooper 2007; Lazarus 2000). It is to these approaches that we now turn.

Surprisingly, but somewhat obscured by the debate surrounding checklists, there is work where researchers have adopted much more of a 'contextual' approach to understanding the process of coping (Lazarus 1990). These approaches – grounded in process-oriented, in-depth, descriptive, holistic person-centred techniques – emphasize the importance of meaning, the reality of the person, the need for synthesis and integration, the significance of the narrative as a primary tool of analysis and the salience of their ecological appropriateness (Lazarus 1990, 1997, 2000; Somerfield & McCrae 2000; Tennen *et al.* 2000). The belief that in-depth descriptions and meanings are as vital a part of our research repertoire as is the exploration of causal links (Lazarus 2000) resonates through the different approaches. Such approaches include, for example, the use of interviews and their thematic analysis (O'Driscoll & Cooper 1994), daily process methods (Tennen *et al.* 2000), person-centred emotion narratives (Lazarus 1999), diary studies (Weber & Laux 1990), personal schemas (Horowitz 1990), process-oriented longitudinal research designs (Lazarus 1999) and ecological momentary assessment (Stone & Shiffman 1994).

It is acknowledged and accepted that these approaches are costly, take considerable time, are generally labour-intensive, frequently require day-to-day monitoring, place considerable demands on both participants and researchers and present their own complexities in terms of data analysis. Nevertheless, the richness in understanding that they can provide is illustrated by their ability to construct a descriptive representation of the coping process (Dewe & Cooper 2007), a sense as to what people thought and did as the encounter unfolded (Folkman & Moskowitz 2000), a capacity to identify aspects of coping not previously described (Erera-Weatherley 1996) and to reveal the significance of events and their meaning and to provide insights and understandings that are likely to reflect what is a more accurate picture of reality than that provided by traditionally used assessment methods (Lazarus 1990).

If we accept the view that coping checklists should be regarded as a 'first generation tool' (Folkman & Moskowitz 2004) and a first step rather than the only step (Lazarus 2000) in advancing our understanding, then researchers should be encouraged to utilize creativity and resourcefulness rather than sheltering behind the convenience of traditional methods and conventional criteria. Those researchers having taken up this challenge have already begun to show the richness of what can be achieved and what can be learnt about a process that is complex and dynamic. There is now an opportunity to move the field forward, acknowledging as we do the contribution that such approaches can add to our understanding of coping as a transactional process (Dewe 2001).

Classifying Coping and Creating Scales

As is clear from the above review on the refining of coping checklists, considerable use has already been made of these instruments. It is something of a tradition in stress research to use checklist data to classify coping strategies. This empirical approach, where a schema for classifying coping strategies emerges from the statistical analysis while aiding our understanding of the different functions coping strategies may play, has yet to provide a universally accepted typology (Cooper, Dewe & O'Driscoll 2001) and continues to challenge researchers to arrive at a common structure of coping categories which allows for meaningful discussion across samples (Folkman & Moskowitz 2004). This is not the only challenge facing researchers when it comes to the classification of coping strategies. Classifying different coping strategies by simply inspecting their structure from analysis has appeared to have emerged as the preferred approach. However, when these descriptors are considered within the context of a stressful encounter, it is clear that the task of classifying coping strategies is not always straightforward (Dewe 2003; Dewe & Cooper 2007). Researchers are faced with two related challenges: operational and interpretive. Operational challenges would include, for example, the utility of different classification approaches, the role of factor analysis in determining coping components and the associated issues of reliability. Interpretive challenges include, for example, interpreting and deriving meaning from coping scores (Dewe 2001; Dewe & Cooper 2007).

Classifying coping strategies has its roots in the work of Folkman and Lazarus (1984). These researchers identified two major process-oriented functions of coping, which they describe as 'problem-focused' and 'emotion-focused'. This classification of coping has provided a broad practical framework for thinking about many different kinds of coping (Folkman & Moskowitz 2004), and a starting point for debate about what falls under each of these headings. As different schemas emerge, support ebbs and flows as to the number of categories, how these categories should be described and whether the underlying complexity of a category gets lost because of a need to classify it as either problem- or emotion-focused. As an aid to classifying coping strategies, Latack and Havlovic (1992) suggest that schemas should account for not just the focus (problem/emotion) of the coping but also the form (cognitive-behavioural).

Irrespective of whether classifying coping strategies is seen as a primary research goal, this is the first issue that most researchers confront when analysing coping data, going some way to help explain the number and range of categories that have been identified. Nevertheless, several themes emerge in respect of the number of categories. A review by Burke (2002) with a focus on work stress suggests four categories (information seeking, direct action, inhibition of action and intrapsychic), whereas Billings and Moos (1981) found support for a three-category solution, including active cognitive, active behavioural (both problem-focused) and avoidance (emotion-focused), while others suggest that the problem- and emotion-focused categories should now be extended to include relationship-focused coping (O'Brien & DeLongis 1996), meaning-focused coping (Park & Folkman 1997) and proactive coping (Greenglass 2002), leaving Folkman and Moskowitz (2004) to suggest a typology which encompasses problem-focused, emotion-focused, social coping and meaning-focused coping.

From their extensive review of the coping literature, Skinner *et al.* (2003) argue that categories like problem- and emotion-focused, for example, fail to capture the complex way coping strategies are used, as any coping strategy is likely to serve a number of functions rather than just one. In their view, 'action types' present the best way forward in categorizing coping. These authors are in no doubt, however, that the richness of coping functions makes categorizing them a challenge, but essential if our understanding of the impact of stress is to be advanced. Lazarus (1999) also points to what he describes as two main errors when distinguishing between problem- and emotion-focused coping. The first is thinking of them as discrete types, where a specific coping strategy falls under one or the other heading. He suggests that 'we should have learned by now that the same act may have more than one function and usually does' (p. 123). Second, when comparing problem- and emotion-focused coping, it should not be assumed that one is better than the other. Only by gathering more data on how, in a particular stressful encounter, the different strategies are used and how they combine together will we be better able to understand how they work and what this means in terms of their effectiveness. The search for the structure of coping continues.

Classifying coping strategies also needs to be considered in the light of how they were statistically derived. For most researchers factor analysis is the preferred tool to create coping components. The benefit of using a technique like factor analysis lies in its ability to produce groups of coping strategies that have a theoretical and observed integrity (Folkman 1992). Nevertheless, researchers have over the years raised a number of concerns about the data-reduction features of this technique. What has emerged as a particular issue for researchers is whether using factor loadings as a method for including or excluding coping items reduces the comprehensiveness of our measures (Folkman 1992), presumes that coping items are used in a way that complies with generally accepted co-variation rules (Aldwin 2000; Billings & Moos 1984; Cooper *et al.* 2001; Dewe & Cooper 2007; Folkman & Moskowitz 2004), ignores the fact that a coping item may serve a number of functions or that a number of coping items fulfil the same function (Stone & Kennedy-Moore 1992; Watson & Hubbard 1996) and limits the meaning and interpretation of factor scores (Coyne & Gottlieb 1996; Coyne & Racioppo 2000; Dewe & Cooper 2007; Zeidner & Saklofske 1996). This is not to say that factor analysis should be abandoned or its benefits underestimated (Watson & Hubbard 1996). However, until we learn more about how coping strategies are used, the roles they play in relation to one another and how and why they combine, factor analysing coping data may need to be treated cautiously (Aldwin 2000).

There is one last issue when it comes to analysing coping data: interpreting the results. Coyne and Gottlieb (1996) neatly capture the essence of the problem by suggesting that scores from coping scales remain somewhat ambiguous statements of what respondents actually think and do. Specifically, by calculating mean scores crucial aspects of the coping process are lost (Coyne & Racioppo 2000). Again, the issue comes down to how different coping strategies are used and the impact this has on how other scale items are endorsed (Dewe 2001; Stone & Kennedy-Moore 1992). The way a coping item is used will vary depending on the stressful encounter the participant has in mind (Zeidner & Saklofske 1996), reducing the likelihood that all scale items will be appropriate and restricting the range of items that can be endorsed (Stone & Kennedy-Moore 1992). Similarly, endorsing one item may inhibit the use of other items, pointing to the need to understand the way in which coping items may combine, form patterns and relate to one another depending on how each is being used. These issues can make comparing mean scores misleading (Coyne & Gottlieb

1996), and identical mean sores may reflect completely different ways of coping (Dewe 2001; Dewe & Cooper 2007).

Abandoning mean scores is not, of course, an option. As we have suggested elsewhere (Cooper, Dewe & O'Driscoll 2001; Dewe 2000, 2001; Dewe & Cooper 2007), we draw attention to these issues in order to raise awareness of the difficulties in interpreting mean scores, what it is that mean scores can and are actually telling us, the complexity with which different coping items are used and relate to one another and the fact that they may not function independently of one another (Folkman & Moskowitz 1994). Coping scales may not operate according to traditional linear-additive assumptions. Scores may limit more 'refined and differentiated analysis' (Zeidner & Saklofske 1996, pp. 510–11) and may 'tend to lump together the idiosyncratic experiences of participants' (Suls & David 1996, p. 998). Acknowledging these issues may represent a first step in motivating researchers to be more careful and thoughtful when constructing coping measures as well as their interpretation of survey responses. But coping research requires refashioning (Coyne & Racioppo 2000), bringing with it a level of conceptual and methodological sophistication that has yet to reflect the field as a whole (Somerfield & McCrae 2000).

The challenge may be to accept the Folkman and Moskowitz (2004) dictum that best practice should now rely less on one single approach and instead involve several different approaches that complement each other, helping to reduce the impression that much research is devoid of theoretical meaning (Dewe & Cooper 2007). This will provide the context for understanding how coping occurs (Folkman 1992), that different research questions require different methods, procedures and approaches (Lazarus 2000) and that it is not a question of replacing one methodology with another but one of a drive towards continuing to develop and search for creative ways that capture the richness of the coping process and aid our understanding of its complexity.

This chapter has reviewed the long and rich history of the meaning and measurement of coping. It is clear that many of the points being raised and the issues discussed are not mutually exclusive. How we define coping will continue to change as our understanding about the nature and modes of coping develop. The chapter should not be seen as one where researchers are continually confronted with stubborn methodological problems. There are issues that must be faced up to (Suls & David 1996). There are also many resourceful and creative researchers already pointing the way forward, offering methods and research pathways that have credibility and an explanatory potential that reflects new opportunities and heralds the next generation of coping research. The issues raised here reflect a field that has matured. This maturity, while expressed through an openness for debate and engagement in controversy, is more about encouraging a creative tension (Dewe 2001) that allows inventiveness to flourish unimpeded by tradition or established conventions. This chapter is also about our social responsibilities as researchers. Here our aim must be to capture the reality of working lives and experiences and use that knowledge to narrow the gaps that link theory, research and practice.

3

New Directions for Coping Research

The last chapter drew attention to a range of issues surrounding how coping is defined and how it is measured. While the debate surrounding these issues has been robust, and has courted controversy, it is clear that change is required and the responsibility for that change rests with all those interested in advancing our understanding of coping. It is also clear that despite the limitations of checklists for assessing coping strategies (which we reviewed in Chapter 2) this has not discouraged researchers from exploring alternative approaches that creatively capture the richness of the coping process. New designs, new ideas and new approaches to old problems are continuing to reflect the contemporary repertoire of coping research, as are methods and techniques that better link theory, research and practice (Tennen et al. 2000). There is a growing confidence (Lazarus 2000) that coping research is emerging with a new-found sense of maturity, where new directions reflecting this spirit of reflection and innovation can be identified as taking the field forward (Folkman & Moskowitz 2004). This chapter turns to these new directions and explores (a) recent advances and developments in our understanding of appraisal and its explanatory potential, (b) the rise of the positive psychology movement and its impact on coping research, (c) new approaches to coping, including relationship coping, meaning-making coping and proactive coping, (d) the effectiveness of coping and (e) leisure as a coping strategy. The chapter concludes with a call for research and theory which extend beyond stress to emotions, and in particular take account of the important role played by positive emotions in workers' health and psychological well-being.

Coping with Work Stress: A Review and Critique, Philip J. Dewe, Michael P. O'Driscoll and Cary L. Cooper, © 2010 John Wiley & Sons Ltd.

New Developments in Appraisal

The transactional model of stress has at its core the cognitive processes of appraisal. However, while work stress researchers acknowledge the explanatory potential of the appraisal process, the need to investigate how individuals evaluate and give meaning to a stressful encounter (primary appraisal) has been given a less than complete treatment in work stress research. To ignore the way individuals appraise and give meaning to a stressful encounter is to ignore the very foundation on which coping decisions are taken and hence the context within which coping occurs. While it is important for work stress researchers to measure the characteristics and qualities of work stressors themselves, when it comes to understanding coping much can be gained from recognizing that the significance of a stressor cannot be understood without also exploring the meanings individuals give to stressors and how encounters are appraised (Dewe & Cooper 2007). A number of developments in our understanding of appraisal are moving the field forward (Folkman & Moskowitz 2004) and, in drawing attention to these, the hope is to encourage work stress researchers to recognize the explanatory potential of meanings and appraisals and to motivate them to contribute to this fledgling line of inquiry so that it becomes as mainstream as identifying stressors themselves.

We begin by first looking at work that extends the appraisal framework to encompass 'benefit'-related appraisals, the distinction between 'benefit-finding' as an appraisal and 'benefit-reminding' as a coping strategy (Affleck & Tennen 1996), positive reappraisals, where stressful encounters are reframed in a positive way (Folkman 1997), and stress-related growth (Park, Cohen & Murch 1996). We extend this discussion on meaning and move beyond appraisals to explore meaning-making coping strategies, where individuals 'search for meaning once a situation has been appraised as stressful' (Park & Folkman 1997, p. 122). We then draw on the work of Lepine, Podsakoff and Lepine (2006), which highlights the importance of exploring whether stressors are appraised as either hindrances or challenges. The concept of appraisal and meaning is at the heart of the stress and coping process. The message is clear for work stress researchers. Exploring the different roles that meaning plays in the stress and coping process is vital if we are to advance our understanding of the dynamics of coping.

In reviewing his early work, Lazarus (2001) describes appraisals in terms of 'harm/loss', 'threat' and 'challenge'. Harm/loss generally refers to something that has already occurred, whereas threat and challenge are mostly focused on the future. The complex relationship between these three types of appraisal means, as Lazarus (2001) suggests, that any encounter may be appraised as having elements of the different types of appraisal, although one appraisal type will predominate. The manner in which individuals appraise and give meaning to an encounter is the trigger that initiates an emotional reaction. The recognition that stress always implies emotion (Lazarus & Cohen-Charash 2001) and the shift in emphasis from stress to emotions (which we discuss later in this chapter) provide a more direct causal pathway for exploring those discrete emotions associated with different appraisals and more particularly their negative *and* positive consequences. This focus on discrete emotions drew Lazarus (2001) towards another kind of appraisal, which he describes as 'benefit' and which he argues distinguishes negative emotions from positive ones. Beneficial appraisals involve appraising an encounter in terms of the benefits accruing to important values, beliefs and goals. Positive emotions could include, for example, relief, pride, joy, hope and gratitude.

Other researchers have also been exploring the nature of appraisal, what may constitute meaning and the adaptive merit of finding meaning in a stressful encounter. While the focus of this work has been on the positive benefits that come out of situations of severe adversity, there is no doubt that these findings have an immediate relevance for work stress researchers. Affleck and Tennen (1996; Tennen & Affleck 2005) extend the concept of benefit to benefit 'finding' (appraisal) and benefit 'reminding' (coping). These authors discuss benefit finding appraisals in terms of a form of selective evaluation, where attention is focused on those beneficial qualities of the encounter as a means of helping the individual adapt and restore their sense of growth and value. Affleck and Tennen (1996) argue that the significance of these benefit finding appraisals lies in their ability to provide positive emotional well-being, making this a good reason to further explore the adaptational emotional outcomes associated with these sorts of appraisals. However, Tennen and Affleck (2005) caution researchers that there is still much to learn about benefit finding and its conceptualization. According to these authors, researchers still need to consider a number of alternative views about the nature of benefit finding, including as a personality characteristic, a reflection on individual growth and development, a statement about individual values and change or as a source of supportive comparison. Similarly, Davis, Nolen-Hoeksema and Larson (1998) suggest that in order to advance our understanding researchers need to distinguish between benefits as personal growth and benefits as defensiveness.

The transactional nature of the stress process means that there is always a fine line between appraisals and coping with the way meanings are constructed, operating at times as one or the other. Tennen and Affleck (2005) draw attention to benefit reminding as a coping strategy, which implies that taking the time to deliberately remind oneself of perceived benefits arising from a stressful encounter is considered to be coping. This effort, suggest Tennen and Affleck (1999), to relish these benefits reflects the strategic intentional qualities of coping and so represents another dimension to the adaptive value of cognitive coping. Others have also pursued the role of meaning-focused coping. The idea that people are motivated to try to make sense of stressful encounters led Davis and his colleagues (Davis, Nolen-Hoeksema & Larson 1998) to refer to the notion of sense making coping. Distinguishing benefit reminding coping from sense making coping led these authors to question just where in the coping process these different types of meaning-focused coping occur and whether positive changes through perceiving benefits, because they may take time, occur later in the coping process.

Folkman (1997) also points to the search for positive meaning as a theme that runs through coping research and draws attention to the idea that in the midst of a stressful encounter individuals instil everyday activities with positive meaning as a means of sustaining them, giving them respite and helping to restore their resources. The importance of this work lies in the fact that coping should be thought of in terms of not just managing stressful conditions but also how during such an encounter coping has the potential to sustain individuals by creating positive psychological states that help them through the experience. In terms of learning more about how coping sustains positive psychological states, Folkman (1997) points to positive reappraisal, where cognitive strategies are used to reinterpret an encounter in a positive way, reinforcing once again the richness and complexity of the coping process.

The potential for growth from stressful encounters has also been examined through the concept of stress-related growth (Park, Cohen & Murch

1996). Running through this concept is a strong developmental theme that raises the question of whether some people grow from demanding encounters (Park, Cohen & Murch 1996), enhancing their coping abilities and skills, their self-confidence, their personal and social resources and their appreciation of those things that are of value and significance in their lives. Understanding the issues surrounding the dynamics of stress-related growth, its structure and its role over time will become more complete as researchers begin to explore this more positive side of the coping process. In summary, we agree with the view expressed by Park and Folkman that 'researchers need to take a broader conceptual view of the various ways that meaning can be involved in the coping process' (1997, p. 132). For work stress researchers, this broader view would involve accepting and recognizing the role played by meanings in the stress process, meanings as appraisals and meaning as coping and the role of positive meanings.

One last point on appraisals, meanings and work stress. While work stress researchers have robustly debated the objective versus subjective measurement of work stressors (Brief & George 1991; Frese & Zapf 1999; Harris 1991; Lazarus 1991; Perrewé & Zellars 1999; Schaubroeck 1999), it is generally agreed that when it comes to measuring work stressors the common concern of most researchers has been to identify their situational characteristics, at the expense of how those characteristics may be appraised. Inconsistencies in the work stressor–strain relationship have, however, led researchers to consider whether this relationship may be better understood by exploring how individuals evaluate stressors. The premise here, as Lepine, Podsakoff and Lepine (2006) explain, is that it is now necessary to explore patterns of appraisals associated with the particular work stressors that are experienced by most workers.

Supporting this idea is the work by Cavanaugh *et al.* (2000, p. 60), who found two underlying appraisals associated with common work stressors. They describe these as 'challenge stressors' ('overcoming demands in order to achieve and gain a sense of fulfilment') and 'hindrance stressors' ('demands hindering or interfering with valued goal achievements'). It is interesting to note how these appraisals capture what Lazarus (1991) describes as threat and challenge appraisals, make it possible to explore how these two appraisals are differently related to both negative *and* positive outcomes and direct researchers away from treating work stressors as if they all have the same (negative) effects.

The Influence of Positive Psychology

It is no coincidence that one of the themes running through new developments in coping research emphasizes positive affect, helping individuals to
achieve, grow and flourish (Folkman & Moskowitz 2000). Nor is it any
coincidence that the year 2000, the beginning of the new millennium,
saw the emergence of the positive psychology movement (Seligman &
Csikszentmihalyi 2000) and the idea that it is now time for psychology
researchers to focus on and give as much attention to human strengths as
it has over its history to human frailty. Seligman and Csikszentmihalyi
(2000) argue that this focus on the science of the positive will not have to
start anew but simply requires that scientific energy and methods be redi-
rected towards a focus that has as its goal an understanding of what makes
individuals flourish. Positive psychology is about positive experiences,
developing an understanding and nurturing of those factors that allow the
individual to flourish. In short, it is about positive human functioning
(Fredrickson 2001). It embraces a number of themes, including what
makes one moment better than the next – the positive experience – the
characteristics of individual strengths, positive contexts and institutions
and how they shape positive experiences, and new ways of thinking about
mental health when viewed through the lens of positive psychology (Seligman & Csikszentmihalyi 2000). Why is positive psychology necessary? The
answer lies in the fact that it is only now that the discipline is beginning to
recognize the value of the question, accepting that little is known about
how individuals thrive and that it is time to adopt a more responsive
approach when considering human capabilities and potential (Sheldon &
King 2001).

The idea of a positive psychology movement has been robustly debated
and so we turn briefly to this debate, moving then to explore the impact
that positive psychology has had on the world of work before turning to
the idea of positive coping and the role of proactive coping. In his target
article leading off the debate in the *Psychological Inquiry*, Lazarus (2003a)
questions whether the positive psychology movement 'has legs' and draws
attention to three themes that raise issues about the nature and conceptual logic of a positive psychology movement. The first of these themes
separating positive and negative experiences leads to an artificial dichot-
omy when each needs to be integrated into a synthesis that captures the
reality of everyday experience. The second theme questions why stress and

coping are seen as a negative psychology, and the third draws attention to whether a positive psychology will succeed if it, like traditional approaches to stress and coping, does not tackle the same methodological problems that face all researchers interested in taking this type of research forward. These views are, of course, vigorously debated in the articles that follow his lead article but need, as Lazarus (2003b) suggests, to be given serious thought.

Workplaces and workplace theories have also come under the influence of the positive psychology movement and this influence has found expression through the work on positive organizational studies. The general concern of positive organizational studies has at its core the belief that to develop a fuller understanding of organizational life research should now engage more with what it is about organizational life that enables individuals to flourish and what can be learnt from this (Roberts 2006). Two themes capture the spirit of positive organizational studies: positive organizational behaviour and positive organizational scholarship. Positive organizational behaviour as discussed by Luthans (2002) refers to those positive individual strengths and capabilities that can be identified, measured and managed as a means of improving organizational performance. Luthans adds that positive approaches must be based on 'sound theory, supported by sophisticated research [that] can be effectively applied to the workplace' (p. 703) and that emphasizing performance improvement sets positive organizational behaviour apart from the more popular but less researched ideas surrounding positive personal development.

Moving on from Luthans' definition, Wright (2003) argues that if positive organizational behaviour is to make an impact then its focus on individual performance must be expanded so that the health, happiness and personal growth of employees become attainable aims in themselves. Bakker and Schaufeli (2008) add that as health and well-being are emerging as strategically important business goals they become an integral part of any description of positive organizational behaviour. Interestingly, when set against the criticism raised by Lazarus (2003a) in respect of positive psychology generally, Bakker and Schaufeli (2008) argue that positive organizational behaviour must not become one-sided but must include positive as well as negative aspects, thereby accepting the argument that the positive and negative are intimately linked and that adaptive strengths flow from both (Fineman 2006). Nevertheless, the enduring emphasis on the negative continues to act as a strong motivational force for those wishing to broaden our understanding of the positive aspects of organizational life. Positive organizational behaviour does not diminish what has gone before, but simply offers a mode of inquiry that not only has the power to expand research horizons but also can be judged against the contribution it makes (Luthans & Avolio 2009; Wright & Quick 2009).

The spirit of positive psychology can also be found in the second strand to the field of positive organizational studies: positive organizational scholarship. The primary focus of positive organizational scholarship is the workplace. Its aim is to study the ways in which organizations and employees 'flourish and prosper in especially favourable ways' and the mechanisms through which this positiveness occurs. Positive scholarship encourages researchers to explore what is 'going right' in organizations, what can be learnt from human flourishing and the possibilities that exist for bringing out the best in employees and organizations (Roberts 2006, p. 293). Concerns are raised about whether positive organizational scholarship depicts a complete picture of organizational life, the sorts of behaviours that may flow from such a focus, their appropriateness and the standards they set (Roberts 2006). The rejoinder emphasizes the developmental theme, that employees and organizations have the capacity for improving, that there is significant value in understanding individual flourishing as well as the dynamics of building capabilities and that growth can flow from adversity.

The importance of these two strands to positive organizational studies lies in the argument that the time has come for work stress researchers to expand their horizons and begin to investigate the positive side of work so that a more complete picture emerges of the nature of work and its meanings (Turner, Barling & Zacharatos 2005). Roberts (2006) reiterates that the positive and the negative are absolutely inseparable, and taken together provide a greater understanding of organizations and those who work in them, so it is now time to give the same emphasis to the positive as has traditionally been given to the negative.

One final issue is the concept of psychological capital described by Luthans and Avolio (2009), which has emerged out of the focus on positive organizational behaviour. Luthans *et al.* (2007) use the term 'psychological capital' to represent those positive resources and 'individual motivational propensities that accrue through positive psychological constructs such as efficacy, optimism, hope and resilience' (2007, p. 542). These authors argue that positive constructs like efficacy, optimism, hope and resilience all have a common positive core that reflects an individual's psychological capital.

Such a resource allows individuals to 'better weather the storm' (Luthans *et al.* 2007, p. 568) and provides organizations with the opportunity to consider how best to invest in such capital.

The concept of psychological capital resonates with the work of Hobfoll (1998) and his conservation of resources theory. Hobfoll (1998) presents a resource-based theory of coping based around the premise that coping strategies can be distinguished from each other depending on whether they generally deplete or accumulate resources. While there is debate around the extent to which Hobfoll's theory adds to our understanding of coping (Lazarus 2001), its importance lies in the fact that it points to the positive nature of resource accumulation as against the more 'negative' aspects of resource depletion/loss and through this distinction the need to explore both types of resources, their relationship with one another and the sort of coping that is associated with each.

From Positive Psychology to Proactive Coping

When thinking about proactive coping and its qualities, it is important to have a context within which to place such ideas. It is possible to identify a number of developments that may have prompted researchers to explore the idea of positive coping as reflected in the concept of proactive coping (Dewe 2008). The theme running through each of the different developments aims to encourage researchers to think more broadly about coping, its nature and those processes through which individuals' lives are enriched. The work on *personal strivings* (Schwarzer & Taubert 2002) and the more recent attention given to positive emotions and the coping strategies that generate them (Folkman & Moskowitz 2003; Fredrickson 2001) all fall under the general rubric of positive psychology and the need to understand more about positive experiences and positive human functioning. The origins of these ideas can, of course, be traced back to developments before positive psychology was more formally inaugurated (Seligman & Csik-szentmihalyi 2000). The term 'proactive coping' was first described by Aspinwall and Taylor in 1997. There is little doubt, however, that much of the interest in positive coping has been stimulated by the interest in positive experiences and factors that allow individuals to flourish, all of which help to define the positive psychology movement. At the same time, Hobfoll's (2001) idea of resource accumulation, described as a strikingly appealing concept that must enhance stress and coping research (Schwarzer

2001), has also helped to broaden our understanding of coping and ener-gize researchers to explore the role of capacity building resources and their positive benefits.

Drawing on these different developments, it is possible to reflect on the qualities that best characterize positive coping (see Dewe 2008). These qualities include positive appraisals and meanings that generate positive emotions, coping strategies that are forward looking and directed towards resource accumulation, personal growth and capacity building, and posi-tive emotions that 'broaden an individual's thought and action repertoire and thereby build the individual's enduring personal resources' (Fredrick-son 2001, p. 219). As has been previously noted (Dewe 2008), while the aim here is to explore new developments in coping and positive coping as one of those new developments, this should not be taken as a criticism that coping research to date has not been positive in its outlook or that elements of positive coping haven't been identified. As Lazarus (2003a) points out, there is no problem with emphasizing the need to focus on the positive, but this should not be done at the expense of the negative since one is intimately linked to the other. Once coping strategies are considered within the context of a stressful encounter, it is somewhat more difficult to determine just how that coping strategy is being used, what the intentions of the individual are and how best to determine whether it was positive or negative. Coping research needs to be investi-gated from a range of perspectives using new and innovative methodolo-gies and new developments. Positive coping should, as Folkman and Moskowitz (2003) suggest, represent more of a catch-up phase for a per-spective that has, in recent years, received a less than complete treatment by work stress researchers.

If proactive coping best reflects positive coping, then what is proactive coping and how does it differ from other coping strategies? Proactive coping has at its core improving an individual's quality of life (Greenglass 2002). It is defined as 'an effort to build up general resources that facilitate promotion towards challenging goals and personal growth' (Schwarzer 2001, p. 406). Essentially, it is the idea that, because proactive coping is oriented to the future, it can be distinguished from the more traditional forms of coping, where the emphasis is on reacting to stressful encounters that have already occurred. A more detailed analysis of proactive coping suggests a number of distinguishing features (Aspinwall & Taylor 1997; Greenglass 2002; Schwarzer 2001, 2004). Set within the idea that proactive copers have a vision where self-initiated constructive actions create opportunities for growth and improvements in their quality of life (Schwarzer 2001), proactive coping is all about positive appraisals involving challenges and goal achievement and strategies that accumulate resources and acquire skills that forearm and prepare (Aspinwall & Taylor 1997), that emphasize goal management rather than risk management (Greenglass 2002) and that result in performance levels that are personally meaningful and provide purpose (Schwarzer 2004). In short, what motivates proactive copers is the belief that change brings with it the rich potential for individual improvement (Greenglass 2002).

When discussing proactive coping, reviewers (e.g. Greenglass 2002; Schwarzer 2001, 2004) generally contrast it to *reactive* coping (dealing with a stressful encounter that has happened) but also with *anticipatory* coping (dealing with an impending demand) and *preventative* coping, where the emphasis is on preparing to deal with possible demands. Anticipatory and preventative coping are, like proactive coping, future-oriented and all three deserve attention (Folkman & Moskowitz 2004). It is interesting to consider the potentially proactive 'capacity building' element of preventative coping (Dewe 2008). While preventative coping is described more in terms of preparing for something threatening that may perhaps happen (Schwarzer & Taubert 2002), it still embodies an element of resource capacity and resilience building captured through such activities as exercise, meditation, relaxation and a more balanced philosophy of life. All of these techniques are designed to create an inner sense of well-being that provides a greater capacity to deal with a stressful encounter should one arise. Whether these techniques share the qualities of resourcefulness, self-improvement and personal growth is a moot point, but they do highlight the need to continue to develop empirically our understanding of these forms of coping, their nature and characteristics and how they are measured (Greenglass 2002; Greenglass & Fiksenbaum 2009; Roesch *et al.* 2009).

Other Developments in Coping

While we have focused on positive psychology, and proactive coping in particular, other forms of coping have also been singled out as representing new developments in coping research. Folkman and Moskowitz (2004) make the point that while traditionally coping research has focused primarily on individualistic approaches the social aspects of coping have not received the attention they deserve. Although there has been much work on social support and its role as a coping strategy (Dewe & Cooper 2007), researchers are now being urged to broaden this work and to explore the whole notion of relationship coping. As this work broadens beyond traditional aspects of social support, terms such as 'interpersonal', 'communal', 'relationship-focused' and 'collaborative' coping all emerge as new developments (Berg *et al.* 2008, p. 505). These types of coping emphasize the social context and developing social interactions into a positive resource. Communal coping, for example, explores how others may be influenced by or react to different coping strategies (Folkman & Moskowitz 2004), whereas collaborative coping looks at the pooling of resources and cooperative ways of problem-solving (Berg *et al.* 2008).

Reviewers have also turned their attention to issues around emotion-focused coping (Folkman & Moskowitz 2004). Pointing to the way emotion-focused coping has been measured, the broad range of strategies it covers and its frequent association with maladaptive outcomes, Stanton, Parsa and Austenfeld (2005) explored the adaptive potential of coping through emotion approach. These authors located their work among the 'newer functionalist approaches' where the emphasis is on the adaptive nature of emotions (Stanton *et al.* 2000, p. 1150). Building on emotion-focused coping, they recommend that researchers now explore the approach-oriented adaptive functions of emotional processing and emotional expression. 'Emotional processing' refers to acknowledging and arriving at an understanding of one's emotions, whereas emotional expression refers to both interpersonal and intrapersonal forms of expressing emotions. A key to both these functions and their outcome is the issue of intention and the requirement that each is used in a conscious and purposeful way (Stanton, Parsa & Austenfeld 2005).

Under the heading of new developments, reviewers also point to the attention now being given to religious coping and its role in providing individuals with the resolve to endure and to find 'meaning and purpose' (Folkman & Moskowitz 2004, p. 759). Meaning and searching for meaning is another aspect of coping that has, as already mentioned, attracted the attention of researchers (Park & Folkman 1997). Many questions still remain for those wishing to explore meaning-based coping, not the least of which include their relationship to positive emotions, how they should best be classified and how they should be measured (Folkman 2008). Seeking meaning is, as Baumeister and Vohs (2005) suggest, an integral part of positive psychology and investigating how individuals search for and find meaning in their lives is fundamental to understanding the human experience. Interestingly, Snyder (1999) suggests that if researchers are to facilitate our understanding of adaptive functioning more emphasis should be given to exploring what it is that seems to block or hinder people from engaging in more adaptive ways of behaving. Snyder argues that such behaviours result in a huge personal and social cost that blights people's ability to develop, flourish and achieve a sense of life satisfaction.

All the new developments we and other reviewers have discussed in respect of coping research acknowledge the need to broaden our understanding of coping by recognizing the importance of meaning and its role as an appraisal, a coping strategy and a reappraisal. This theme of broadening our understanding of coping extends still further to exploring both the positive as well as the negative, what type of coping generates positive emotions, growth, fulfilment and purpose and how individuals flourish, accumulate resources and maximize their potential. Development also requires new questions to be asked that go beyond how frequently coping strategies are used to how they are used, why they are used in that way and what they are trying to achieve. Underlying all of this is the need to constantly ask where our traditional methodologies are taking us and how, if we wish to capture the richness and complexity of the coping process, we must now become creative and innovative in the methods we use to capture this diverse and powerful construct.

Running almost in parallel to work stress and coping research is the work on leisure as a coping strategy. While leisure, stress and coping have been described as 'an important area of enquiry' (Iwasaki & Schneider 2003, p. 108), this field has developed a sense of vibrancy and importance simply because leisure plays an important part in people's lives, has clear associations with health and well-being, and has significant theoretical and practical implications for coping research (Iwasaki 2003). Much can be gained through collaboration between leisure, stress and coping researchers. Considerable discussion surrounds the term 'leisure' and its meaning since it was first defined in terms of free time (Brightbill 1960; Cushman & Laidler 1990; Gray 1974; Trenberth & Dewe 2005). While definitions have moved between the objective nature of leisure based around different types of leisure activities and its subjective nature as a state of mind or meaning, more contemporary definitions prefer to define it more broadly so as to provide a definitional context where leisure can be explored in terms of its function, relevance and meaning in people's lives (Parr & Lashua 2004). In getting to grips with the nature of leisure, researchers have explored how individuals construct different meanings of leisure (Watkins 2000; Watkins & Bond 2007), its role as a resource in overcoming negative life events (Kleiber, Hutchinson & Williams 2002), its spiritual functions (Heintzman & Mannell 2003) and the insights that emerge from viewing leisure as a coping strategy (Schneider & Wilhelm Stanis 2007).

The view that leisure has an important coping function is well supported in the leisure literature (Coleman & Iso-Ahola 1993). In attempting to understand the different ways leisure may help people cope, Iwasaki and Mannell (2000) suggest a two-dimensional approach, distinguishing between 'leisure coping beliefs' and 'leisure coping strategies'. The former describes more general beliefs about how leisure helps in coping with stress, whereas leisure coping strategies are context-specific coping behaviours or cognitions derived through leisure activities. In this way leisure acts as a coping resource as well as a coping strategy (Iwasaki & Schneider 2003). Reinforcing the role of leisure as both a coping strategy and a coping resource, Kleiber, Hutchinson and Williams (2002) distinguish between the benefits of leisure as a coping strategy and the value of leisure as a coping resource, where leisure operates as a means of positive transformation which provides opportunities for self-development.

The complexity and multifaceted role of leisure as a coping strategy is further illustrated by the meanings individuals give to active leisure when describing it within a stress context. Active leisure is seen as something more than just physical activity and embraces a wide range of less physical forms, including spiritual, social, cultural and empowerment activities, suggesting that less physical aspects of leisure should not be underestimated in the role that they play in helping to define active leisure (Iwasaki *et al.* 2006). Similarly, Iwasaki, Mactavish and Mackay (2005, p. 81) identify a number of roles leisure plays in coping with stress, including acting as a 'positive diversion or time-out', an opportunity for energizing and renewal, the promotion of life balance and as a facilitator of 'resilience and the capacity to proactively cope with or counteract stress'. Trenberth and Dewe (2002) explore different reasons for using leisure as a coping strategy and the relationship between leisure and different emotions. They suggest that leisure may be used in a compensatory, distracting or intrinsically motivating way. More recently, the role of leisure as a coping strategy has been discussed by those involved in providing therapeutic recreation services. These services help clients to

learn more about the coping benefits of leisure, to develop their repertoire and range of leisure activities that are agreed as personally beneficial and to show how these activities help to build up their resources
(Hutchinson, Bland & Kleiber 2008).

It is clear that many similarities exist between the work on leisure and
coping and mainstream work stress and coping research. It is also clear
that leisure coping research faces the same methodological and conceptual
issues in terms of how coping should be measured, the meanings given to
different leisure activities and how they are used to cope with stress. As
work stress research expands its focus to embrace work–life balance and
work–non-work spillover (see Chapter 5) then the idea that coping with
work stress is not simply something that occurs at work will gain even
greater significance and draw researchers towards exploring coping from
these different perspectives. To advance our understanding of the depth
and range of coping strategies and the various roles they perform, it is
clearly essential for researchers to investigate interactions between various
forms of coping.

Progress towards Understanding Coping Effectiveness

Somerfield and McCrae (2000) state that the aim of coping research must
be to identify those ways of coping that 'are best' for managing stressful
encounters. While researchers have not ignored the issue of coping effectiveness, it seems that one way to explain the variability across findings is
to reflect on whether current research pays too little attention to the transactional nature of stress, particularly the role of primary appraisal (Cooper,
Dewe & O'Driscoll 2001; Dewe & Cooper 2007), relies somewhat too much
on inference, describing implicitly different coping strategies as being more
or less effective (Dewe & Cooper 2007), fails to consider the context within
which coping takes place (Folkman & Moskowitz 2000) and ignores the
knowledge that can be gained by looking to other areas of psychology
(Somerfield & McCrae 2000).

Current research may also have failed to sufficiently acknowledge the
role of individual differences not just in terms of predispositions but also
in terms of goals and values (Coyne & Racioppo 2000; Suls, David &
Harvey 1996), sets unrealistic expectations about just how effective coping
strategies may be (Somerfield & McCrae 2000) and over-emphasizes the
search for universally effective coping strategies (Lazarus 1999). Neverthe-

less, two approaches guide researchers in relation to coping effectiveness (Folkman & Moskowitz 2000, 2004). The first focuses on the link between positive outcomes and effective coping. The second centres on the 'goodness of fit' between characteristics of the encounter and coping. In this case, the better the fit, the more effective the coping.

The first issue confronting researchers is what is meant by 'coping effectiveness'. That is, what criteria do individuals use to judge coping effectiveness, do such judgements change from encounter to encounter, when are those judgements made, are such judgements different from reappraisals and what contextual and personal factors influence such judgements? There is also the need to distinguish between resolution and conclusion (Folkman & Moskowitz 2004) and what that means when evaluating effectiveness. In many ways the issue of what is effective coping is captured in the dictum of effectiveness 'for whom' and 'at what cost'. Researchers have had respondents indicate, across a range of possibilities, whether coping helped to resolve the encounter (Koeske, Kirk & Koeske 1993) and asked respondents to distinguish between using a coping strategy and judging how effective it was (Bar-Tal & Spitzer 1994). This work points to individuals being able to make judgements as to effective coping but still leaves open the issue of what is meant by an encounter being resolved or in what way coping is being used effectively. Of course, there is also the question of who is best placed to make a judgement about coping effectiveness (Folkman & Moskowitz 2004). If coping measures do not distinguish between coping effort and coping effectiveness, and that they may need to be redesigned to 'reflect the quantitative manner' in which a strategy is used (Aldwin 2000, p. 158), this may prompt research to adopt more of an emotional narrative approach (Lazarus 1999), letting participants themselves describe what they mean by effective coping, thereby providing insights into the nature of coping effectiveness.

Coping effectiveness must inevitably be judged in terms of the context within which it occurs. Viewing coping effectiveness in this way requires researchers to consider a number of issues that surround the outcome being measured and expectations about what outcomes can be achieved (Dewe & Cooper 2007). It is important to determine the appropriate outcome in terms of the coping strategies being used (Aldwin 2000). This concern emerges from what reviewers refer to as the uncritical approach to selecting outcomes, where there is little attempt by researchers to consider just how appropriate such outcomes may be (Somerfield & McCrae 2000), a practice undoubtedly encouraged by the way in which researchers have interpreted the rather blunt term of 'being under stress' as providing a licence to measure any outcome that falls within that general rubric (Dewe & Cooper 2007). Hence the call for researchers to give more attention to discrete emotions as a more focused pathway to understanding the dynamics of coping (Lazarus 2001; Lazarus & Cohen-Charash 2001), recognizing that coping effectiveness promotes both positive and negative emotions (Lazarus 2000), accepting the need to be more selective and discriminating when considering which outcome to measure (Dewe & Cooper 2007). Researchers need also to consider as an alternative to outcomes the goal or goals an individual has in mind when coping with a stressful encounter (Aldwin 2000) and to acknowledge that how a stressful event is appraised and given meaning will influence not just coping but also what outcomes are trying to be achieved (Dewe 2001).

The dynamic nature of coping adds a further complexity when considering outcomes. Patterns of coping strategy may support one another or provide correcting, adjusting, fallback or inhibiting functions (Dewe 2003). It is also the case that a coping strategy may influence one but not another outcome (Zeidner & Saklofske 1996). So when patterns of coping activities are explored in relation to a particular outcome, the way coping patterns are formed and the nature of the relationship between the different coping strategies makes understanding coping effectiveness more complex. The richness of the coping process expressed through various contextual influences also makes determining coping effectiveness difficult. Individual differences will, for example, influence not just the choice of a strategy but also how competently it may be used (Suls, David & Harvey 1996). Different situations require different types of coping, suggesting that coping flexibility also must be part of any judgement evaluating effectiveness (Folkman & Moskowitz 2004) and that to understand coping effectiveness requires a careful analysis of the situation itself (O'Brien & DeLongis 1996), not just in terms of goals, values, supports and controls but also, as mentioned, in terms of appraisals and meanings against which coping is initiated. Much of this complexity will require new methods and new ways of evaluating coping effectiveness.

Nevertheless, if our understanding of coping effectiveness is to be advanced, it is important to acknowledge that describing coping strategies as either problem- or emotion-focused is substantively different from determining their effectiveness, that the issue is not about whether one coping strategy is better than another, that the same coping strategy can produce both positive and negative outcomes, that coping and outcomes need to be more carefully thought through and that coping effectiveness should best be investigated within the context of a stressful encounter. Somerfield and McCrae (2000) suggest that it is just as important to move towards more realistic expectations about coping and coping effectiveness, accepting that individual efforts alone may not always solve problems, that people spend years learning how to cope and that how people cope has a lot to do with who they are.

From Stress to Emotions to Positive Emotions and Coping

It is clear by now that emotions are assuming an increasingly important role in the study of coping. A number of reasons account for this: the concern and critical debate that constantly surrounds the term 'stress' and its meaning, its usefulness as anything other than a general rubric and its bluntness in respect of explaining affective responses (Cooper, Dewe & O'Driscoll 2001), the fact that emotions profoundly influence behaviour at work (Pekrun & Frese 1992), that emotions best capture and reveal the dynamics of the coping process (Lazarus & Cohen-Charash 2001), the influence of the positive psychology movement with its focus on positive emotions (Seligman & Csikszentmihalyi 2000), the growing understanding of positive affect and positive emotions (Fredrickson 2001) and the growing awareness of the presence of positive emotions in the coping process (Folkman & Moskowitz 2004). In summary, stress generates emotional consequences – 'stress always implies emotions' (Lazarus & Cohen-Charash 2001, p. 53). In terms of potential causal pathways, it is now more useful to explore the role of discrete emotions in the coping process, since emotions offer a rich source of information about what is actually happening to a person (Lazarus 2001). The 'implacable logic' of the transactional nature of stress is, as already discussed, that it is emotion centred in the sense that at its core is the link between what one is thinking (meanings/appraisal) and the emotion being experienced (Lazarus 2001). To conclude this chapter, we now turn to explore the nature of positive emotions and the role of these emotions in the coping process.

Fredrickson (1998, 2005) suggests that positive emotions not only contribute to the richness and quality of people's lives but also have an adaptive significance, facilitating approach behaviours that energize individuals to engage with their environment. These qualities distinguish them from negative emotions (Fredrickson 2001). To better capture the nature of positive emotions, Fredrickson (2001) developed the *broaden-and-build theory* of positive emotions. According to this theory, positive emotions have the ability to 'broaden people's momentary thought-action repertoires' motivating them to engage in a wider range of 'thoughts and actions than is typical' (Fredrickson & Branigan 2005, p. 314). Broadening these thought-actions is important because it builds lasting personal resources, which have the capability to function as reserves that can be drawn on at a later stage to enhance coping and build capacity in a way that allows people to transform themselves (Fredrickson 2005). Positive emotions also aid in helping to undo lingering negative emotions, build resiliency and improve well-being (Fredrickson 2001). Fredrickson (2005) positions her theory alongside the transactional ideas of Lazarus (1999) by referring to these emotions as being initiated by the meanings (appraisals) individuals give to an encounter.

Taking up the argument for investigating positive emotions, Lazarus and Cohen-Charash (2001) illustrate that positive emotions must be considered a discrete group, since contrasting them with negative emotions diminishes the distinctive qualities of these emotions particularly in terms of their antecedents, subjective experience and behavioural consequences. They suggest that positive emotions include happiness, pride, relief, hope, love, gratitude and compassion. The importance of exploring positive emotions as discrete entities becomes even more significant when these emotions are considered in relation to the transactional nature of stress. As Lazarus (2001) argues, how one appraises a stressful encounter operates as the link between this meaning and how one acts or feels, in this way uniting coping with the emotion process. The link may, as Lazarus suggests, be so strong that each emotion comes with its own core relational theme or meaning, making the study of appraisals a fundamental part of any investigation involving coping and emotions.

The manner in which individuals use meaning as part of the coping process has, as we discussed earlier, highlighted the significant adaptational qualities of positive emotions and that even in the most dreadful encounter positive emotions do co-occur with negative emotions, imbuing such encounters with positive meaning (Folkman & Moskowitz 2000). Evidence also suggests that in such dreadful encounters people consciously search out meanings that lead to positive emotions, providing not just a breathing space but also the opportunity to rebuild resources that maintain coping (Folkman & Moskowitz 2004). Learning more about the adaptational qualities of positive emotions, asking 'what are the coping processes that people use to generate positive affect in the midst of stress' (Folkman & Moskowitz 2000, p. 652) and investigating the crucial role of meanings, appraisals, coping and positive emotions are all necessary if coping research is to move forward.

Underlying the issues we have discussed in this chapter is the inescapable demand to develop new, innovative and creative ways to explore the wealth of what coping research has to offer. Researchers have responded to this demand and in doing so have offered explanatory pathways that call for our understanding of what constitutes coping to be broadened to allow a range of new types of coping to emerge that better capture the notion of problem- and emotion-focused coping, recognizing that only by examining these strategies in context can we begin to move from mere description to asking new questions that tackle issues like 'Why is the strategy being used?', 'In what way (how) is it being used?', 'What is expected to be achieved?' and 'How is its effectiveness assessed?'. Within that context of the coping process researchers, particularly those exploring a work setting, need to recognize the fundamental role of meanings generally and their particular significance in helping to define and describe appraisals, coping and reappraisals. In addition, coping research can only benefit by emphasizing the role of emotions, exploring the role of both positive and negative emotions and giving now as much attention to how people thrive and flourish as has been given to anxieties and illness. It is clear from the history of coping research that none of this will be easy, but it is equally clear that this broader perspective is critical for developing more comprehensive models of work-related stress, coping and well-being.

4

Coping with Specific
Work-Related Stressors

In previous chapters we have discussed the nature and major functions of coping and how coping operates in work settings, emphasizing the important relationship between coping behaviours and emotions. The present chapter addresses the question of how individuals attempt to deal with specific kinds of stressor that they encounter in their work lives. Clearly, coping behaviours are not enacted in isolation and, while the social psychological literature on coping is very pertinent to an understanding of coping with work stressors, we need to investigate the specific forms of coping that people utilize when they confront particular stressors at work.

There have been several efforts to develop classifications of the different kinds of work stressor that individuals may be exposed to. As has been described earlier, Lazarus and Folkman (1984) argue that strain (or distress) arises when environmental demands, pressures or constraints are perceived (appraised) by the person as exceeding his or her resources or capacities to manage them. Research on job-related stressors or hazards, to use the terminology favoured by Cox and his associates (see, for example, Cox et al. 2007), has built upon this perspective, along with others such as Karasek's (1979) job demands/control model. These and other accounts of the stress coping process illustrate the importance of exploring the nature and scope of environmental factors which impinge upon individuals and hence potentially induce strain and diminish psychological well-being. A schema of occupational stressors proposed initially by Cooper and Marshall (1976) and later updated by Cartwright and Cooper (1997) offers a useful classification framework which includes six general categories of work-related stressors:

Coping with Work Stress: A Review and Critique, Philip J. Dewe, Michael P. O'Driscoll and Cary L. Cooper, © 2010 John Wiley & Sons Ltd.

1. Factors intrinsic to the job itself. These include the physical environment, workloads, working hours, use of technologies, and exposure to risks or hazards.
2. Roles in the organization, which encompass variables such as role responsibilities, role ambiguity, role conflict and role overload.
3. Social relationships at work, such as those with supervisors, colleagues and clients or customers.
4. Career development. This category includes job insecurity, perceived under- or over-promotion and feelings of lack of achievement of one's career goals or ambitions.
5. Organizational factors. These can be wide-ranging, encompassing the formal structure of the organization, the political climate within the firm or company, organizational policies (e.g. on hiring and promotion) and their impact on perceived justice in the organization. The lack of effective participation in decision-making processes is a frequently cited organizational stressor, along with overly bureaucratic structures which inhibit flexibility and innovation. Inappropriate and ineffective communication strategies (especially on the part of management) have also been reported as significant contributors to employee strain. The above factors are often considered aspects of either the culture or the climate of the organization.
6. The work–home interface. Conflict or interference between work and (for instance) family life has been consistently found to be a major stressor for many workers.

The above categories of stressors (hazards) provide a valuable starting point for explorations of coping with work-related difficulties and problems. In the present chapter we will focus on stressors which belong in the first five of these categories. The final category (the work–home interface) is dealt with separately in Chapter 5, given its prominence in recent literature and evidence that managing the work–home interface is an increasing challenge for workers in the twenty-first century. The present chapter concentrates on coping with potential stressors which reside in the workplace itself, rather than those which intersect work and 'non-work' domains.

To develop this chapter we conducted an extensive search of the empirical research on coping with specific work-related stressors. Our expectation was that we might construct a matrix of stressors × coping strategies, to identify the kinds of strategy which had been most frequently studied in relation to each of the above stressor categories, as well as any evidence on their effectiveness. This proved to be an unrealistic goal, since much of the research in this field did not describe the specific nature of the stressor(s) investigated or did not align the coping strategies with specific stressors. For instance, there have been numerous studies of work demands and pressures, often based upon Karasek's job demands/control model, but frequently work 'demands' are treated as a global construct, rather than as differentiating various types of demand. Nevertheless, some stressors have been systematically explored in relation to coping, and we will discuss these later in the chapter. We begin, however, with an overview of coping models and typologies which have been utilized in research on coping with work stressors.

Types of Coping

As we have discussed previously in this book, the transactional model of stress coping, outlined initially by Lazarus (1966) and further elaborated upon by Lazarus and Folkman (1984), has been a major platform for empirical research on coping with work-related stressors. In Chapter 1 we explained the basic dynamics of the transactional model, including its emphasis on cognitive appraisal as a core component of coping. To restate briefly, Lazarus and Folkman suggest that there are two dimensions of appraisal, the first (primary appraisal) being an assessment by the individual of whether an event, person or object poses a potential threat to their well-being, and the second (secondary appraisal) being the person's evaluation of the resources available to them to deal with the threat and what possible courses of action they might take. The essence of the transactional approach to stress is that 'stress relates to those *transactions* where environmental demands are perceived as challenging or taxing the individual's ability to cope, thus threatening well-being and necessitating individual effort to resolve the problem' (Dewe, Cox & Ferguson 1993, p. 6, italics in original).

Cognitive appraisal provides stressful encounters or transactions with meaning. Primary appraisal is essentially a process by which the person determines what is at stake for them in the situation. Is the transaction one which will threaten their (physical, psychological or social) well-being or does it, conversely, offer them a challenge which they can confront with some level of confidence and which may enhance their well-being? Or is it one which does not impinge in any way at all on their functioning, in other words is neutral in respect of their well-being? People therefore infuse meaning into their transactions with their environment. Meaning is also a major issue in respect of secondary appraisal, especially as the choice of coping reactions will shape the nature of the transaction between the person and his/her environment, and will have significant implications for their subsequent levels of stress and well-being.

Dewe, Cox and Ferguson (1993) note an important distinction between coping *behaviours* (or strategies) and coping *styles*. Coping strategies are behaviours directed towards specific stressors. For example, one may endeavour to manage excessive work demands by using time management (see later for a discussion of this strategy) or delegation of tasks to other people. These are very specific behaviours intended to reduce the particular stressor (overload). Coping styles, on the other hand, reflect relatively consistent or habitual ways of dealing with stressors generally. For instance, some people may generally deal with stressors in their work-life by confronting them head-on, using a problem-focused approach to resolve the problems they are dealing with. Others may take a more hands-off approach, perhaps using various kinds of emotion-focused coping to assuage their concerns about the significance of the issues. There is some evidence that individuals do display coping styles, although strategies may also vary depending on the nature of the specific work-related stressors (O'Driscoll, Brough & Kalliath 2009).

In a relatively recent review and critique of coping research in general, Folkman and Moskowitz (2004) note that several different typologies or models of coping behaviours (strategies) have been constructed over the years. Some of these have been based on empirical research on actual behaviours of people dealing with stressors, for example using the critical incident methodology elucidated by Flanagan (1954), whereas others have been theoretically generated in the first instance and then tested empirically. The Lazarus–Folkman model, which as noted earlier provided a launching pad for much of the following research on stress coping, identifies two primary coping strategies: problem-focused coping and emotion-focused coping. These were discussed in some detail in Chapter 2. The primary distinction between them is that problem-focused coping endeavours to change the situation, whereas emotion-focused coping focuses on modifying the person's perceptions, cognitions and emotions. As we described in Chapter 2, neither strategy is inherently more valuable or effective than the other, and each may be more appropriate for different circumstances. Folkman and Moskowitz suggest that problem-focused coping is more advantageous when the situation is (at least to some extent) controllable, but when the person cannot exert significant control over the stressor, that is their efforts may not effect much if any change in the stressor, emotion-focused coping may be more effective.

An intriguing notion is that some forms of coping may have both positive and negative outcomes for a person. For instance, Folkman and Moskowitz cite research by Wu *et al.* (1993) which found that doctors who coped by accepting responsibility for their actions were more likely to change their practices (i.e. use problem-focused coping) which led to improved performance, but at the same time this problem-focused coping induced more strain in the physician. By way of contrast, it is sometimes suggested that emotion-focused coping (or variants of it) is ineffective in the longer term, because it leads to no change in the stressor which is threatening the person's well-being. However, in uncontrollable situations where endeavouring to change the stressor may further frustrate the person and lead them to feel incompetent, an emotion-focused strategy may indeed be an effective way of coping. Based on this and other evidence of the mixed effects of coping strategies, it would be too simplistic to argue that one strategy (e.g. problem-focused coping) leads to uniformly better outcomes than another (e.g. emotion-focused coping).

Other coping researchers have developed alternative typologies to the problem-focused/emotion-focused duality proposed by Lazarus and Folkman. Many of these alternative models have been attempts to expand the range of coping behaviours included or to elaborate on the kinds of behaviour that may be classified as problem-focused or emotion-focused, and they are not necessarily incompatible with the problem-focused/ emotion-focused distinction. For instance, Billings and Moos (1981, 1984) suggested a tripartite conceptualization of coping:

- *Active cognitive coping:* adopting a positive outlook on the situation; thinking about alternative courses of action.
- *Active behavioural coping:* consulting with other people about how to handle the situation; trying to find out more about the situation; taking positive steps to address the problem.
- *Avoidance:* ignoring the situation; deflecting attention to other issues; engaging in distracting activities.

Clearly, the first two of these strategies are variants of problem-focused coping, whereas the third is a form of emotion-focused coping, which entails trying to ignore the impact of the stressor. Folkman and Lazarus (1985) had themselves subdivided emotion-focused coping into subtypes, including wishful thinking, distancing (psychologically isolating oneself from the stressor), emphasizing positive aspects of the situation, self-blame and use of tension reduction to alleviate strain. Different types of problem-focused coping were also identified, such as confrontive coping, seeking social support, planful problem-solving (Folkman *et al.* 1986). Similarly, a frequently utilized instrument (aptly named the COPE) developed by Carver, Scheier and Weintraub (1989) also embodied aspects of both problem-focused and emotion-focused coping:

- *Active coping:* planning, acting on the stressor.
- *Avoidance coping:* as described above, but also including mental disengagement.
- *Support:* seeking instrumental or socio-emotional support.
- *Positive cognitive restructuring:* positive reinterpretation of the meaning of the situation; using humour; acceptance of the situation.

Whereas the above categorizations were derived predominantly from theoretical arguments, other researchers have developed models of coping based upon empirically derived categories of coping behaviours. A good example of this approach is research conducted by Amirkhan (1990), who factor analysed people's responses to 161 coping items and from this analysis came up with a three-factor solution which incorporated problem-solving, seeking social support and avoidance. Again, the first two categories can be viewed as subsets of problem-focused coping, whereas avoidance is clearly a form of emotion-focused coping.

Another form of coping which has received considerable attention is what has been referred to as 'proactive coping' (Aspinwall & Taylor 1997). Aspinwall and Taylor suggest that this type of coping 'consists of efforts undertaken in advance of a potentially stressful event to prevent it or modify its form before it occurs' (p. 417). This function therefore distinguishes proactive from other (reactive) forms of coping which are enacted after the person has encountered a stressor. The aim of proactive coping is to either prevent the stressor from occurring in the first place and/or to reduce its potential impact on the person. Typically, this is achieved through the acquisition of resources and skills which will prepare the person to tackle stressors when they arise. According to Aspinwall and Taylor, proactive coping is therefore almost always 'active' rather than 'passive'. Interestingly, despite its intuitive appeal and the persuasive arguments advanced for the efficacy of this coping approach, very few empirical studies have investigated the utilization of this form of coping with work-related stressors. Although numerous studies have examined 'active' coping, this is not synonymous with proactive coping.

In a systematic review of stress coping typologies, Skinner *et al.* (2003) analysed 100 different measures of coping behaviours, which included around 400 different coping behaviours. From this analysis, they derived a number of 'families' of coping responses. Several of these were derived from the Ways of Coping Checklist which Lazarus and Folkman had developed to assess problem-focused and emotion-focused coping. Major elements of problem-focused coping are planning and decision-making, problem-solving, seeking social support (especially practical assistance) and taking direct action to address the stressor. Emotion-focused coping, on the other hand, is characterized by a variety of features, some of which may be positive and others negative in their effects. Emphasizing positive aspects of the situation and positive reappraisal of the meaning and significance of the stressor exemplify emotion-focused strategies that may generate positive outcomes from a stressful transaction. Potentially less efficacious strategies are escape-avoidance, wishful thinking, self-blame and suppression. A final type of emotion-focused coping is acceptance/resignation, which may or may not be effective, depending on the controllability of the stressor. In most cases it may be argued that such an approach would not represent an effective strategy for dealing with stressors; however, in a situation such as terminal illness or chronic disability, where the individual has no influence over the source of stress (e.g. an unremitting illness or disability), acceptance and resignation may indeed be valuable devices for coming to terms with the reality that one is confronting.

From their review and analyses, Skinner *et al.* (2003) recommend abandonment of the three most common distinctions between coping strategies, that is problem-focused versus emotion-focused, approach versus avoidance and cognitive versus behavioural. In their view, coping is more complex and intricate than is implied by these distinctions and (as noted above) several different kinds of behaviour may fit into each of these labels. Instead, Skinner *et al.* suggest a hierarchical system of categories of coping which encompasses 13 higher-order categories (or 'families') of coping behaviour: problem-solving, support-seeking, escape, distraction, cognitive restructuring, rumination, helplessness, social withdrawal, emotional regulation, information-seeking, negotiation, opposition and delegation.

(Curiously, 'delegation' included maladaptive help-seeking and self-pity, which on the surface would not appear to belong in this grouping.)

It is evident from the above brief overview of various models of coping that a large array of coping behaviours has been identified and studied and that, while there is some overlap in typologies of coping responses, there are also significant differences in the ways in which researchers have approached this topic. This is to be expected, given that (a) theoretical perspectives on coping vary considerably between researchers and (b) the differential nature of stressors and situations is likely to elicit markedly different kinds of responses from people. In the present context, our focus is on work-related stressors. Although many of the coping strategies mentioned above may well be applicable in this context, others may be totally irrelevant, even though they could be pertinent in other situations (e.g. coping with illness). The above discussion illustrates that uniformity does not exist in definitions and categorizations of coping strategy, which hinders our ability to draw definitive conclusions about the relative utility and effectiveness of different types of coping.

Coping with Work Stressors

Following on from the above general discussion of coping behaviours, we now turn to research which has examined how individuals attempt to deal with work-related stressors. As mentioned earlier in this chapter, initially our aim was to provide a review of specific stressors and how they are confronted, along with an assessment of the effectiveness of different approaches to dealing with these stressors. However, such a review proved to be unrealistic, as there has been insufficient research on the relationship between some major stressors and coping behaviours. For instance, the literature has identified role variables (ambiguity, conflict and overload) as major stress factors for a variety of workers, and has consistently demonstrated a significant association between levels of these role stressors and increased psychological strain and reduced subjective well-being (e.g. Beehr & Glazer 2005; Glazer & Beehr 2005; Ortgvist & Wincent 2006). Nevertheless, despite the prevalence of role stressors and their effects on individuals at work, there is surprisingly little empirical evidence on how these stressors are coped with. Numerous studies have examined work–family inter-role conflict, which we discuss in detail in Chapter 5, but there have been few direct investigations of coping with conflict occurring within the work role itself (i.e. intra-role conflict). Tidd and Friedman (2002) note that both problem-focused and emotion-focused coping may be either beneficial or detrimental, depending on how much control the person has over the extent of role conflict they are experiencing. Overall, active problem-focused coping was linked with reduced negative impact of role conflict on uncertainty and (indirectly) work-related strain. In contrast, Day and Livingstone (2001) found that negative coping styles (such as venting of negative emotions and denial) were linked with higher strain when military personnel experienced role stressors. In 2007, Pomaki, Supeli and Verhoeven observed that health-promoting behaviours moderated the relationship between job/role conflict and emotional exhaustion and depression among medical doctors. With a few exceptions, however, evidence on the effects of coping on the relationship between specific role stressors and psychological strain is very sparse indeed. Instead, many reported studies on this topic have combined work demand variables into a generic work stressor variable, rather than assessing the specific stressors separately.

Owing to the lack of comprehensive studies of coping in relation to all of the specific categories of stressors listed on page 67, our approach here is to provide some examples of different coping strategies which have been examined in respect of various types of stressor, to draw a few inferences about the kinds of coping which may be effective in dealing with these stressors and to offer some suggestions for further investigation of coping with work-related stressors. For this purpose, we have selected the following stressors (or risk factors) as examples of research on coping with work stress: work demands, boredom at work, organizational change, job insecurity, and bullying and aggression. The choice of these specific areas is not because they necessarily create greater strain for individuals but simply because there has been some focus on these stressors in job stress coping research.

Coping with work demands

As we have discussed throughout this book, demands from the job can pose significant challenges and pressures for workers, and are frequently cited as major causes of strain and reduced well-being (e.g. Daniels *et al.* 2008; Ganster 2005; Tucker *et al.* 2008). Karasek's (1979) job demands/control model of strain accords work demands with high potentiality as stressors, and there is no doubt that excessive demands tax a person's resources and can lead to deleterious outcomes, including reduced well-being and health, along with reduced satisfaction with the job and commitment to the organization (Fox, Dwyer & Ganster 1993; Glazer & Kruse 2008). Therefore, how individuals endeavour to cope with excessive work demands is an important issue. However, as we discussed above in relation to role stressors, surprisingly little research has directly investigated how people cope with time demands at work.

One relatively obvious coping response is time management, which intuitively would appear to be an effective strategy for managing competing demands in the work context. Time management entails several activities, including defining one's goals and what one wishes to achieve in a specified time period, deciding on the tasks to be performed in order to accomplish these goals, prioritizing tasks to ensure that important (or urgent) ones receive appropriate attention and planning how to effectively utilize the time available (e.g. in a given day) to ensure that planned goals are achieved. In addition to these behaviours, a review of achievements at the end of a set time period is also an important activity, to determine whether goals have been achieved or, if not, the impediments to goal achievement. Although in principle these tasks seem relatively straightforward, it would appear that their enactment in practice can often be far from simple.

Nevertheless, research has typically illustrated that use of time management can alleviate symptoms of strain arising from high work demands. For instance, Jex and Elacqua (1999) observed that time management behaviours were positively related to psychological well-being, partially mediated by feelings of control. That is, time management behaviours led individuals to experience greater feelings of control, which in turn reduced psychological strain. However, the predicted moderator effect of time management on the demands–strain relationship was not statistically significant. A possible reason proffered by Jex and Elacqua for this finding was that there was insufficient variability between people in the amount of time management utilized (all scored relatively high on the measure of time management). They recommend that future studies attempt to secure samples which have a range of time management levels. There may also have been some positive self-report bias in reports of the utilization of time management, with individuals' self-reported usage of this strategy perhaps being higher than their actual usage.

A more recent study by Peeters and Rutte (2005) examined the effects of time management in relation to burnout among elementary school teachers in the Netherlands. They hypothesized a three-way interaction of work demands, time management and autonomy on burnout. High work demands and low autonomy were predicted to lead to burnout among teachers who reported low usage of time management. This hypothesis was confirmed in respect of emotional exhaustion, the major component of burnout. The authors suggest that 'time management compensates for low autonomy whether work demands are high or low, but it does so more strongly when work demands are high' (p. 72). Interestingly, the interaction effect was not significant for personal accomplishment, another major dimension of burnout, suggesting that the effects of time management may not always translate into higher levels of achievement. Nevertheless, Peeters and Rutte suggest that time management can be an effective strategy for reducing the negative impact of high work-related demands.

The overall utility of time management as a stress coping mechanism in relation to excessive work demands may be determined by other characteristics of both the situation and the person. For instance, if the situation is one that the person has little control over (and therefore limited autonomy), time management may not always be feasible or practical. Similarly, individuals vary in terms of their ability to effectively engage in time management behaviours, which require a degree of self-discipline and a focused approach to task completion. Hence the impact of time management may be moderated by both situational and dispositional factors.

Boredom at work

On the other side of the coin to excessive work demands are situations where individuals have to deal with insufficient demands or stimulation in their job. Boredom at work is a factor which has long been recognized as a potential stressor (Guest, Williams & Dewe 1978) and a significant contributor to job dissatisfaction in particular, and it has been suggested that a relatively high proportion of workers experience boredom in their work, at least from time to time (Fisher 1998). Curiously, therefore, there have been very few studies of how individuals cope with work-related boredom. While changing the characteristics of the job to make it more stimulating, challenging and meaningful has been touted as an antidote to boredom, for some jobs it is not always possible to make substantial changes which would make them more interesting. In any event, by themselves these modifications are unlikely to significantly alleviate workplace boredom, if the inherent nature of the job renders it lacking in intrinsic interest for the person. Under these circumstances, individual coping strategies may play a critical role in determining whether the person continues to be bored or can find ways to extract some level of interest from their work. One recent study which explored this issue is by Game (2007), who surveyed and then interviewed workers in a chemical processing plant in the United Kingdom. Given the nature of the work performed, a high priority was placed by the organization on compliance with rules and regulations regarding safety, and individual workers had little opportunity to use discretion in how they performed their jobs, therefore making this an appropriate location for the investigation of boredom. Using critical incident methodology and a structured questionnaire (Flanagan 1954), Game assessed arousal, job-related well-being, job satisfaction and strategies for coping with boredom. Boredom coping was operationalized as engagement with tasks and maintaining concentration. As anticipated, high levels of coping with boredom were associated with greater satisfaction and higher well-being, as well as higher self-reported arousal, suggesting that workers who actively tried to engage with their work and retain their task focus were less likely to experience the negative consequences of boredom. More research is required, however, to determine just how individuals can develop and maintain this approach under conditions which would seem to militate against active engagement.

Organizational change

Another potential stressor which has received some attention in the coping literature is organizational change, which typically entails a range of adjustments from both the organization as a whole and individuals affected by the change. In the current economic and political climate, numerous organizations are facing considerable challenges to their modi operandi and are being forced to deal with substantial threats to their productivity and profitability, especially in the face of an economic downtown which has been rated as being on a par with the Great Depression of the 1930s. Some of the issues accompanying these changes fall more appropriately under the topics which we discuss below (uncertainty and job insecurity). For the present, we focus on more general issues of change that organizations contend with on a continuing basis. In addition to the strain induced by threats to job security, organizational change in general can create feelings of uncertainty and possible threats to people's well-being, often owing to forebodings about what the change may imply for the nature of their work and work relationships (Rafferty & Griffin 2006).

Several researchers have explored how individuals endeavour to cope with organizational change and the potential outcomes of such coping efforts. A series of studies in Australia by Terry and Jimmieson (2003) reflect the overall thrust of this line of research. Terry and Jimmieson (2003) summarize evidence from separate field studies of change in three Australian organizations, including an airline merger, restructuring in a public sector organization and the introduction of a new pay scheme in a public utility company. These studies were based upon the Lazarus–Folkman transactional model (Lazarus & Folkman 1984), with a strong emphasis on people's cognitive appraisals of the meaning of the change and their potential responses to it. In the airline merger study, there was evidence that situational appraisals and coping resources were associated with employee adjustment to the merger. The second study, on the restructuring of a public sector agency, found that individual levels of self-efficacy mediated the relationship between change-related information and employee adjustment during the early phases of the change implementation, although not at later stages. Terry and Jimmieson (2003) suggest that, especially in the early stages of an intervention, organizations should endeavour to enhance workers' perceptions of self-efficacy and control over the change process and outcomes. The findings and conclusions of their third study (focusing on the impact of a new pay scheme for managers which directly linked bonuses to their unit's performance) were somewhat different from those derived from their second study. In the third study, Terry and Jimmieson found that self-efficacy was a less critical factor in relation to the introduction of the new pay scheme than was the provision of information about the change. They suggest that in this context the manner in which the organization implemented the intervention was more critical than individual coping mechanisms for employee adjustment (well-being).

A systematic investigation of how employees cope with organizational change was reported recently by Fugate, Kinicki and Prussia (2008). These researchers note that employees often have negative perceptions of organizational change, appraising change as potentially harmful or threatening. Based on the Lazarus–Folkman appraisal model of coping (Lazarus & Folkman 1984), Fugate and his colleagues examined a model which proposed that negative appraisals of change will be associated with both positive and negative emotional reactions, which in turn will induce either control-based coping, which focuses on proactive behaviours to reinstall a feeling of control over events, or escape coping, which comprises avoidance behaviours. Fugate *et al.* hypothesized that escape coping would lead to a greater use of sick leave and higher intentions to quit the job, which in turn would lead to higher voluntary turnover later on. Their longitudinal results illustrate support for a partial mediation effect of coping and emotions. The above relationships were obtained, but in addition there were direct relationships between negative appraisals of change and both sick leave (days absent) and voluntary turnover.

In addition to the mediation effects of coping, Fugate, Kinicki and Prussia tested possible moderating (buffering) effects of control coping and escape coping. Whereas escape coping was proposed to interact with threat appraisals to increase employee withdrawal, control coping should have the opposite effect. The findings demonstrated no support for the moderating effect proposition: neither the control coping × threat appraisal nor the escape coping × threat appraisal interaction terms were significant. Fugate *et al.* conclude that their data support the mediational model but not the moderator model of coping effects. They argue that their findings confirm the importance of appraisals (of change) as a mechanism underlying individuals' responses to organizational change, but also that 'it is not simply one's appraisal of changes that influences turnover but also how one copes with and reacts emotionally to these changes' (p. 28).

The above research highlights the critical role of emotions in the stress coping process. Furthermore, it illustrates some important coping processes that workers may engage in when confronted with the possibility of changes that may be threatening to their well-being or security. As noted by Fugate, Kinicki and Prussia (2008), the use of escape (or avoidance) coping is unlikely to generate positive outcomes either for individuals or for their organizations. One practical implication for management is that they should endeavour to reduce this coping strategy among their employees and foster the utilization of more proactive (e.g. control-based) coping strategies. This is entirely consistent with Terry and Jimmieson's (2003) recommendation that management has a responsibility to provide information about the change process and potential outcomes of organizational change, so that workers are informed about the implications for themselves. The management of change is a shared responsibility between management and employees, and reliance solely on personal coping mechanisms will normally be insufficient for people to adapt to organizational changes which impinge upon their work lives.

Job insecurity

Another potentially major source of stress for many people is insecurity surrounding their job, which may be related to organizational change, as discussed above. Job insecurity can be manifested in various ways, including threat of job loss, actual unemployment, redundancy or simply modifications to the nature of one's work which change the job, work hours or working conditions. All of these issues have been found to have a significant impact on people's levels of strain and well-being (Probst 2009).

A comprehensive model of coping with employment uncertainty or insecurity was developed by Latack and her colleagues (Latack, Kinicki & Prussia 1995), based on the control theory of coping outlined by Edwards (1992). According to control theory (also referred to as the 'cybernetic theory of coping'), job loss creates a disequilibrium between a current state (unemployment) and a desired state (employment), and this disequilibrium induces various coping behaviours in people. The nature of the coping behaviours engaged in will, in turn, influence the causes of the disequilibrium, and then the new level of disequilibrium leads to modified coping responses. Hence there is a feedback loop in the process which can explain the relationship between people's experiences (e.g. of uncertainty), their responses to these experiences (coping) and outcomes such as well-being. A modified and simplified version of the Latack model is presented in Figure 4.1.

One key element of the Latack *et al.* model is the efficacy of coping with job loss. Coping efficacy (or effectiveness) is clearly associated with improved functioning and overall well-being, hence it is critical to determine which coping strategies are likely to generate positive outcomes for the person who is confronted with job loss. As noted by Latack, Kinicki and Prussia (1995), 'high coping efficacy in the face of job loss translates into the perception that one has control. As such coping strategies differ based on the extent to which individuals perceive they can change the situation' (p. 322). Perceptions of control are, at least to some extent, based upon attributions made to explain how and why the job loss occurred. Internal attributions tend to lead to self-blame, which, as noted earlier, is a form of emotion-focused coping linked with less positive outcomes for the person. On the other hand, external attributions (e.g. that the cause of unemployment is not linked to personal characteristics but rather environmental factors) may generate more active, problem-solving coping approaches which can produce desirable outcomes, such as re-employment.

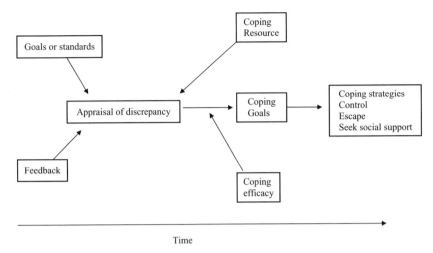

Figure 4.1   Modified version of the Latack, Kinicki and Prussia (1995) model of coping with job loss.

Related to, but distinct from, the experience of job loss is long-term unemployment, which can also have substantial deleterious consequences for individuals and their families. These negative effects have been well documented (Probst 2009), and can be even more severe than those associated with (initial) job loss. There has also been considerable research on the methods used by people to deal with long-term unemployment, and several studies have reported the effectiveness of various coping strategies. An example of these is an investigation conducted by Patton and Donohue (1998), which explored the relationship between different coping responses and well-being among long-term unemployed (over 12 months) people undertaking employment training in Australia. Strain was gauged via the General Health Questionnaire (GHQ-12), while coping responses were identified via interviews with respondents. Coping strategies linked with high GHQ scores (i.e. high strain) included keeping busy, emotional release and psychological withdrawal. Interestingly, keeping busy was also associated with positive well-being, along with maintaining a positive outlook, religious faith and re-evaluation of expectations. As noted earlier, emotions played a key role in the development of effective coping responses. Individuals who utilized ineffective coping responses indicated an awareness of more constructive approaches, but said that negative feelings and cognitions prevented them from engaging in these strategies. Patton and

Donohue conclude that 'cognitive strategies are important in sustaining the experience of long-term unemployment' (p. 341) and that a variety of coping mechanisms contributed to heightened well-being, whereas others were ineffectual or even counterproductive.

Confirmation of the above findings was obtained in a comparative study of employed versus unemployed high-technology workers in Canada (Mantler *et al.* 2005). This study, which examined coping with the stress associated with employment uncertainty, was interesting in that the employed sample were being confronted with uncertainty as well, owing to the potential threat of job loss and loss of career opportunities in the industry. Mantler *et al.* found that emotion-focused coping responses, especially emotional avoidance, increased the link between employment uncertainty and perceived stress, whereas problem-focused coping (which comprised problem-solving, seeking social support, cognitive restructuring, active distraction and use of humour) was related to reduced stress, although it did not significantly buffer the relationship between uncertainty and stress. Employment status (employed versus unemployed) was not related to the choice of coping responses, but both groups benefited from the use of proactive coping strategies.

In summary, job insecurity or uncertainty is clearly a significant work stressor, and in the current economic climate one which increasing numbers of people are having to cope with. Evidence suggests that proactive coping strategies are most likely to be effective, including making active efforts to scope out alternative job opportunities, setting goals and priorities, planning and decision-making. Augmenting perceptions of control and hence self-efficacy would also appear to be important for enhancing coping effectiveness when the person is confronted with job insecurity. Some forms of emotion-focused coping, on the other hand, especially avoidance (or escape) coping and psychological withdrawal, have been found to be counterproductive and are associated with increased rather than reduced strain.

Interpersonal conflict at work

Interpersonal difficulties (e.g. conflict with other people) represent another class of stressors that can be prevalent in work settings and can generate considerable stress (Liu, Spector & Shi 2007). There is an extensive literature, especially in social psychology, on coping with interpersonal stress generally, but fewer studies have been conducted on coping with interpersonal conflict (and related interpersonal stressors) in work environments.

De Dreu and colleagues in the Netherlands have reported several studies on conflict management and well-being in work settings (for a review, see De Dreu, van Dierendonck & Dijkstra 2004). Their research revealed that yielding to the other person and trying to avoid dealing with them were predictors of lower subjective well-being, and that problem-solving did not necessarily enhance well-being. The latter finding could be due to the lack of effectiveness in some cases of problem-solving in actually reducing the conflict. In another study (Van Dierendonck & Mevissen 2002), trolley car drivers who used forcing behaviour or conflict avoidance experienced higher burnout as a result of experiencing conflict with their customers, again confirming the ineffectiveness of either avoidance or dominance approaches to conflict management. Finally, Dijkstra, van Dierendonck and Evers (2005, p. 123) observed that escape coping (which they refer to as 'flight') mediated the relationship between interpersonal conflict and stress among healthcare workers. Use of escape coping was associated with increased stressors and reduced well-being.

Portello and Long (2001) also explored how individuals cope with interpersonal stressors at work, in a sample of Canadian female managers. These researchers assessed two types of coping which have been referred to above: engagement and disengagement coping. Engagement coping did not significantly predict reduced distress as Portello and Long had expected, but disengagement predicted greater daily hassles and more distress. Consistent with our earlier comments about the critical role of appraisals in the selection of coping strategies, in this study primary appraisal of the stressor as being upsetting was significantly associated with greater use of disengagement coping. Clearly, utilization of disengagement as a coping mechanism was not effective in reducing strain (in fact, quite the contrary), although the anticipated positive benefits of engagement coping were not realized in this study. Interestingly, women managers who used disengagement coping were also likely to use engagement coping. It is possible that the interpersonal stressors confronted by the women in this setting were not amenable to resolution via engagement coping, even when they felt they had some degree of control over the situation. For instance, some research on coping with bullying (see discussion below) has suggested that endeavouring to engage directly with the bully may be a counterproductive strategy and can lead to an escalation of conflict (Zapf & Gross 2001).

A final illustration of research on coping with interpersonal conflict is a study conducted among nurses in Israel by Tabak and Koprak (2007), based on a model of conflict resolution developed by Rahim and Bonoma (1979). Tabak and Koprak note that one frequent source of interpersonal conflict for nurses in hospital settings are their interactions with physicians, and that five alternative types of coping may be salient: integrating, dominating, compromising, obliging and avoidance. Their correlational data indicated that integrating was negatively associated with stress and positively with job satisfaction (as would be predicted), while avoidance showed the opposite pattern of relationships with these criterion variables. A combination of integrating and dominance strategies was also significantly related to both reduced stress and increased satisfaction, whereas a combination of obliging and avoidance strategies was linked with higher stress and less satisfaction. However, regression analyses indicated that, when all five strategies were analysed together, only integrating was a significant predictor of both stress and job satisfaction.

The above brief overview of coping with interpersonal conflict in work contexts provides no clear-cut evidence on effective strategies for dealing with this stressor. Clearly, there are several moderating influences on relationships between coping strategies and affective outcomes such as strain and job satisfaction. Although direct (integrating) strategies would appear overall to be the most effective approach to conflict management, this conclusion would appear to be applicable only under certain conditions. Specifically, when the individual has some degree of control over the situation and when the person with whom they are in conflict is amenable to constructive resolution of the conflict, the likelihood of integrating strategies achieving positive outcomes increases. Unfortunately, however, these conditions do not always exist in work situations, in which case the effectiveness of integration strategies may be undermined. On the other hand, it is evident that avoidance or disengagement approaches are unlikely to yield desired outcomes, and may even exacerbate the level of strain the person experiences as a result of interpersonal conflict.

Bullying and aggression at work

Above we discussed interpersonal conflict in general, but there are some specific forms of conflict which have received considerable attention recently in the literature. Workplace bullying, harassment and aggression have become increasingly of concern for employers, unions and workers, and there is mounting evidence that these forms of 'violence' have a very substantial impact on individuals' well-being as well as on their job performance (Porath & Pearson 2009). There have also been suggestions that the prevalence of antisocial behaviours may be increasing, although it is difficult to confirm this empirically, as reporting rates can vary over time for a number of reasons. It is also difficult to completely differentiate between terms such as 'bullying', 'mobbing' and 'harassment', which share some common features, although they are typically regarded as separate (albeit related) behaviours. Here we focus specifically on bullying, which has received considerable attention in the literature over the past 15 years, and has been consistently demonstrated to have a close association with job-related stress (Hauge, Skogstad & Einarsen 2007). Definitions of bullying are somewhat variable, and different kinds of behaviour have been labelled 'bullying'. However, a typical characterization is that bullying entails repeated and enduring negative acts towards an individual, such as teasing, harassment, aggression, social exclusion, insults and victimization, and where the target feels unable to defend him/herself against this antisocial behaviour (Einarsen 2000).

The prevalence of bullying has been investigated in several studies in different countries, and estimates vary, but typically between 1 and 4% of employees report having been bullied at work, by their supervisor/manager, work colleagues or clients/customers. Although this incidence rate may not seem very high, the psychosocial effects of bullying on individuals is substantial, including heightened stress, reduced job performance, increased absenteeism and intentions to leave the job, along with an overall decline in well-being (Einarsen *et al.* 2003). Considerable international research has been conducted to establish both the causes and the outcomes of workplace bullying, but relatively less attention has been given to how individuals cope with this experience or organizational efforts to address bullying problems. Below we describe three examples of research on coping with bullying.

Zapf and Gross (2001) argue that bullying is a subset of interpersonal conflict, where the two parties are in positions of unequal power, there is a series of conflict episodes which continues for a (relatively) long period of time, and where one party feels harassed or victimized by the other. They conducted two studies in Germany to explore what the 'victims' of bullying do in escalated conflict situations. In their first study Zapf and Gross interviewed victims of bullying and in the second study they distributed structured questionnaires to both people who had been bullied and those who had not. In the qualitative interviews, most victims of bullying reported that they endeavoured initially to use constructive conflict-resolution strategies, but that these were often ineffective in removing or reducing the bullying, hence they turned to less proactive approaches and eventually even left the organization as a way of avoiding the bullying. In the quantitative study avoidance coping was also the most prominent strategy utilized. Those who were classified as 'successful victims' (i.e. the bullying reduced) were less likely to use direct-action strategies, such as trying to confront the perpetrator. In fact, confronting the bully tended to be used more often by 'unsuccessful victims', indicating that direct action may be counterproductive in these situations. Avoidance of further conflict escalation seemed to be the only effective method for ameliorating the negative outcomes of bullying. Zapf and Gross suggest that frequently the only realistic choices for the target are either to be separated (physically) from the bully or to leave the organization entirely.

Olafsson and Johannsdottir (2004) also examined coping strategies employed to deal with bullying behaviours, in a sample of store, office and bank workers in Iceland. They identified four potential clusters of coping strategies, which they label 'assertive response', 'seek help', 'avoidance' and 'do nothing', although differences between the last two categories are not entirely clear. In general the strategies aligned along two continua: active versus passive and emotional versus detached. Olafsson and Johannsdottir note that individuals exposed to bullying may modify their approach if bullying is prolonged, perhaps starting out with active attempts to remove or reduce the bullying, but ultimately adopting a more resigned or passive acceptance approach, accompanied by psychological and ultimately physical withdrawal from the situation. In their study, although there were no significant gender differences in levels of bullying reported, women were more likely to report seeking outside help, whereas men more often reported confronting the bully. Unfortunately, Olafsson and Johannsdottir did not explore the relative effectiveness of active versus passive coping strategies.

Finally, Hogh and Dofradottir (2001) used a structured questionnaire to assess coping with bullying in a large sample of Danish workers, whom they classified as 'non-exposed', 'somewhat exposed' and 'very exposed' to bullying. In this study, respondents indicated that the source of the bullying was most often a work colleague (rather than a supervisor or manager). There were no differences in the coping strategies reported by the somewhat exposed and very exposed groups, but (as one might expect) these two groups differed significantly from the non-exposed sample of workers.

Specifically, people subjected to negative acts were less likely to use problem-solving coping to address the stressors. The authors suggest that problem-solving may be functional only when people believe they can do something constructive to resolve the problem; if they feel they have little influence or control, they may resort to passive avoidance, even though this does not reduce the stressor. Hogh and Dofradottir also found that people who were somewhat exposed to bullying, but not those very exposed, were more likely to report using humour as a strategy for relieving tension. As with the Olafsson and Johannsdottir (2004) approach, however, Hogh and Dofradottir (2001) did not assess whether certain types of coping were more effective in either reducing bullying or alleviating its impact on the person's well-being.

In summary, there is considerable evidence that interpersonal conflict and conflict-related behaviours such as bullying and aggression are significant sources of psychological (and sometimes physical) strain for many individuals in their workplaces. Dealing with these issues is not always straightforward, and there is relatively little consistent data on the effectiveness of different types of coping approach. While for conflict in general it is typically recommended that problem-solving collaboration is the most valuable strategy, leading to positive outcomes and a reduction in conflict, the enactment of this strategy can be difficult and time-consuming, requiring willingness and energy to resolve conflict issues. Often a compromise approach is more realistic, even though this may not always fully resolve the conflict. On the other hand, effective strategies to manage more escalated forms of conflict, such as bullying and aggressive behaviour, typically require joint involvement of both individuals and managers; the studies cited above illustrate that it can be difficult, if not impossible, for individuals themselves to reduce antisocial behaviours that constitute bullying.

Coping Strategies Used by Specific Occupational Groups

Rather than examining coping in relation to specific stressors, some researchers have focused on specific occupational groups whose job entails dealing with people and events which have high stressor potential. Two occupational groups which have received considerable attention in the stress coping literature are police officers and nurses, who are recognized as experiencing substantial stress and even burnout owing to various facets of their work. Although there has also been empirical investigation of the coping strategies used by other occupations, we limit our attention here to these two groups, simply to provide an illustration of research on coping by members of these occupations. The discussion below intended to imply that other occupations do not experience considerable stress. As with the issues covered above, our intention is not to include an exhaustive review of studies on this topic, but rather to provide some examples of the types of research conducted and conclusions about the types of coping utilized by members of these two occupational categories.

A study by Burke (1998) of police officers found that escape coping behaviours (such as withdrawal, use of alcohol and drugs, and excessive sleeping) were significantly linked with greater work–family conflict and more psychosomatic symptoms, as well as reduced job satisfaction, whereas active coping (talking with others, problem-solving, minimizing concerns) was associated with higher job satisfaction, although it was not significantly related to work–family conflict or reduced psychosomatic symptoms. Furthermore, escape coping and active coping were negatively related to each other. Perhaps the most interesting finding from this study, however, is that police officers who reported more work stressors also reported greater use of escape coping, suggesting that their personal coping efforts were largely ineffective in promoting well-being and reducing strain.

Hart, Wearing and Headey (1995) also examined how police officers cope with the stressors encountered in their role. They propose that emotion-focused and problem-focused coping behaviours are associated with either hassles or uplifts, which in turn influence psychological distress and well-being. Their investigation of police officers in Australia found that the indirect effects of coping, via hassles and uplifts, were more prominent than direct effects on strain and well-being. In addition, and supporting Burke's conclusions, emotion-focused coping strategies were maladaptive in terms of well-being, whereas problem-focused strategies were adaptive. Hart *et al.* conclude that 'when police officers attempt to cope with stressful work experiences by managing or dealing with their emotional response, the likely result is an increase in work hassles. When, however, police officers attempt to cope by managing or dealing directly with the stressful event, they are more likely to experience work uplifts' (p. 151). They further suggest that their findings challenge the conventional view that effective coping is directly associated with reduced stress and improved well-being; rather, hassles and uplifts at work play a mediating role in the link between coping and well-being.

Another occupational category which has also been the subject of considerable research on stress and coping is the medical profession, in particular nurses. This group has been documented as experiencing a range of stressors at work, including role stressors, interpersonal conflict (with both patients and other staff), bureaucratic hassles as well as (in some areas of nursing) the strain arising from dealing with acutely and chronically ill people. The risk of burnout among nurses has been reported as being relatively high (Innstrand *et al.* 2008). Several studies have examined how nurses attempt to cope with the stressors encountered in their job and whether these coping efforts led to positive outcomes. Above we referred to a study by Tabak and Koprak (2007), which examined the tactics used by nurses in Israel to resolve conflict with physicians, and whether these tactics were linked with reduced stress and increased job satisfaction. They observed that integrating (problem-solving) and dominance (attempting to get one's own way) coping strategies were related to low occupational stress and higher levels of job satisfaction among these nurses, whereas obliging and avoidance strategies showed the opposite patterns of relationship with stress and job satisfaction. As might be anticipated, senior nurses and those with higher status were more likely to engage in either integration or dominance than were their lower-status counterparts.

Welbourne *et al.* (2007) examined the relationship between coping strategies, attributions concerning the causes of stress and job satisfaction among nurses in the United States. Their results illustrate that a positive attributional style, that is viewing favourable events as under one's personal control and unfavourable events as externally controlled, was linked with the greater use of problem-solving and cognitive restructuring coping, less use of avoidance and higher job satisfaction. In addition, the relationship between attributional style and job satisfaction was mediated by the use of problem-solving and cognitive restructuring. Support-seeking and avoidance coping, on the other hand, did not significantly predict job satisfaction. Welbourne *et al.* recommend that organizations should assist nurses to develop positive attributional styles and effective approaches to coping, such as problem-solving and cognitive restructuring.

A study by Niiyama *et al.* (2009) assessed how nurses in Japan deal with traumatic stress arising in their workplace. Nurses who indicated that they had experienced any one of four threatening events at work and who scored highly on a questionnaire tapping traumatic stress reactions were classified as suffering from post-traumatic stress disorder (PTSD). Six coping strategies were investigated in this study: positive action (which is similar to problem-solving assessed by Welbourne *et al.* 2007), positive thinking (akin to cognitive restructuring), emotional avoidance, uncontrolled thinking, talking with others and distraction. Comparisons were conducted of nurses classified as experiencing ongoing trauma and those designated as being in recovery. Somewhat surprisingly, the trauma group reported greater use of positive action, positive thinking, avoidance, uncontrolled thinking and talking with others than did the recovery group, while the latter reported more use of distraction. Niiyama *et al.* (2009) suggest that perhaps after trauma the use of direct coping strategies such as positive action may serve to prevent stress reactions from diminishing, whereas distraction may (under these circumstances) be an effective device for dealing with traumatic stress. Alternatively, it may be that the recovery group no longer needed to use strategies such as positive action, positive thinking and talking with others.

The studies mentioned above yield a brief snapshot of the variables which have been explored in respect of two specific occupational groups. As noted earlier, police officers and nurses are frequently exposed to potentially stressful situations and events, hence assessing how they cope with stressors in their work environment is an important research issue. Our (admittedly selective) choice of studies provides some interesting information on coping strategies utilized by these occupations. Overall, the findings suggest that active coping (such as problem-solving and seeking support) is more likely to achieve positive outcomes for both police and nurses, although in some circumstances (such as the traumatic stress situation examined by Niiyama *et al.* 2009) there may also be potential negative side effects of this approach to coping. It is clear from the above studies, however, that avoidance coping typically does not generate positive outcomes.

Future Directions in Research on Coping with Specific Work Stressors

Our discussion of specific work-related stressors in this chapter is intended to provide a broad overview of the various forms of coping strategy which have been investigated in relation to a range of different work stressors. At the beginning of the chapter we acknowledged that our goal was not to generate a comprehensive review of all work-related stressors, or of all the research which has been conducted on stress coping, but rather to selectively examine a few, relatively major work stressors and how they are confronted by individuals. A concomitant aim was to assess the effectiveness of different strategies for coping with work-related stressors.

It is evident from the research discussed in this chapter that numerous typologies of coping have been proposed, although many of these have built upon the transactional framework developed by Lazarus and his associates (e.g. Lazarus & Folkman 1984). The transactional model positions cognitive appraisal and emotions at the heart of stress coping, suggesting that responses to stressors arise from the individual's primary appraisal of the meaning of the stressor to their well-being along with their secondary appraisal of coping options and resources available to them. As further discussed by Folkman (2008), emotions (both positive and negative) also play an integral role in the stress coping process, as they lie at the heart of concepts such as psychological strain and subjective well-being.

Despite the plethora of research conducted on coping strategies and (to a somewhat lesser extent) their effectiveness in dealing with specific work stressors, there are several issues that remain unresolved in this field of exploration. For instance, as we noted earlier, studies of coping have not always clearly specified the nature of the stressor(s) being investigated, and frequently have combined stressors rather than differentiating the type of coping which is used to address specific stressors. This is most evident when we consider research on work demands, including factors such as role ambiguity, role conflict and role overload. This line of research has often concatenated these stressors, hence there is a paucity of information on whether the strategies used by people to attend to one stressor are similar to or distinct from those used for other work demand stressors. Previously we discussed the difference between coping *styles* and coping *strategies*, yet there is little confirmatory evidence about whether individuals do indeed adopt the same (or similar) approaches when attending to different work demands or, on the other hand, if distinctly different approaches are utilized depending on the kind of stressor.

Similarly, more attention needs to be accorded to how individuals cope with short-term versus long-term stressors. Folkman and Moskowitz (2004) comment, for example, that emotion-focused coping may be adaptive in the short term but less effective for longer-lasting stressors, such as incessant work demands. In contrast, they suggest that proactive and problem-focused coping may be more effective long-term coping strategies. Unfortunately, much of the research on coping has tended to use cross-sectional studies which do not consider the duration of stressors, therefore Folkman and Moskowitz's suggestion remains largely untested. On a more general note, there is a dire need for longitudinal investigations of coping processes, first to assess both the short-term and longer-term impact of different coping methods and, second, to examine how coping behaviours evolve over time. For instance, as we noted in the section on coping with interpersonal conflict and bullying, a person exposed to bullying behaviour may initially endeavour to confront the bully to ascertain whether a resolution can be achieved, but if these efforts are unsuccessful may then resort to psychological withdrawal or other forms of avoidance coping. Only longitudinal research which examines the development (and change) in coping strategies over time can systematically address these questions.

More research is also required on the conditions or circumstances under which different forms of coping will be effective. In Chapter 5 and earlier in this chapter we discuss the importance of personal control as a critical moderating variable in the relationship between coping behaviours and psychological health and well-being. The contribution to well-being of control (or at least *perceived* control) over the stressor has been underlined in numerous studies of stress and well-being, although moderating (buffering) effects of this variable have not always been established (e.g. Siu *et al.* 2002). In addition to control, other variables may also influence the effectiveness of different coping strategies, such as the level of responsibility and accountability the person has for outcomes such as performance, the social environment in which the individual operates and dispositional factors, but there has been little systematic research to determine which variables have the most significant moderating effects. Dispositional variables, including positive and negative affectivity, core self-evaluations and hardiness, have been explored in some research, and clearly can exert a substantial influence not only on an individual's choice of coping modality but also on the potential outcomes of coping. The exact role of dispositional variables, especially personality, warrants further examination – recent research on core self-evaluations has generated some promising information, but conceptualizations of this construct and its operationalization in research need further development (Johnson, Rosen & Levy 2008).

Another individual difference variable which has received some attention in research on coping is gender. Whether systematic differences exist between men and women in their selection of coping strategies, and even their coping styles, has been debated in the literature over many years, without any definitive resolution. In the literature on coping with work-related stressors, there has been very little attention to gender similarities and differences. In the social psychological literature, however, this issue has been more prominent. A meta-analytic review by Tamres, Janicki and Hegelson (2002) found that women tended to use almost all types of coping more than men, although the nature of the stressor was also important in differentiating men's and women's coping behaviours. Specifically, as might be expected, women engaged in more support-seeking behaviours, especially emotional support. Tamres *et al.* report that to some extent gender differences were accounted for by differences in stressor appraisals (i.e. women tended to evaluate stressors as being more severe than did men). There is clearly a need for more research on gender differences in coping with work-related stressors, and whether these differences are associated with differing appraisals and perceptions of the environment, including control.

Another issue which has received surprisingly little attention in research is the potential impact of coping strategies on people's physical health and well-being. Almost all studies of stress coping at work have focused solely on psychological strain or distress. Although the more general coping literature has described some possible effects on physical health, and there have been studies on coping and ill-health, this interest has not spilled over into research on coping with work-related stressors. Day and Livingstone (2001), whom we referred to earlier in this chapter, examined self-reported health symptoms among military personnel, finding that only negative coping styles (venting of emotions, denial and disengagement) were significantly related to physical health outcomes, and these coping behaviours exacerbated rather than alleviated health problems. Positive coping, such as problem-solving and seeking informational and emotional support, had no significant effects on physical complaints. These are intriguing findings, but unfortunately there have been few other studies of coping and physical health to substantiate or disconfirm Day and Livingstone's results.

Finally, as we have noted previously in this book and elsewhere (Cooper, Dewe & O'Driscoll 2001), managing stressful work environments is a joint responsibility of individuals and organizations. Many stress management interventions (SMIs) are unfortunately targeted solely towards changing individual workers' appraisals and/or their coping strategies. Although it is vital for individuals to develop and maintain constructive personal coping strategies, in many situations work-related stressors can be beyond the person's control. In these cases, the organization (e.g. a person's immediate manager) has a responsibility to endeavour to alleviate strain arising from work stressors. Primary intervention is most often needed to deal with the causes of stress at work, although secondary interventions (e.g. stress management training) and tertiary interventions (e.g. employee assistance programmes) are also valuable. Whichever approach or combination of approaches is taken, there needs to be collaboration between individuals and their employer to ensure that optimal mechanisms are developed for confronting work-related stressors.

5

Coping with Work–Life Conflict

In the previous chapter we discussed how people endeavour to manage stressors in their work environment in order to minimize stress and preserve their well-being. We examined a range of different work-related stressors and described specific strategies that may be utilized to deal with each of these stressors. The present chapter focuses on one particular kind of stressor: the experience of conflict or interference between demands at work and responsibilities and commitments outside of the work setting, especially in respect of family life and one's personal life. Referred to as 'work–family conflict' or (more recently) 'work–life conflict', this stressor has been demonstrated in research since the 1990s to exert a considerable impact on individuals' well-being along with other areas such as family functioning and even performance on the job. In contrast to the *intra*-role conflict, which we describe in Chapter 4, which refers to interference between roles within a single domain (e.g. the work context), work–family (or work–life) conflict is a form of *inter*-role interference which occurs when there is conflict across domains. In the 1980s and 1990s, research and writing in this area focused predominantly on work versus family, but in recent years the 'non-work' component has been expanded to include other aspects of people's lives. For simplicity, we will refer to the two major spheres as the 'work domain' (i.e. a person's paid employment) and the 'life domain' (which comprises all other dimensions of life, including family, recreation, community activities and personal life). Although this classification is not entirely appropriate, as clearly 'life' includes work, it is commonly used in the literature and enables differentiation between the two spheres.

Coping with Work Stress: A Review and Critique, Philip J. Dewe, Michael P. O'Driscoll and Cary L. Cooper, © 2010 John Wiley & Sons Ltd.

Greenhaus and Beutell (1985) outline three ways in which work demands and life commitments and responsibilities may interfere with each other. The most obvious of these is 'time-based conflict', arising from competing demands and time pressures in the two domains. For instance, being required to invest long hours at work inevitably will mean fewer hours available to spend time with one's family or on recreational and other personal activities. Time-based conflict would appear to be a major source of stress for an increasing number of people (Hammer *et al.* 2005). A second form of inter-role conflict is what Greenhaus and Beutell (1985) refer to as 'strain-based conflict', which they define as a spillover of stress from one setting to another. Parents, for instance, frequently experience this form of interference; the need to juggle multiple family responsibilities can generate a considerable amount of psychological strain for a parent, which is then transferred into their work life. Alternatively, when people experience high levels of strain at work, perhaps owing to intense time pressures, role ambiguity or role conflict, this strain can be carried over into their lives away from the job. Like time-based conflict, strain-based conflict has also been illustrated to have significant negative effects on individuals and their significant others (both at home and at work). Finally, 'behaviour-based interference' refers to the display of specific behaviours in one domain which are incongruous with expected behaviours within the second domain. For example, at work an individual may be expected to be aggressive, ambitious, hard-driving and task-oriented. Successful job performance may depend on these behaviours. In contrast, at home being loving, supportive and accommodating may be regarded as essential to developing and fostering a happy and healthy family life. A person may experience considerable difficulty switching between roles which have conflicting expectations of their behaviour (O'Driscoll, Brough & Kalliath 2006).

The bulk of research conducted on work–life (or work–family) conflict has built upon this tripartite model of inter-role conflict, and a frequently used measure of between-domain conflict (Carlson, Kacmar & Williams 2000) clearly differentiates between the three forms. More recently, debate about the importance of inter-role conflict for well-being has been broadened to consider work–life *balance*, a somewhat nebulous concept which has attracted enormous attention in the media and is now beginning to be researched empirically. Definitions of 'balance' vary, with some researchers (Greenhaus, Collins & Shaw 2003) focusing on the balance of time commitments between work and other roles, while others concentrate more on the subjective experience of balance (Frone 2003). Frone, for example, suggests that balance arises when the person experiences relatively low levels of inter-role conflict and high levels of *facilitation* (or enrichment) between their work and their family/personal life.

Although we recognize the salience of inter-role facilitation and work–life balance for the development and maintenance of individual well-being, given that this book is about coping with stress, and stress is likely to be generated by the experience of conflict between roles, we limit our attention to conflict, rather than incorporating facilitation and balance. We begin with an overview of two major factors which have been found to alleviate the stress arising from work–life conflict: social support and control (or autonomy). The reason for opening with a review of research on these two variables is that, as discussed in Chapter 4, there is strong evidence that social support and control have both direct and indirect (i.e. moderating) effects on strain and well-being. This research evidence also highlights how support and control can be utilized as coping strategies, which are the focal point of this chapter. For simplicity, and to be consistent with a distinction which we will elaborate on in Chapter 6, we differentiate between individual (or personal) coping and organizational approaches to dealing with work–life conflict. Under each heading we describe various types of strategy or intervention, and assess their effectiveness in reducing the impact of work–life conflict on strain and well-being.

Social Support

Research on the role of social support (from other people) in mitigating the negative impact of stressors on personal well-being is voluminous and generally attests to the importance of this factor. However, the exact way in which social support functions to reduce strain and enhance well-being is not entirely clear-cut and different mechanisms have been proposed. The direct effects hypothesis proposes that social support directly reduces strain, that is people who have access to and use support from other people in their environment are less likely to experience strain and have greater well-being. This hypothesis has frequently been confirmed in empirical research, although it does not by itself provide an explanation of how social support operates to reduce strain. The key to understanding the direct effects of support probably lies in the nature of support provided and the

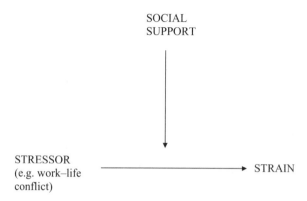

Figure 5.1   Moderating effect of social support.

kind of support desired or needed by the individual. For example, in some circumstances practical help or assistance may be needed to deal with a potentially stressful situation, such as a technical problem that the person cannot resolve by themselves. Similarly, informational support or advice may serve to reduce ambiguity or uncertainty for an individual and hence pre-empt the development of strain, especially in an unfamiliar task or situation. In respect of emotional support, however, the reasons for a direct impact on strain are less clear, although they may be linked to the individual's emotional needs. It is evident, for instance, that people vary in the level and kinds of emotional support desired and that a high level of comforting and sympathy will be effective in reducing strain for some people but not others. In other words, while overall emotional support may be beneficial, it is likely to have a more positive impact when it is congruent with the individual's needs and desires.

A second major explanation for the effects of social support is what is referred to as the buffering hypothesis, where support operates as a moderator of the relationship between stressors and strain (or well-being). This effect is depicted in Figure 5.1. According to the buffering hypothesis, individuals who receive social support will experience less strain (and higher well-being) than their counterparts who do not receive support from others, because support shields or protects people from the potentially harmful consequences of aversive events and circumstances. The buffering effect may occur because support helps the person change their perception that the stressor is damaging to their well-being, that is it influences the appraisal process which we discussed in Chapter 3.

Figure 5.2   Social support as a mediating variable.

A final explanation that has been proffered is the mediation hypothesis (Figure 5.2), which proposes that the acquisition of social support may be triggered by encountering a stressor. This is really a variant of the direct effects hypothesis, as the impact of social support on strain is the same as that posited in the direct effects explanation. The only difference between them is that in the mediation model stressors are assumed to induce the person to seek support from others, whereas the direct effects model makes no assumptions about when social support is activated.

Irrespective of which theoretical mechanism is favoured, as mentioned above there is considerable evidence that the utilization of social support from others has beneficial effects. In Chapter 4 we discussed how social support can alleviate strain arising from stressors in the work context, such as role ambiguity, role conflict and role overload. Here we reflect on its influence in respect of work–life conflict as a stressor and overview findings from the research on this issue.

One of the earliest, and most cited, studies of the impact of social support on reduced work–life conflict is an investigation conducted by Thomas and Ganster (1995), who explored the effects of organizational policies and practices which support employees' family commitments. (We discuss the role of these policies later in the chapter.) As a result of their research, Thomas and Ganster conclude that, while organizational policies are valuable, having a supportive supervisor is also a critical factor in reducing work–family conflict. In particular, supervisors can provide employees with the opportunity to exert greater control over their work scheduling, which will enable them to better balance their work and family commitments.

Other investigations around the same time also highlighted the importance of social support in reducing levels of work–life conflict experienced by workers who have family responsibilities. Kirchmeyer and Cohen (1999), for example, examined worksite support, consisting of flexible work schedules and accommodating needs. They differentiate this kind of support from more formal organizational policies, as it reflects more the behaviours of immediate managers and supervisors rather than broader organizational support. Kirchmeyer and Cohen also distinguish between two directions of conflict: work → family interference and family → work interference. Although these two directions are typically linked (Kirchmeyer and Cohen found a correlation of 0.43 between them), they are also conceptually and practically distinct. In their study, worksite support was directly related to lower levels of work → family interference but not to family → work interference. Kirchmeyer and Cohen did not explore possible buffering (moderating) effects of worksite support.

Recent studies have further illuminated the direct impact of social support on levels of work–life conflict as well as its potential buffering effects. Most research has focused on support provided in the work context, for example from supervisors and work colleagues. One possible reason for this is that typically levels of work → family interference have been found to be significantly greater than family → work interference (e.g. Anderson, Coffey & Byerly 2002; Lapierre & Allen 2006; O'Driscoll *et al.* 2003; Rotondo, Carlson & Kincaid 2003) and hence are more likely to exert a negative effect on individuals' lives. Second, from a practical perspective it may be believed that modifying the work environment is more feasible and may benefit a greater number of people. However, this does not undermine the importance of developing effective family support.

Ayman and Antani (2008) note that work-related support can be provided by (at least) three sources: the person's immediate manager/supervisor, their work colleagues and the organization as a whole. We discuss the effects of organizational support a little later in this chapter, and for the moment will concentrate on supervisory and collegial support. There is substantial evidence that these sources of support can help to reduce work–life conflict, over and above any formal policies and practices that the organization has instituted to assist work–life balance. For example, various researchers have demonstrated that having an understanding and supportive supervisor can be very beneficial (e.g. Frye & Breaugh 2004; Grandey, Cordeiro & Michael 2007; Lapierre & Allen 2006), although there are some caveats.

First, there is no one-size-fits-all model of supervision which will be appropriate in all situations and for all individuals. The type, extent and duration of support provided by supervisors must be attuned to the individual's needs and preferences. On some occasions, targeted instrumental support from supervisors may be required to alleviate work → life interference (O'Driscoll *et al.* 2003), whereas at other times it may be more appropriate for supervisors to provide emotional support and understanding of the worker's situation. Furthermore, as observed in research on social support and stress generally, sometimes extensive and intensive support from a supervisor can be perceived as intrusive and perhaps even controlling. Ayman and Antani (2008) comment that under some conditions receiving help or assistance from a supervisor can threaten a person's self-esteem (mainly because they may feel an inability to cope on their own) and increase a feeling of indebtedness to the supervisor.

Overall, however, the evidence suggests that the availability and utilization of supervisory support is negatively associated with work–life conflict and psychological strain. Hammer *et al.* (2007) developed a model which illustrates the various mechanisms by which supervisory behaviours can influence levels of work–family conflict (and enrichment). They observed that worker perceptions of supervisor family-supportive behaviours will be shaped by the organizational context, especially the overall culture of the organization (which we review later). Hence, to understand the role of supervisors in helping to reduce work–life conflict for workers under their jurisdiction, we also need to examine the broader organizational environment, including formal policies as well as the attitudes and behaviours of higher-level managers.

Fewer studies have considered the effects of support from work colleagues on work–life conflict. Although it is clear that collegial support can be a significant contributor to stress reduction (Fenlason & Beehr 1994), as with supervisory support the effects are not entirely clear-cut. Kirby and Krone (2002), for instance, note that co-workers may in fact be resentful of a person taking time off work to attend to family responsibilities, as the co-workers may have to 'pick up the slack' and as a result develop a feeling of injustice or unfairness. This is a phenomenon sometimes referred to in the work–life literature as 'backlash'. On the other hand, having co-workers who share a belief that work–life balance is important and who are willing to assume additional responsibilities so that their colleague can experience reduced work–life conflict will be beneficial. Again, however, the type and extent of support provided by work colleagues must be perceived by the person as appropriate and wanted, otherwise a reverse buffering effect (Fenlason & Beehr 1994) may occur.

Three other studies we will mention here examined support from the family environment rather than from work. In a survey of Japanese married working women, Matsui, Ohsawa and Onglatco (1995) found that emotional and practical support from their husbands buffered the impact of parental demands on levels of work–family conflict experienced by women in their sample. However, this research did not differentiate between work → family interference and family → work interference. It may be anticipated that husband support could have more influence in respect of family → work interference rather than work → family interference.

Aryee *et al.* (1999) also examined the effects of spousal support, in a sample of male and female Hong Kong dual-earner parents. In their study, separate measures of work → family and family → work interference were collected. Consistent with Matsui *et al.*'s findings, Aryee and his colleagues observed that spousal support had a moderating effect on work–family conflict, but only in relation to family → work interference, that is spousal support buffered the impact of parental demands on family → work interference. They conclude that 'this finding may be reflective of the effectiveness of within-domain support on the perceived spillover from that domain' (p. 273). As noted above, support from one's partner/spouse or other family members is unlikely to have a significant bearing on levels of conflict emanating from work demands, as people outside the work context have little if any influence over these demands.

Lapierre and Allen (2006) also observed that support from family members is related to reduced levels of both time-based and strain-based family → work interference. In their study, however, only instrumental assistance contributed significantly to reduced conflict. Lapierre and Allen suggest that instrumental help from family members may be of more benefit than emotional assistance, although in their study there was a relatively strong correlation (r = 0.61) between these two kinds of assistance.

So far we have focused predominantly on work-related sources of support, especially from supervisors and work colleagues, although we have also briefly referred to support from family sources (such as partner/ spouse and other family members). Research evidence to date indicates that work-related support is more likely to reduce work → life (especially work → family) interference, whereas family support has more impact on family → work interference. Later in the chapter we discuss the effects of support provided by the organization as a whole, including formal policies. We now turn to a second variable which has been found to play a substantial role in alleviating work–life conflict.

Personal Control

In addition to social support, another factor which has a marked influence on people's well-being and stress reduction is the extent of control they feel they can exert over their circumstances. In the stress literature generally, perceived control has consistently been associated with lower levels of psychological strain and higher well-being (e.g. Hatinen *et al.* 2007; Spell & Arnold 2007), as well as moderating (buffering) the effects of work-related stressors on strain and well-being (e.g. de Jonge & Dormann 2006; O'Driscoll & Beehr 2000). There is substantial evidence, therefore, that personal control plays a pivotal role in the alleviation of stress, either as a direct predictor of reduced strain or as a buffering variable (as hypothesized by the well-known Karasek (1979) job demands/control model of strain).

Perceived control has also been found to be an important variable in respect of work–life conflict, and there have been numerous empirical studies examining its role in reducing the negative impact of work–life conflict on well-being and life satisfaction. Researchers have uniformly concluded that providing workers with the opportunity to exercise greater control and have more autonomy, especially in terms of their work schedules, will yield positive benefits for individuals, as well as potentially for the organization. For instance, Allen (2001) and Shockley and Allen (2007) suggest that a major benefit of 'family-friendly' policies occurs when they offer increased flexibility in work scheduling, which enables individuals to better accommodate their family commitments. The benefits of this increased flexibility may be two-fold: on the one hand, they allow parents to take more direct control over their work time (and, increasingly, workplace) so that family responsibilities can be attended to and, on the other, they increase feelings of autonomy and control, which are important components of well-being (Warr 2005). This line of thinking is also consistent with the general approach advocated by Hobfoll's (1989) Conservation of Resources theory of stress, which posits the acquisition of personal control (over one's environment) as a valued resource. Efforts to increase levels of personal control are likely to generate greater resilience and resistance to stress.

Similar themes have been echoed by other researchers. From a very comprehensive review of the literature on organizational work–family policies, Kelly *et al.* (2008) conclude that being able to exert some level of personal control over work time, in particular, is a major predictor of reduced work–family conflict and enhanced work–life balance. For instance, Anderson, Coffey and Byerly (2002) argue that formal policies regarding flexible work schedules are most effective (for both men and women) when they are supported by informal workplace practices which allow individuals to exert control and autonomy. In their pioneering research on the effects of organizational initiatives, mentioned earlier, Thomas and Ganster (1995) reflect that increased flexibility and control are key ingredients for ensuring that organizational policies concerning work–life balance have positive outcomes. Similarly, Behson (2002) encourages managers to modify informal work practices in order to allow greater employee control over their work schedules.

Moderator effects of personal control have also been illustrated, although perhaps surprisingly there have been relatively few direct explorations of the moderator effects of perceived control on the relationship between work–family conflict (as a stressor) and psychological strain or well-being. In a study of coping with work–family conflict among Hong Kong workers, Aryee *et al.* (1999) observed that active attempts to deal with work–family conflict issues are only effective when individuals feel that they have some degree of personal control over the work environment, especially their work schedule. Thomas and Ganster (1995), on the other hand, suggest that perceived control may be a mediator (rather than a moderator) of the relationship between flexibility and outcomes of work–family conflict. In other words, the reason why flexibility in work schedules is valuable is that it can afford individuals more personal control, which in turn generates positive outcomes for them.

In sum, it is very clear that perceptions of having control over one's work schedule and even place of work can have a substantial bearing on either directly alleviating work–life conflict or indirectly reducing the negative impact of this form of inter-role conflict. Increased control can be beneficial in that it will enable individuals to better balance the demands and commitments of their work and non-work roles, but also there is a psychological benefit in that feeling greater control over one's life in itself generates positive well-being. Individuals and organizations should therefore continue to explore ways in which personal control can be enhanced. Although clearly there are practical constraints on how much autonomy and control can be afforded to individual workers, depending on the work context and the nature of their job, a general principle is that permitting workers to exercise an appropriate amount of control over their work schedule will yield beneficial results in terms of reduced inter-domain conflict and greater well-being. A major challenge, of course, is to determine how increased autonomy and control over work schedules can be implemented in ways that are both feasible for the organization and beneficial for employees. Unfortunately, research to date has offered little guidance on how this might be achieved (Kelly *et al.* 2008).

Above we have outlined the salience of these two general factors (social support and personal control). We now turn to individual strategies for dealing with work–life conflict, which will be followed by a discussion of organizational initiatives designed to alleviate work–life conflict and promote greater work–life balance for organizational members.

Personal Coping Strategies

Since the 1980s, there has been ongoing debate about the mechanisms used by individuals in their efforts to achieve greater work–life balance, although there would appear to be relatively few empirical studies testing the impact of different coping strategies (Drach-Zahavy & Somech 2008). As with more general research on coping with stress, the predominant theoretical perspective adopted by work–family conflict researchers is Lazarus' differentiation between problem-focused and emotion-focused coping (see Chapter 2 for an overview of this model). An early typology of coping strategies was proposed by Hall (1972), who outlined three broad types of coping that a person might engage in to reduce the impact of work–life conflict. The first type, structural role (re)definition, entails changing other people's expectations about one's role, either at work or in the family. An example of the use of this approach would be negotiating with one's partner/spouse about who will undertake different household chores. Personal role (re)definition, the second strategy, involves modifying one's own expectations and goals. For instance, one might decide to prioritize certain tasks both at work and at home and to focus only on those that are highly important. Finally, reactive role behaviour means endeavouring to fulfil all obligations, without changing anything, and reflects a relatively passive (if demanding!) approach to accommodate role demands. Although this strategy may be functional in the short term, ultimately it is unlikely to be very adaptive, and can heighten strain and reduce overall psychological well-being. On the other hand, a combination of the first two types of coping is likely to generate benefits for people wishing to achieve a better balance between their work and family lives.

There are several examples of research which have explored people's use (or attempted use) of problem-focused and emotion-focused coping strategies in relation to work–life conflict.

For instance, Aryee *et al.* (1999) examined problem-focused and emotion-focused coping behaviours associated with the experience of work–family conflict among Hong Kong Chinese employed parents. They hypothesized that these coping behaviours would moderate the relationship between inter-role conflict and three criterion variables: job satisfaction, family satisfaction and life satisfaction. However, problem-focused coping was found to be ineffective in buffering the impact of both work → family interference and family → work interference on these indicators of well-being, and emotion-focused coping served to moderate only one relationship, that between family → work interference and job satisfaction. Aryee *et al.* suggest that the lack of effects for problem-focused coping in particular may be due to workers feeling that they had little control over their work schedules; under these conditions, efforts to modify the situation may simply have been ineffectual.

Parallel findings to those of Aryee *et al.* are reported by Pinquart and Silbereisen (2008) from a study of almost 2000 workers in Germany. These researchers investigated the relationship between demands from both work and family life and depressive symptoms, along with problem-focused coping. In this study, problem-focused coping moderated the relationship between family-related demands and depression, but not the relationship between work demands and depression. Pinquart and Silbereisen comment that 'stress-buffering effects of problem-focused coping would more likely occur if stressors are changeable' (p. 219), and that their respondents perceived higher levels of control over family demands than work demands.

Jex and his colleagues (Adams & Jex 1999; Jex & Elacqua 1999) examined the effects of one type of problem-focused coping: time management. Because time-based conflict is one of the major forms of interference between work and family (Greenhaus & Beutell 1985), Jex *et al.* hypothesized that using time management should buffer the relationship between work–family conflict and strain. However, although time management may assist in reducing work–family conflict, Jex and Elacqua did not find support for the moderation hypothesis. Once again, it is likely that the extent to which individuals can exert control over their work and family demands will affect the relative influence of time management strategies. Similarly, time management may only be effective in respect of reducing time commitments, and may not necessarily reduce other sources of inter-role conflict, especially strain-based conflict.

More recently, Lapierre and Allen (2006) examined time-based and strain-based work → family and family → work interference, and found that problem-focused coping (such as setting priorities at home and work, seeking assistance and being organized) was negatively related to strain-based family → work interference, although this coping had no significant relationship with other forms of work–family conflict. Lapierre and Allen conclude that 'such coping skills could help family stressors from draining energy that is needed at work but may be of little if any help in terms of securing more time for work activities' and that 'situational constraints at work (e.g. externally imposed deadlines) may make it difficult for problem-focused coping to be of significant value in that role' (p. 178). This is consistent with the notion that problem-focused coping is only effective when the individual can exert some degree of control over the environment. If work demands and schedules are not under the person's control, setting priorities and other forms of problem-focused coping may have little impact on work → family interference.

A somewhat different approach is that adopted by Baltes and Heydens-Gahir (2003), who outline a model of coping with work–family conflict based upon goal-setting, which parallels the Conservation of Resources theory (Hobfoll 1989) referred to earlier in this chapter. The Baltes and Heydens-Gahir model incorporates three distinct forms of coping, all of which may be construed as variants of problem-focused coping. The first of these is *selection*, which entails identifying and setting life goals, which serve to channel one's efforts and energies. In respect of work–family conflict, a person may determine to concentrate their attention on a small number of activities or commit themselves to achieving one or two important goals. The second component of this model is *optimization*, which refers to developing ways of achieving one's goals, such as maintaining a sustained effort and devoting oneself to the achievement of goals. Finally, *compensation* is a coping strategy utilized if optimization is not successful, and involves setting alternative goals which are more achievable. In their study, Baltes and Heydens-Gahir found that these strategies were associated with reduced job-related stressors and family-related stressors, which in turn led to a reduction in work → family interference and family → work interference. However, in the work context, selection coping appeared to be the most viable strategy (e.g. refusing to take on additional work assignments so that family responsibilities could be attended to), whereas in the family setting only optimization was linked with a reduction in family stressors, but selection and compensation did not have the hypothesized stressor-reduction effects. This research is of particular interest as it illustrates that the effects of coping strategies may vary depending on the context. Again, the extent to which a person can exert control over his or her courses of action would appear to be a major determinant of whether or not a particular coping behaviour will be effective.

While there has been considerable research on organizational policies and initiatives designed to assist workers to achieve reduced work–family conflict and better work–life balance, with an emphasis on increasing flexibility and personal control, Behson (2002) comments that 'little empirical research has been conducted on the types of informal behaviors employees use to balance work and family concerns' (p. 324). Whereas formal approaches involve arrangements such as job sharing with a colleague, use of flexitime or parental leave, Behson developed a set of 16 items to assess informal work accommodations to family (IWAF) as a mechanism for coping with work → family interference. These accommodations were based on Lazarus' differentiation of problem-focused and emotion-focused coping, and include behaviours such as leaving work early to fulfil a family responsibility, arranging for a colleague to cover work tasks so that the person can accommodate a family need, taking some time off during the day to deal with a family matter, working through the lunch hour in order to be able to leave work early, and even taking children to work occasionally. These are not formally organized practices, but rather ad hoc arrangements that a person may make to enable him or her to attend to non-work issues. In his research on the benefits of IWAF, Behson found that, while there was no direct relationship between IWAF and strain, job satisfaction or organizational commitment, use of IWAF served as a buffer between work → family inference and psychological strain. In a second investigation, he observed that IWAF was positively linked with seeking social support and negatively related to emotion-focused coping. Behson concluded that informal accommodations can play a very valuable role in alleviating work–family conflict, and that organizations should encourage their employees to exert greater control over their work schedules.

Rotondo and her colleagues (Rotondo, Carlson & Kincaid 2003; Rotondo & Kincaid 2008) examined four different coping styles in relation to work–family conflict (both directions). Consistent with the notion that problem-focused coping may be more beneficial in alleviating the negative impact of work–family conflict, Rotondo, Carlson and Kincaid (2003) found that seeking assistance and direct action at home (trying to be more efficient, working harder) were associated with lower family → work interference, whereas avoidance/resignation was linked with greater conflict between domains. In their more recent study, Rotondo and Kincaid (2008) concluded that emotion-focused coping (such as positive thinking and cognitive reappraisal of the situation) had little influence on either work → family or family → work interference, and problem-focused coping also did not alleviate work → family interference although (consistent with their previous findings) it was related to reduced family → work interference. Together, the two studies illustrate that coping strategies which may reduce one direction of conflict, for instance family → work interference, do not necessarily ameliorate the other direction of conflict. This suggests that further investigation is needed of the conditions under which various coping strategies are most likely to be effective.

In a reflective review of the literature on coping with work–family conflict, Jennings and McDougald (2007) note four other coping styles that people may engage in: *segmentation* (deliberately separating work from life off the job), *compensation* (getting highly involved in one domain to compensate for dissatisfaction or lack of fulfilment in the other), *accommodation* (limiting psychological or behavioural involvement in one domain in order to meet the demands of the other) and *boundary management* (developing a strategy for creating, maintaining and crossing borders between domains). Segmentation could be viewed as an extreme form of boundary management, where the person maintains a strict isolation between work and non-work domains. Jennings and McDougald observed that the choice of coping strategies will be influenced by a number of factors, including work schedule autonomy (or control) and flexibility and household/family demands and responsibilities. They also discuss possible gender differences in the selection of coping strategies. For instance, there is evidence that women have less boundary separation between work and family domains than do men, and hence tend to experience more spillover from family to work (Williams & Alliger 1994). As a result, they are also more likely than men to express a desire for segmentation (Rothbard, Philips & Dumas 2005).

Some researchers have utilized an inductive approach to determining how individuals cope with work–life conflict, rather than assessing strategies derived from a priori theoretical models of coping. An example of this is research conducted by Wiersma (1994), who set out to describe specific behaviours engaged in by dual-career couples to deal with work–home conflict issues. Wiersma interviewed males and females who were in a dual-career relationship, using the critical incident technique, which focuses on specific events or incidents and asks the individual how he or she behaved in each situation, and the results (outcomes) of their behaviour. From interviews with 24 respondents (9 males, 15 females), Wiersma developed 130 critical incidents, 99 of which were retained and categorized into six different areas of work–home conflict. Independent judges then classified the behavioural responses into the six categories. Some of the major coping mechanisms reported by these dual-career workers included hiring domestic help, dividing household chores among family members, setting priorities (at both work and home), cognitive reappraisal (evaluating the importance and meaning of what they were doing), maintaining social relationships, role cycling (including delegation of tasks), mutual sharing (such as celebrating each other's accomplishments) and ignoring negative comments (about their arrangements) from other people. Most of these strategies could be described as either problem-focused or emotion-focused coping behaviours.

A more recent illustration of the inductive approach is reflected in two studies reported by Somech and Drach-Zahavy (2007). In their first study, these researchers conducted focus group interviews with employed parents, who identified eight distinct strategies relevant to coping with work → family and family → work interference. Somech and Drach-Zahavy labelled these eight strategies 'super at home', 'good enough at home', 'delegation at home', 'priorities at home', 'super at work', 'good enough at work', 'delegation at work' and 'priorities at work'. Clearly, there are parallels between these coping behaviours and the typology developed by Hall (1972), which was discussed earlier. There is also some overlap with Lazarus' notion of problem-focused and emotion-focused coping. In their follow-up study, Somech and Drach-Zahavy (2007) observed some gender role differences, with women who were more 'modern' in their ideology and men who were more 'traditional' both reporting that they tried to achieve a better work–life balance by exerting additional effort in their job (i.e. being super at work) and by delegating household chores to others (i.e. using delegation at home and the 'good enough' approach). Traditional women and modern men, on the other hand, apparently endeavoured to use a segmentation approach to their work–life balance, by delegating work responsibilities and setting priorities at work so that sufficient time was available to devote to their home lives.

Findings from the above studies seem to suggest that problem-focused coping approaches are more likely than emotion-focused approaches to be effective in reducing either work → family or family → work interference. By and large, this is consistent with findings from the more general literature on stress coping, but again we would emphasize that the benefits of problem-focused coping rely heavily on the person having the capacity to exert at least some influence over the stressor(s). If a person is not able to change their environment, for example their work demands or their family responsibilities, problem-focused coping is unlikely to be effective and could in fact have some negative implications, for instance by creating a sense of inefficacy in the person and hence lowering their self-esteem. In these situations, it may be more beneficial for a person to utilize some form of emotion-focused coping, especially re-evaluating the importance of different aspects of their lives and perhaps even accepting that some demands and responsibilities are inevitable. Innstrand *et al.* (2008), for instance, suggest that psychologically distancing oneself from work pressures and problems may be an effective emotion-focused strategy for reducing work–family conflict. However, Pinquart and Silbereisen (2008) found that distancing amplified, rather than reduced, the effects of work-related stressors, again attributing this to the relative lack of control that individuals often experience in relation to work demands.

Most of the research described above has focused on strategies that may be regarded as forms of active coping, where the individual deliberately takes some action in their efforts to reduce or even pre-empt work–life conflict. As we know from the more general coping literature, however, often individuals are less proactive (or even reactive) in their responses to stressors and engage in various forms of avoidance coping. Interestingly, while this is recognized in stress research as a commonly used approach, there has been relatively little systematic empirical research on avoidance coping in relation to work–life conflict. Avoidance is typically viewed as a type of emotion-focused coping, and sometimes has been subsumed under that more generic label, but this obscures its specific impact and it is preferable to explore it separately from other types of emotion-focused coping (such as reappraisal of the importance of a stressor).

Some studies of work–life conflict have investigated the specific use of avoidance strategies. Two examples are Snow *et al.* (2003) and Rotondo, Carlson and Kincaid (2003). Using a longitudinal methodology (which is relatively rare in this field of research), Snow *et al.* (2003) explored the use of avoidance and active coping among female secretaries in the United States. Avoidance coping operated as a 'risk factor' in that it was related to higher levels of anxiety, depression and somatic complaints four months later and, to some extent, mediated the relationship between stressors and strain. However, its potential buffering (moderating) role was not investigated by Snow and his colleagues. In their research, Rotondo, Carlson and Kincaid (2003) explored avoidance and resignation conjointly, predicting that the use of this coping style would be associated with higher levels of work → family and family → work interference. This hypothesis was confirmed for both time-based conflict and strain-based conflict. Interestingly, females reported greater usage of avoidance/ resignation than did males, which Rotondo, Carlson and Kincaid argue is of concern, given that women often experience higher levels of work– family conflict than do men (Williams & Alliger 1994). From the above two studies, it is clear that use of avoidance as a coping strategy is not likely to generate beneficial outcomes, in either the short term or the longer term.

In the above section we have endeavoured to provide an overview of major themes emerging from over 30 years of research on how people attempt to cope personally with problems related to work–life conflict. Our review has been necessarily selective and we have not attempted to cover all the studies which have been reported but rather to focus on some of the key issues emerging from research in this area. A major theme is that the choice of coping strategy and the effectiveness of coping behaviours are contingent upon the extent to which individuals can exert some degree of control over their environment, whether at work or outside of work. In particular, the utilization and effectiveness of active, problem-focused coping strategies is highly dependent on some level of personal control. Second, it is evident that there are individual differences in both usage and benefits of different forms of coping, and that these individual differences may reflect variations in the environmental demands faced by different people. For instance, some studies have noted distinct gender or gender-role differences in coping behaviours, which may be attributable to the differential expectations and demands confronted by men and women. Personality factors may also play a major role in this regard, and there is some evidence that choice of coping strategy may be influenced by certain personality characteristics, such as neuroticism or extraversion (Norlander, Von Schedvin & Archer 2005). Third, as we have noted several times in this book, the appraisal process undertaken by individuals will have a substantial impact on the selection of coping method(s) and their outcomes. For instance, appraising an incident or event as a challenge stressor versus a hindrance stressor will largely determine the manner in which a person approaches that incident or event, and consequently the impact of the stressor on their well-being.

Before moving to a discussion of organizational initiatives and interventions to reduce work–life conflict and assist with work–life balance, for further reading on personal coping we recommend recent chapters by Drach-Zahavy and Somech (2008) and Thompson *et al.* (2007). Each of these chapters reviewed research on coping with work–life conflict, and Thompson *et al.* provide a useful table summary of some of the major studies and their findings. These authors also developed a valuable model of the coping process, which includes primary and secondary appraisal of stressors (relating to work–family conflict) and potential consequences of problem-focused and emotion-focused coping behaviours.

Organizational Strategies to Ameliorate Work–Life Conflict

In contrast to the relative paucity of research on the use and effectiveness of personal coping efforts to reduce work–life conflict, there has been a plethora of research in recent years on the benefits and limitations of organizational policies and practices which are designed to improve work–life balance for organizational members. The importance of reducing conflict between work and non-work among workers has become increasingly recognized as an issue not just for individuals themselves but also for their organization. For instance, many organizations realize that where their employees experience excessive conflict between their work and family lives this is likely to lead to dissatisfaction, strain, absenteeism, intentions to leave and perhaps even performance deficits (Perry-Smith & Blum 2000). For this reason, organizations often institute policies and strategies that are intended to help employees reduce inter-domain conflict. These approaches are a form of organizational stress management intervention (SMI), which we discuss in more detail in Chapter 6.

A basic premise underlying organizational strategies is that individuals cannot, by themselves, resolve all the difficulties associated with conflict between work and family (or non-work), especially if they have little influence over the factors (stressors) which lead to work–life conflict. Hence there is a need for the organization to take some responsibility for addressing these factors. Research in this field has examined two major issues: (a) the nature of policies and practices implemented by organizations and (b) how effective these strategies are in reducing work–life conflict and resulting strain. Below we report a selection of studies which have investigated these issues. As with our review above of the literature on personal coping strategies, our intention is not to provide an exhaustive review of all the research which has been reported but rather to summarize the major themes and conclusions emerging from this line of investigation, and to highlight some critical issues surrounding the implementation of so-called family-friendly (or worker-friendly) policies.

There have been many investigations of the possible effects of specific policies or initiatives designed by organizations to help reduce work–family conflict or alleviate its negative consequences. However, findings from these studies have been very inconsistent, and have not always indicated that specific policies yield positive outcomes for employees. For instance, Goff, Mount and Jamison (1990) found no support for the prediction that use of a work-based childcare centre would reduce either work–family conflict or absenteeism among employed parents, although supervisor support was related to less work–family conflict. Goff *et al.* suggest that what is critical is parents' satisfaction with their childcare arrangements, rather than whether these are located on- or off-site.

Anderson, Coffey and Byerly (2002) used data from a US-wide survey of over 2000 workers which asked about the availability of services to help find childcare, information about eldercare services, employer-sponsored or -operated childcare centres and direct or indirect financial assistance with childcare. The survey also questioned respondents about their perceptions of schedule flexibility, manager support and career consequences of using work–family policies. Anderson and her colleagues found that negative career consequences (from using policies) and lack of managerial support were major predictors of work $\rightarrow$ family interference, which in turn was linked with job dissatisfaction, turnover intentions and strain. Although schedule flexibility did have some relationship with the outcomes, its contribution was not substantial. The availability of dependent care benefits was essentially unrelated to all of the outcome variables.

Unfortunately, much of the research on the relationship between organizational family-friendly policies and work–family conflict has been cross-sectional in design, which severely limits conclusions which may be drawn about the effects of these policies. There have, nevertheless, been a few longitudinal studies. A good illustration is a US national survey conducted by Hammer *et al.* (2005), who investigated the impact of couples' utilization of workplace supports on their levels of work–family conflict (both directions) and job satisfaction one year later. They distinguish between *policies* (such as flexible work arrangements), *services* (e.g. providing information about dependent care options) and *benefits* (e.g. childcare subsidies or on-site childcare facilities). They also note that often research has focused on the availability of organizational policies, services and benefits rather than on their actual usage. In their research, Hammer *et al.* explored utilization of 13 different workplace supports, grouped into two categories: alternative work arrangements and dependent care supports. As anticipated, wives were more likely to utilize workplace supports than their husbands were. Paradoxically, however, the availability and usage of organizationally family-friendly benefits led to higher rather than lower work–family conflict, for women at least. Hammer *et al.* suggest that 'using supports may serve to exacerbate wives' own work–family conflicts by enabling wives, the traditional caregivers, to take on even more family care responsibilities rather than increasing their own ability to manage existing work and family demands' (pp. 805–6).

Blair-Loy and Wharton (2002) argue that analysis of the use of workplace family-friendly policies must consider the social context of work groups. In most work settings, individuals do not function in isolation from work colleagues and the attitudes and behaviours of the latter can have a substantial bearing on whether a person avails themselves of an organizational policy. As noted above, the formal existence of a particular policy does not necessarily mean that it will be utilized by employees. There are several reasons for this, including that it may not meet an individual's specific needs, and that the person may be concerned about their colleagues' reactions and the impact that their use of a policy might have on their colleagues' workload. Therefore, as illustrated in a follow-up publication by Blair-Loy and Wharton (2004), organizations must be aware of some of the potential constraints upon usage of policies that may have been designed with good intentions but do not necessarily 'fit' well in the work context. Again, support from the immediate supervisor is highlighted by

Blair-Loy and Wharton as a key factor affecting individuals' decisions about whether or not to utilize family-friendly policies.

Kirby and Krone (2002) also discuss organizational factors which may inhibit employees from taking advantage of family-friendly policies. In particular, they observed that the absence from work of a team member may impinge upon the other team members' ability to complete all the work required and lead to an increase in their workloads. According to Kirby and Krone, the discourse which surrounds policy implementation can play a crucial role in whether policies are practical and usable. At an informal level, despite the existence of formal policies which seem to promote work–family integration, the team culture may make it very difficult for an individual to actually take advantage of the policies. In particular, team members' communications about what is and what is not acceptable will contribute significantly to decisions about whether or not to use a policy, such as taking time off to attend family matters.

Other studies have, nevertheless, confirmed the efficacy of family-friendly policies in reducing work–family conflict. For instance, Thomas and Ganster (1995) examined the direct and indirect benefits of organizational policies and practices which are supportive of family responsibilities. They found that flexible work schedules and supervisor support were both directly associated with greater feelings of personal control among workers, and that control was negatively related to work–family conflict. In addition, supervisor support showed a direct (negative) relationship with work–family conflict. As we discussed earlier in this chapter, Thomas and Ganster suggest that personal control is a key factor in the reduction of work–family conflict and that the benefits of organizational policies will be most evident when they enhance levels of personal control among workers.

Frye and Breaugh (2004) found that a global measure of the usefulness of family-friendly policies was significantly related to lower levels of work → family interference (although not, predictably, to family → work interference). Kirchmeyer (1995) reports that policies which increase flexibility in the work/non-work boundary and provide employees with resources that assist them in fulfilling non-work responsibilities are likely to be effective. On the other hand, there is also some evidence that suggests a *positive* relationship between organizational work–family initiatives and work–family conflict. For example, in a longitudinal investigation, Brough, O'Driscoll and Kalliath (2005) observed that use of workplace supports was associated with greater family → work interference, although it was unrelated to work → family interference. As suggested by Hammer *et al.* (2005), it may be that using resources from the organization may exacerbate family → work interference because it confirms to the person their reliance on extra help and an inability to manage things by themselves.

Whereas some studies have indicated that family-friendly initiatives yield positive benefits for individual workers, in terms of reducing levels of work–family conflict, other researchers have suggested that the availability and even usage of such policies may not be sufficient to significantly alleviate the strain arising from work–family conflict. In addition to specific policies or programmes, support from managers and supervisors is needed for individuals to experience any meaningful reductions in work–family conflict. Furthermore, Allen (2001) suggests that a more fundamental consideration is whether the organization is perceived as being supportive of employees' family needs and responsibilities. She developed a measure (containing 14 items) of family-supportive work environments, and examined this construct as a connecting link between work–family conflict (in the work → family direction) and possible work-related outcomes: job satisfaction, organizational commitment and turnover intentions. Allen's work extended earlier research by Thompson, Beauvais and Lyness (1999), who had designed an instrument to assess work–family culture, which focused on 'shared assumptions, beliefs and values regarding the extent to which an organization supports and values the integration of employees' work and family lives' (p. 392). Allen's measure is an extension of the Thompson *et al.* approach in that it specifically assesses perceptions of support provided by the organization (note that supervisor support was ascertained separately). Perceptions of organizational support for family were directly related to reduced work–family conflict, increased job satisfaction and organizational commitment, and lower turnover intentions. In addition, perceived organizational support completely mediated the impact of supervisor support on work–family conflict, that is supervisor support induced perceptions of organizational support, which in turn were linked with reduced conflict. Perceived organizational support also mediated the relationship between family-friendly benefits and reduced conflict, increased satisfaction and increased commitment.

Similar findings are reported by O'Driscoll *et al.* (2003). In a study of managerial personnel in New Zealand, the availability of specific organizational policies (such as flexitime, compressed work schedules and on-site childcare centres) bore no direct relationship to reductions in work → family interference, family → work interference or psychological strain. Instead, these relationships were fully mediated by perceptions of organizational supportiveness. It would seem that the key to helping workers reduce work–life conflict and enhance their psychological well-being lies not so much in the provision of specific policies but rather in the development of a culture which is perceived to be family- or worker-supportive. O'Driscoll *et al.* also found that supervisor support moder-ated (buffered) the relationship between levels of work → family interference (but not family → work interference) and psychological strain, highlighting the importance of having support from one's imme-diate supervisor.

Thompson and her associates (Kopelman *et al.* 2006; Thompson *et al.* 2004) report results which are congruent with those reported by O'Driscoll *et al.* (2003). In their first study, which collected data at two time periods separated by an interval of 18 months, Thompson *et al.* (2004) found that intangible (emotional) support from the organization was related to later (reduced) work → family interference, but tangible support (information and instrumental support) did not. In their second study (Kopelman *et al.* 2006), there was a significant link between the number of work–family initiatives offered by an organization and employee perceptions of organi-zational support and their affective commitment to the organization. However, the number of work–life programmes offered was essentially unrelated to work → family interference or family → work interference. Kopelman *et al.* comment that one possible reason for this apparent anomaly is that work–life initiatives may have some remedial impact on the availability of more time to attend to family matters (e.g. via flexitime) but often do not really change basic work demands. In other words, unless work-related demands can be substantially reduced, organizational policies and practices are unlikely to generate systematic reductions in work–life conflict.

A multi-national study by Lapierre *et al.* (2008) also confirms the impor-tance of a family-supportive work environment. Specifically, perceptions of organizational support were linked with lower levels of both work → family interference and family → work interference (although the relationships were generally stronger for the former), which in turn were associated negatively with job, family and overall life satisfaction. Interest-ingly, perceived organizational support was equally related to reduced time-based work → family interference and strain-based work → family interference, suggesting that the positive effects of these perceptions generalize across forms of work → family interference. Lapierre *et al.* suggest that overall perceptions of the organization as being supportive of individuals' family needs is a critical factor in promoting better work–life balance. This conclusion is consistent with Grandey, Cordeiro and Michael's (2007) suggestion that key ingredients for alleviating work–family conflict may be the provision of supervisor support and personal autonomy to manage work–family issues.

Conclusions

Overall, it is evident from the above summary of research on the management of work–life conflict that there is no clear-cut answer to the question: 'Do organizational policies work?'. Some specific initiatives, such as offering flexibility in work schedules, do have positive outcomes for workers, whereas the effects of others (e.g. on-site dependant care facilities) are not uniform. Several key themes emerge from a review of the literature. First, it is not necessarily the specific policies per se which are responsible for any reductions in work–life conflict, at least not directly. They may help, but only if they contribute to an organizational culture which is viewed as supportive of work–life balance or integration. There can be many constraints or barriers to individuals attempting to take advantage of specific policies or programmes. Growing evidence indicates that a supportive organizational environment, which includes organizational values which are family-friendly or worker-friendly, plus supportive supervision, is critical for reducing conflict between work and 'non-work' life and enhancing work–life balance.

Ultimately, organizational initiatives to assist individuals to better balance their work and non-work lives, especially family commitments and responsibilities, will be effective in reducing the negative effects of work–life conflict only if they provide flexibility and enable individuals to take personal control over the nature and timing of their work. As we have outlined earlier in this chapter, several studies have illustrated the vital role played by flexibility and personal control in helping individuals cope with the strain associated with work–life conflict. Similarly, feeling supported (both instrumentally and emotionally) by one's supervisor, work colleagues and family members, as well as by organizational management, is an important ingredient for reducing work–life conflict and enhancing work–life balance. As with the other stressors we have reviewed in this book, managing the work–life interface is a joint responsibility of both the individual (and their family) and the organization. Unilateral efforts to reduce interference between the two domains (work and 'life') are likely to have limited effectiveness; rather, collaboration between workers and their organization is needed to address the fundamental causes of inter-role conflict and to generate conditions which foster balance between the work and non-work domains.

6

Stress Management Interventions

As we have discussed throughout this book, the cost (both financial and human) of stress is substantial for individuals, their families and work colleagues, as well as for employers. There are also signs that levels of work-related stress generally may be increasing in society, imposing additional burdens on the societal infrastructure needed to deal with the aftermath of stress. Nevertheless, despite widespread recognition that stress is a significant issue and of its potential disruptiveness to people's lives and their work performance, the level of attention accorded by organizations to addressing stress-related issues is still relatively small when compared with their investments in other areas, such as financial budgeting, marketing and technological development (Beehr & O'Driscoll 2002; Cooper, Dewe & O'Driscoll 2001). Many possible reasons have been cited for this relative lack of attention, and some of these will be outlined shortly. We begin this chapter with a definition of the term 'stress management intervention' (SMI) and a discussion of the importance of such interventions. This will be followed by an overview of different perspectives on stress management, and a critique of efforts to evaluate the effectiveness of SMIs. We conclude the chapter with some recommendations for more efficacious implementation of interventions, along with some further issues that need to be considered in the stress management process within work settings.

Coping with Work Stress: A Review and Critique, Philip J. Dewe, Michael P. O'Driscoll and Cary L. Cooper, © 2010 John Wiley & Sons Ltd.

Conceptual Framework for Stress Management Interventions

Various definitions of SMIs have been proposed by stress researchers, varying in terms of their degree of specificity, hence it is critical to be clear on the conceptualization of these interventions. Broadly speaking, an SMI is any activity which is designed to reduce or eliminate stressors and/or their effects on strain (Burke & Richardsen 2000; Murphy & Sauter 2003). Some of these activities, such as job design, may directly remove or reduce work stressors (e.g. role ambiguity, role conflict or work overload), whereas others, such as stress management training, are intended to mitigate the impact of stressors on individual workers, and yet others, such as employee assistance programmes (EAPs), aim to rehabilitate individuals who have experienced unmanageable strain. Similarly, some approaches (*individually focused* interventions) may be targeted at the individual, whereas *organizationally focused* interventions endeavour to change the work environment or other aspects of organizational functioning in order to reduce stressors or resultant strain.

Individually focused (or person-focused) interventions typically attempt to achieve one of two goals: (a) modifying people's appraisals of stressors, so that individuals are not as strongly influenced by the stressors, or (b) change people's ways of responding to stressors, that is their coping behaviours. One of the earliest classifications of individual-level coping strategies (Newman & Beehr 1979) grouped coping behaviours into four categories:

1. Behaviours aimed at the person's own psychological state, such as forward planning and assessment of one's aspirations.
2. Health-related behaviours, such as diet, exercise and sleep, which are designed to improve one's physical status.
3. Changing one's behaviour and activities to improve life generally, for example by engaging in relaxation, taking more holidays or developing close friendships to increase social support.
4. Behaviours intended to change the work environment, such as reducing one's workload, delegating some tasks to other people or even changing to a less demanding job.

Research evidence for the effectiveness of these approaches in reducing work-related stress in the longer term is mixed, although some techniques may have positive benefits. A potential limitation is the inherent assumption that individuals can control and change the circumstances which have produced strain for them. Although this may be true for some external factors, in other cases elimination or even modification of the stressors may be beyond the person's immediate control, in which case individual coping behaviours may have little impact on the situation(s) which created strain (Cooper, Dewe & O'Driscoll 2001; Semmer 2003).

Organizationally focused interventions are based on the assumption that the responsibility for stress management is shared by the employer and management. A plethora of different types of intervention have been promoted in the popular literature and, compared with the 1980s, organizations are certainly more receptive these days to investigating work-related sources of stress and endeavouring to make the workplace more 'healthy' for their employees (Noblet & LaMontagne 2006; Semmer 2008). Some of these efforts are directed towards stressors directly or the alleviation of strain, whereas others are targeted at more general 'health promotion'. Newman and Beehr (1979) suggest that there are three categories of the stressor-reduction approach:

1. Changing people's tasks, such as designing jobs to better match workers' abilities and preferences or providing training to increase workers' capacity to complete tasks.
1. Changing role characteristics, which may mean reducing workload, increasing involvement in decision-making or reducing role conflict.
2. Changing characteristics of the organizations, such as communication or management structures, and processes that may affect people directly (e.g. the reward system, training and development, supervision styles).

While it is evident that these can be distinct strategies, they also overlap considerably and changes at one level can have a marked impact on other levels. For instance, increasing employee participation in decision-making can influence the ways in which people interact with their supervisors and their perceptions of their role in the organization.

Another way of considering interventions is to reflect on the *level* of intervention, that is, what is the intervention attempting to achieve? A conceptual framework for SMIs which has been frequently utilized is that presented in Table 6.1, which depicts three distinct levels of intervention.

Table 6.1   Typology of stress management interventions

Primary Interventions
Scope: Preventive: Reduce the number and/or intensity of stressors
Target: Work environments, technologies or organizational structures and functions
Underlying assumption: Most effective approach to stress management is to remove stressors
Examples: Job redesign, role restructuring, management development (e.g. communication)
Secondary Interventions
Scope: Preventive and/or reactive: Modify individuals' responses to stressors
Target: Individual person
Underlying assumption: May not be able to remove or reduce stressors, so best to focus on individuals' reactions to these stressors
Examples: Stress management training, 'wellness' programmes
Tertiary Interventions
Scope: Reactive: Minimize the damaging consequences of stressors by helping individuals cope more effectively with the outcomes of stress
Target: Individual person
Underlying assumption: Focus is on 'treatment' of problems once they have occurred
Examples: Employee assistance programmes, counselling

Source: Adapted from Cooper, Dewe and O'Driscoll (2001), p. 189.

Primary interventions build upon an assumption that the most valuable way to reduce strain in the work environment is to eliminate or at least reduce the sources of strain (i.e. the stressors) themselves. This is sometimes referred to as the *preventive model* of stress management (Tetrick, Quick & Quick 2005), which suggests that proactive strategies for dealing with stressors will be more valuable than reactive (after-the-event) approaches. It is clear that such models derive from the more general person–environment fit perspective (see, for instance, Edwards & Cooper 1990), where the focus is on modifying the environment to meet workers' needs. Primary interventions are, therefore, intended to change environmental contingencies which exert a negative impact on people, rather than expecting individuals to modify their appraisals or reactions. Elkin and Rosch (1990), among others, summarize some of the major primary interventions that may be conducted to reduce workplace stressors, such as reducing workload, increasing employee participation in relevant decision-making and redesigning work to enhance worker autonomy and control.

Secondary interventions, on the other hand, do not aim to deal directly with the stressor(s) but rather to modify the reactions of people to those stressors. The most prominent example of this approach is stress management training, which typically entails assisting individuals to enhance their coping skills or to modify their appraisals of stressors. This is the approach most frequently utilized by organizations (Cooper, Dewe & O'Driscoll 2001; Noblet & LaMontagne 2006), even though (as noted above) it is not always effective in reducing stress levels. In addition, often it is implemented *after* the organization has detected that its employees are experiencing high levels of strain, which means that it is a reactive strategy to managing stress levels rather than an attempt to prevent undue strain from developing in the first place. Nevertheless, stress management training can have beneficial effects, especially if it enables individual workers to constructively modify their attitudes and behaviour. For instance, under certain circumstances the following techniques may be efficacious in reducing high levels of strain: cognitive restructuring (Welbourne *et al.* 2007), time management (Jex & Elacqua 1999), conflict resolution (Behfar *et al.* 2008) and meditation and relaxation training (Mackenzie *et al.* 2007).

A somewhat more recent technique, emerging especially from clinical psychology, is mindfulness training. Mindfulness is a derivative of meditation and cognitive restructuring, referring to 'a state of kind and benevolent attention to all contents which arise in the mind' (Walach *et al.* 2007, p. 189). In essence, mindfulness entails focusing on one's cognitions about events, people and situations in a neutral, non-judgmental and non-emotive manner, simply acknowledging their existence without an appraisal of their goodness or badness. Proponents of this technique contend that neutralizing one's emotions about these cognitions eventually creates a more balanced affective state, which enables the person to become more resilient and resistant to the impact of stressors. Connections with Zen Buddhism are immediately evident. Recent evidence for the positive benefits of mindfulness training has been presented by Walach and his associates, who found that workers allocated to a mindfulness-based stress reduction programme showed an increase in positive coping strategies and reduced negative coping, along with greater feelings of self-efficacy in dealing with work-related stressors.

Also under the umbrella of secondary interventions, increasing numbers of organizations have introduced various health promotion activities, sometimes referred to as 'wellness programmes', for their employees. A growing body of research literature has developed on the efficacy of this approach to stress management. The underlying rationale is that individuals who are generally healthy (both physically and psychologically) will be better equipped to confront the stress of daily life, including work life. However, although there is some evidence that such initiatives may be beneficial for employee well-being (Parks & Steelman 2008), a review by Harden *et al.* (1999) concludes that only 25% took explicit account of employees' expressed needs and just 14% involved employee participation in the design and implementation of the health promotion programme. These figures suggest that in many organizations the decision to provide a wellness programme may be based more on ideology than on a systematic analysis of worker needs and desires. There is clearly a need for more systematic evaluation of the benefits of the health promotion programmes provided by organizations (Noblet & LaMontagne 2008).

Whereas primary interventions are by definition proactive, secondary interventions may be either proactive or reactive. For instance, assisting workers to develop skills in handling conflict resolution may prevent conflict from occurring or escalating, but providing such training after conflict has developed between employees would illustrate a more reactive approach to conflict management. In reality, proactive and reactive approaches may complement each other and both can have value. An investigation of the combined approach to SMI was conducted by Brough and Biggs (2008). These investigators are engaged in a longitudinal implementation of a stressor reduction and stress management training intervention within the Corrections Services Department in one state of Australia. Initially, pilot studies were conducted to ascertain workers' perceptions of the factors contributing most to their levels of stress, such as violence from offenders and lack of consultation and participation in decision-making, along with an assessment of other indicators of severe stress, including grievance reports, critical incidents and patterns of absenteeism. An intervention was then designed to enhance the ability of corrections personnel to deal with stressors and to reduce overall levels of strain. This intervention contained elements of both primary and secondary techniques, including recommending to management various changes in job design and workshops for staff on stress management training. The effects of the interventions are being evaluated using a quasi-experimental, longitudinal design.

Overall, stress management training and other forms of secondary intervention have exhibited very mixed results. It is clear that these interventions can be valuable for some kinds of stressors (Dewe 1994), particularly when the individual has some degree of discretion in their work environment and can exert at least a moderate level of control over the stressors (such as work demands). Techniques such as mindfulness, time management and other kinds of personal stress management rely upon the person being in a position to modify their cognitive and behavioural responses to the situation. If problem-focused coping is not a viable strategy, the individual may invoke emotion-focused coping but, in the longer term, an inability to influence the nature or intensity of a stressor may result in these coping efforts being ineffectual.

Similarly, an exclusive focus on secondary interventions may shift attention from management responsibility to individual worker responsibility for stress management. Managers often exhibit a tendency to attribute the causes of strain to individuals' own cognitions and behaviours, and hence to view the responsibility for stress management as lying predominantly with the individual worker (Cooper, Dewe & O'Driscoll 2001). Murphy and Sauter (2003, p. 153) state, for instance, that '*stress management* interventions are more prevalent than *stressor reduction* interventions' (italics added). Reasons for this include (a) a prevailing belief that stress is an individual problem, rather than a work design or work environment issue, (b) the substantial cost (in time and money) of redesigning jobs or the work environment, (c) that environmental factors (stressors) may have differential impact on different people (some may experience strain and others may not) and (d) a reluctance by management (based partly on concerns over legal liability) to accept direct responsibility for levels of stress experienced by individual workers.

The third 'level' presented in Table 6.1 comprises *tertiary interventions*, which largely reflect a rehabilitation approach to stress management. Interventions at this level are based on a 'treatment' rather than a preventive philosophy (Cooper, Dewe & O'Driscoll 2001). Perhaps the most well-known example is the EAP, which normally involves some type of counselling for workers who report strain or other difficulties (including performance problems). EAPs may be provided in-house (e.g. by human resources personnel), although more frequently the organization will hire off-site EAP consultants. Since the 1980s, the use of EAPs worldwide has expanded enormously, especially with the advent in many countries of health and safety legislation which acknowledges work stress as a hazard which employers need to address (Berridge & Cooper 2000). The organizational response to this legislation is frequently to engage external consultants to providing (employer-funded) counselling services for workers experiencing excessive strain. This may be viewed by employers as a cost-effective and relatively non-disruptive method for meeting their legal obligations and (hopefully) assisting the employee to better manage their work-related strain. Unfortunately, however, rigorous evaluations of the effectiveness of EAPs are rare (Kirk & Brown 2003), and their long-term efficacy is often questioned (Cooper, Dewe & O'Driscoll 2003). As with stress management training, a fundamental limitation in EAPs and other tertiary interventions is that they do not (and perhaps cannot) directly address sources of strain, as they focus entirely on the individual and not on changing the work context per se. Nevertheless, there is some evidence that EAPs may be at least partially beneficial and can lead to improved well-being among workers and cost-savings for employers.

The tripartite typology presented in Table 6.1 provides a summary of different types of organizational SMI and a useful classification of different approaches and their underlying rationale. The three levels range from totally proactive or preventive (primary interventions) through to totally reactive (tertiary interventions). In reality, however, this classification is a simplification of the often multifaceted approaches taken by organizations to deal with stress-related issues. Normally some combination of the above (and other) methods is utilized by a particular firm or company, although the predominant emphasis is still on secondary- and tertiary-level interventions which attempt to modify individuals' coping strategies rather than making changes to work environment factors which create or exacerbate strain (Giga *et al.* 2003; Murphy & Sauter 2003). An ongoing major challenge for stress researchers and practitioners is to develop and promote the implementation of proactive, stressor reduction interventions. In this respect, the risk-management paradigm outlined by Cox and his colleagues (e.g. Leka, Griffiths & Cox 2005) presents a valuable platform for the development of effective stress management programmes.

Evaluating Stress Management Interventions

A key issue in determining whether an SMI is achieving what is intended is the evaluation of its effectiveness. Unfortunately, as observed by several commentators (e.g. Cooper, Dewe & O'Driscoll 2001; Cox *et al.* 2007;

Murphy & Sauter 2003), evaluations of SMIs are frequently unsystematic and contain methodological flaws which detract from our ability to draw valid conclusions about the impact of an intervention. Beehr and O'Hara (1987) differentiate between three types of validation issue: (a) internal validity, (b) construct validity and (c) external validity. They note that there are many factors which can influence the outcomes of a stress management programme, and it is virtually impossible to take all of these into account when conducting an evaluation. Some of these factors have been elaborated upon by Burke and Richardsen (2000), who suggest that while organization-level interventions may be successful in reducing either the stressors or resultant strain, there are several methodological issues which cast doubt on their validity. One issue is the very relationship between work-related stressors and well-being. As pointed out by Burke and Richardsen, it is extremely difficult to demonstrate conclusively that work stressors are a direct cause of psychological strain and reduced well-being, especially since many other (e.g. off-the-job) factors also contribute to a person's level of strain and overall well-being. Second, individual stressors by themselves may not exert a significant influence but in combination can be very deleterious to well-being. A prime example of this combined effect can be seen with workload. Although studies have often found that work overload contributes to psychological strain (Glazer & Beehr 2005; Greenglass, Burke & Moore 2003), the effects of overload may be compounded by other stressors, for instance role conflict, interpersonal conflict with supervisors and colleagues and work–family conflict. An intervention which addressed only workload issues may therefore have a limited impact on reducing an individual's strain level.

Most SMI evaluations are field studies, where there is often limited control over critical variables which can affect the validity of the evaluation, such as random assignment to intervention versus control groups. Because of these limitations, the positive effects of an intervention on variables such as strain, job satisfaction and burnout (all of which have been used as indicators of well-being) may be due to other (uncontrolled) factors rather than the intervention per se. In addition, as Burke and Richardsen (2000) point out, different evaluation studies have focused on a range of different 'outcomes' and there is little standardization of measures of these outcomes, further contributing to the inconclusive evidence for intervention effectiveness. Reliance solely on self-report measures of outcome variables has also been regarded as a limitation, in that self-report biases may distort individuals' responses to measures of strain and well-being, although Spector (1994) argues that (a) mono-method bias is not necessarily a problem in this line of research and (b) self-report is really the only viable way to assess some variables, such as job satisfaction and subjective well-being. Finally, while there have been calls for greater utilization of longitudinal research designs, these can be difficult to enact in practice and the time periods covered by longitudinal studies vary substantially. In fact, 'little is known about the optimal time span required to permit changes in outcomes … to occur' (Burke & Richardsen 2000, p. 203), limiting conclusions about whether a particular intervention is effective over time.

Two relatively recent commentaries on evaluation research have been by Giga *et al.* (2003), who examined SMI evaluations in the United Kingdom, and Murphy and Sauter (2003), who reviewed the situation in the United States. Giga *et al.* conducted an extensive review of evaluations in the United Kingdom published since 1990, reporting that the majority of these focused on individually focused interventions, such as relaxation and meditation, cognitive-behaviour treatment, time management and EAPs. A smaller number assessed interventions which focused on both individual- and organization-level activities, including role stress management, increased autonomy and participation in decision-making, and the provision of co-worker support groups. Finally, very few studies tested the effects of organizationally focused strategies, such as changing the work environment, enhanced communication systems and job redesign. Giga and colleagues conclude that, despite repeated calls for more comprehensive approaches to stress management which include both individual- and organizational-level strategies, evidence from the United Kingdom indicates that interventions which target individual coping rather than modification of the work environment are predominant.

A similar picture is painted by Murphy and Sauter (2003) in the United States. They observed a preponderance of individually targeted interventions (e.g. muscle relaxation, meditation, health promotion) which may reduce worker strain and enhance well-being, but do not deal directly with the causes of strain. Unfortunately, for reasons articulated above, interventions which directly target the work-related sources of stress have not been consistently demonstrated to be effective. Murphy and Sauter advocate more comprehensive and systematic approaches which complement, and are integrated with, other human resource functions routinely carried out in organizations (e.g. selection, training, performance management). In addition, following National Institute for Occupational Safety and Health guidelines, they suggested that 'stress be viewed within a healthy work organization perspective that fosters both worker wellbeing and organizational effectiveness' (p. 155).

One area which has received considerable attention in the evaluation literature is health promotion. As we commented earlier, health promotion initiatives reflect a philosophy that efforts to enhance worker wellbeing (physical and psychological) will be beneficial not just to the individual but also to the organization. In a twist on the adage dating back to the human relations school of thought in the 1950s that 'a happy worker is a productive worker', the modern mantra adopted by advocates of health promotion programmes is 'a *healthy* worker is a productive worker'. In other words, it is assumed that high levels of physical fitness and psychological well-being will uniformly lead to better individual performance and ultimately organizational productivity. Thus it is in the organization's interest to promote physical and psychological well-being among its employees.

Data on the efficacy of health promotion programmes are generally supportive of this assumption, although again researchers have cautioned about limitations in the evaluations conducted and the conclusions which are sometimes drawn. For example, from a review of evaluations of health promotion programmes in the United Kingdom, Harden *et al.* (1999) conclude that many efforts to assess the effectiveness of these initiatives are not sufficiently rigorous, and evaluations often are conducted on the short-term effects of health promotion rather than on its longer-term benefits. Hence, as discussed above in relation to SMIs, evaluations of health promotion programmes also suffer from (sometimes relatively serious) methodological limitations. Interestingly, however, and in contrast to most commentaries on the importance of evaluation methodology, in a recent meta-analysis of approximately 100 evaluation studies Parks and Steelman (2008) found that the methodological rigour of the evaluation did not significantly moderate the relationship between participation in an organizational wellness programme and absenteeism and job satisfaction.

Reviewers have decried the lack of attention to *process* issues in most evaluations of SMIs and health and well-being promotion initiatives undertaken by organizations (Noblet & LaMontagne 2008). The manner and timing of an intervention implementation can exert a significant influence on its effectiveness, and the same applies to evaluations of interventions. For instance, Nielsen and her colleagues in Denmark (Nielsen *et al.* 2006; Nielsen, Randall & Albertsen 2007) observed that several processes may affect the quality of an evaluation, including (a) poor implementation of the intervention, and inconsistent implementation across different groups, (b) 'contamination' of the control group (e.g. by being exposed to elements of the SMI), (c) loss of participants from either the intervention group or the control group and (d) incomplete follow-up measures of effectiveness. All of these factors may undermine the credibility and validity of the evaluation, and potentially lead to inaccurate and inappropriate conclusions about its benefits and limitations. In addition, typically SMIs are not carried out in isolation from other programmes or activities (such as skill-based training) within an organization, and these other initiatives may influence the outcomes of an SMI, either augmenting or diminishing its effect (Nielsen *et al.* 2006).

In contrast to conclusions drawn from some studies and earlier reviews of the impact of SMIs, Richardson and Rothstein (2008) conducted a meta-analysis of 36 experimental studies (including 55 interventions) and reported a medium to large effect for the interventions evaluated in these studies. Using the typology outlined in Table 6.1, Richardson and Rothstein classified interventions as primary, secondary or tertiary. The most common forms of intervention were secondary, that is targeted towards individual attitude and behaviour change to assist individuals to better cope with stress. Of these secondary interventions, the authors reported that while relaxation and meditation were the most popular activities (used in 69% of the studies), cognitive-behavioural interventions (designed to modify individuals' appraisals of stressful events and their reactions to these events) yielded the most benefits. Other initiatives, such as time management and goal-setting training and exercise programmes, were generally less effective in promoting better stress management. Whereas multimodal approaches have sometimes been recommended as being most beneficial (Semmer 2008), Richardson and Rothstein advise (2008) against combining cognitive-behavioural interventions with others, on the grounds that other activities may dilute the positive effects arising from a cognitive-behavioural intervention. Their overall conclusion is that there is value in providing secondary-level stress management training, although they (like others) note the very limited number of studies which have focused on organizational-level (primary) intervention outcomes.

In an effort to reconcile the inconsistent conclusions which have been drawn in the literature on SMI evaluation and the seemingly incompatible requirements of conducting controlled (quasi)experiments in a sometimes erratic and unpredictable real-life setting, Cox *et al.* (2007) propose an innovative solution to the problem of carrying out practically viable yet scientifically valid evaluations of SMIs. They note that the reality of organizational life means that experimental or even quasi-experimental longitudinal evaluation studies are often simply unrealistic to conduct. For instance, the random assignment of employees to a control group (or even a wait-list control group) may not be acceptable to management, who typically want all their employees to receive immediate exposure to a stress management workshop or other form of intervention. Similarly, longitudinal evaluation designs entailing a pre-test and perhaps two or even three post-intervention assessments may be difficult to implement in practice. To address these challenging issues, Cox and his associates propose that evaluations need to be *fit for purpose*, which they define as 'the correct approach to obtaining data of appropriate quality ... judged against the purpose of obtaining the data' (p. 350). In other words, rather than slavishly adhering to a methodological paradigm developed from experimental psychology, which may not be workable in a real-life setting, decisions need to be made about the most appropriate yet manageable approach to the collection of evaluative information about a stress management programme, based on the purpose for which the information will be used.

The 'adapted study design' utilized by Randall, Griffiths and Cox (2005) represents a good illustration of adapting the evaluation approach to meet the contingencies of the situation in which the evaluation is being conducted. Whereas many evaluations have concentrated primarily on intervention outcomes, Randall *et al.* recommend a flexible approach that focuses on both the process through which the intervention has been implemented as well as its outcomes. Similarly, rather than simply assigning participants to groups (e.g. an intervention group or a wait-list control group), which as noted above can be problematic, in an adapted design a decision about whether employees have been exposed to the basic elements of the intervention is made after rather than before the intervention has been implemented. Based on their research findings, Randall *et al.* conclude that awareness of the nature of an intervention and involvement in the intervention process are important elements to assess during evaluations. They also argue that 'adapted study designs built around process evaluation appeared to offer a means of strengthening the evaluation of stress management intervention in complex and unpredictable environments' (p. 38).

From the above discussion, it is clear that generally evaluations have illustrated that SMIs and health promotion (or wellness) programmes can be beneficial, although evidence on their long-term effectiveness is still required. There is no doubt that systematic and rigorous evaluation of SMIs is a challenging exercise, and many studies have (sometimes severe) methodological limitations. However, it is important to acknowledge the accumulated evidence rather than data from single studies. Similarly, the notion of 'fit for purpose' developed by Cox *et al.* (2007) and the concept of adapted study design which they advocate (Randall, Griffiths & Cox 2005) provide a valuable platform for the design of useful yet manageable evaluation research. These ideas do not undermine the desirability of utilizing quasi-experimental designs and longitudinal studies to evaluate the long-term impact of SMIs, nor are they contradictory to the evaluation principles outlined by earlier reviewers (e.g. Beehr & O'Hara 1987; Ivancevich & Matteson 1987) which called for greater use of experimental research designs. However, Cox *et al.* have injected a note of realism into the field of SMI evaluation, which will enable researchers to conduct more ecologically valid evaluations of the effectiveness of these programmes.

Factors Influencing the Effectiveness of Stress Management Interventions

A significant issue in both research and application in the field of stress management concerns the effective implementation of these programmes and endeavouring to ensure that they are beneficial. To achieve this, we need to understand the range of factors which can affect the way in which stress management and health promotion programmes operate in organizations, as well as how to optimize their contribution to reducing stress levels and enhancing worker psychological well-being. Here we reflect upon a few major factors which have been discussed in the literature, grouped under three headings: (a) involvement and participation of workers (employees) in the design and implementation of SMIs, (b) the role of management and supervisors and (c) the impact of the organization's climate on both intervention processes and outcomes. Following this discussion, we present some guidelines for the practical implementation of SMIs to maximize their benefits.

Worker involvement and participation

One issue which has been noted frequently is the participation of workers in the design and implementation of SMIs. Numerous authors have argued that simply being exposed to an intervention may not generate significant benefits in terms of reduced stress and increased well-being, as lack of involvement in intervention design and implementation can undermine the consequences of a stress management programme. Active engagement (participation) of affected workers in the development of a stress management programme is a key element for various reasons, including that these people are typically in the best position to determine the nature of the stressors being encountered and to judge what would be most useful in terms of addressing these stressors and meeting workers' health and well-being needs (Grawitch, Trares & Kohler 2007). Second, involving employees in the design and implementation of SMIs can facilitate their own perceptions of discretion and control over their job and work environment, which is well known as a prerequisite for enhanced well-being (Creed & Bartrum 2008). In fact, Morrison and Payne (2003) contend that increased control is *the* major contributor to reduced stress and heightened well-being, suggesting that 'job control is pivotal to the preventive management of job strain' (p. 136).

Similarly, having input into the content and enactment of a stress intervention will promote feelings of commitment among workers to the intervention, along with their appraisals of its effectiveness. Nielsen, Randall and Albertsen (2007) observe that appraisals of the quality of an intervention and that it will create sustainable benefits can be critical to stress management effectiveness, hence strategies to enhance these appraisals can have a positive impact on the intervention process. Nielsen *et al.* also note, however, that participation is a necessary but not sufficient condition for SMI effectiveness.

The role of management and supervisors

Managers and supervisors can also make a significant contribution to the impact of stress management and health promotion programmes. The importance of managerial support for these programmes has been underlined by several authors. For example, from their review of a range of work stress interventions, Giga, Cooper and Faragher (2003) conclude that commitment to the goals of the intervention from top management is critical for the successful achievement of programme benefits. Management must be willing to provide financial and other forms of support to enable an intervention to be properly designed and implemented, and to ensure that essential follow-up activities are carried out. Without such commitment, it is likely that (a) the intervention may not be offered sufficient resources for it to be systematically applied, (b) ongoing stress prevention and stress management processes may be relegated to a secondary priority and (c) individual employees will perceive a lack of interest on the part of management in their psychological health and well-being. According to them, 'the viability and success of an intervention is dependent on senior managers sending clear signals demonstrating their intent and long-term support' (Giga, Cooper & Faragher 2003, p. 291).

In addition to top-management commitment, front-line supervisors also play a major role in the success of SMIs and health promotion initiatives. Several studies have demonstrated that the absence of supervisor support can both diminish the effects of an intervention and increase worker stress levels (either directly or indirectly). Morrison and Payne (2003), for instance, argue that supervisors have a marked influence on workers' perceptions of their jobs, especially the amount of discretion and control (or autonomy) available to them in carrying out job-related tasks. The extent to which supervisors enable their employees to exert appropriate levels of control over their work can therefore have a considerable effect on levels of strain and well-being (Gilbreath & Benson 2004). Furthermore, supervisors can (either intentionally or unintentionally) undermine stress management approaches in a variety of ways. These include very simple actions, such as not permitting an employee to take time off work to attend a stress management workshop, or not addressing stressors that the supervisor may be able to modify (e.g. work demands), through to more subtle behaviors, such as disparaging remarks about a person's capabilities if that individual participates in a stress management training session. Finally, given that supervisor behaviours can themselves be a major source of strain for employees (O'Driscoll & Beehr 1994), organizations need to invest time and effort into appropriate supervisory training and development (Morrison & Payne 2003).

Organizational climate

As outlined by Reichers and Schneider (1990), the term 'climate' refers to collective perceptions of the psychological, cultural, social, political and physical environment which exists in an organization. In other words, it reflects views of what it is like to work in an organization, including communication and decision-making processes, social interactions, perceptions of justice and a variety of other elements which are psychologically meaningful to employees within an organization. When these perceptions are widely shared by organizational members, we can refer to a 'collective climate'.

The collective climate may shape people's views of human resource interventions, including stress management and health promotion. For instance, Nytro *et al.* (2000) discuss how various elements of an organizational climate may impact on the implementation of job stress interventions. These include whether management and supervisors treat mistakes and failures as learning opportunities rather than as limitations and are aware of the effects of their interactional style on the willingness of individuals to (a) acknowledge their need for assistance and (b) engage in developmental activities. In some organizations there is a climate of fear and mistrust, which can lead to heightened anxiety (about job performance and even job security), subversion of organizational goals and even (active or passive) sabotage of regular operations. Nytro *et al.* contend that these counterproductive attitudes and responses emerge from a dysfunctional climate, which is not conducive to the development and maintenance of health and well-being. In such environments, it is unlikely that useful stress management and health promotion programmes could be successfully implemented. To counteract these problems, it is critical to develop more open communication systems (Giga, Cooper & Faragher 2003) and more supportive management styles (Barling & Carson 2008).

A final important element of organizational climate that must be explored when considering the introduction of interventions is the organization's readiness for change. Nytro *et al.* (2000) point out that both managers and employees can resist efforts to change 'for fear of adverse consequences to them or their colleagues' (p. 221). This fear can apply as much to initiatives whose intention is to improve well-being as it does to others aimed at other areas, such as performance management. Frequently, people persist with courses of action, even in the face of evidence that these are 'unhealthy', simply because they are afraid of the implications of changing their behaviour or patterns of activity. This resistance to change is well-known in the literature on organizational change and development. The limited success of SMIs and health promotion programmes may be due, in part, to the lack of prior assessment of the organization's readiness to embrace these initiatives and whether individuals (both managers and employees) are willing to modify their modi operandi.

Some Guidelines for Effective Interventions

In light of the key issues outlined above, we will now develop some recommendations for the effective implementation of SMIs and, more generally, health promotion within organizations. These recommendations are not intended to be prescriptive or exclusive of other considerations, but rather are offered as guidelines to stimulate creative solutions to the substantial and ongoing challenge of counteracting the problems associated with work-related stress. We would also note that some of the suggestions below have been raised on previous occasions by stress researchers, but would appear to have largely fallen on stony ground. Despite the development in many countries of health and safety legislation which incorporates stress as a potential health hazard, organizations still frequently appear to adopt a simplistic approach to stress management which continues to place the weight of responsibility on individuals to deal with stress-related problems (Cooper, Dewe & O'Driscoll 2001; Murphy & Sauter 2003; Noblet & LaMontagne 2008). Clearly, a one-sided approach to stress management will yield only limited, usually short-term, benefits and more comprehensive approaches will be required to successfully address the seemingly increasing levels of stress experienced by many workers.

Combining stress management with stress prevention

One conclusion emerging from over 30 years of research on occupational stress interventions is that a strategy which puts all the emphasis on stress *management* is unlikely by itself to yield substantial benefits in many work situations. As outlined earlier, SMIs are frequently categorized as primary-, secondary- or tertiary-level approaches, with the two latter approaches based predominantly on a 'stress management' philosophy. In and of themselves, these intervention strategies can be (at least somewhat) effective in reducing levels of strain among many employees, especially in situations where the individual has a reasonably high level of control over their environment. As suggested by Morrison and Payne (2003), however, often workers have little if any control over their conditions of work, in which case secondary-level (e.g. stress management training) and tertiary-level (e.g. EAPs) interventions may have very limited effects on a person's overarching stress and well-being.

In many (if not most) situations, therefore, a combination of preventive and management approaches is needed to effectively deal with work stress-related problems. Although a certain amount of stress (or stimulation) may be beneficial and contribute to an individual's subjective well-being, there is evidence that a growing proportion of the working population experiences stress levels that are not entirely manageable at the individual level (Giga, Cooper & Faragher 2003). To adequately address this problem, it is important to conduct systematic diagnoses of levels of stress and their potential causes. We will discuss diagnostic procedures shortly. A basic consideration is whether a work-related stressor can be prevented from developing in the first place, can be modified when it does exist or is immutable, in which case the focus should be on trying to enhance people's capacity to cope with and manage the negative outcomes of the stressor.

As outlined earlier, the philosophy underlying the preventive model of stress management is that the responsibility for stress management lies not just with individual workers but also with organizational managers and supervisors. Based on the relatively new discipline of preventive medicine, 'preventive management is an organizational philosophy and set of principles which employs specific methods for promoting individual and organizational health while preventing individual and organizational disorders, distress and illness' (Tetrick, Quick & Quick 2005, p. 213). This suggests that, rather than simply trying to address the consequences of stress (such as dissatisfaction, strain and a decline in physical and psychological well-being) after they have developed, organizations should endeavour to prevent the circumstances which create these dysfunctional experiences from occurring.

Although it is clearly not always possible to anticipate events or occurrences which may induce strain in certain individuals, and it is recognized that people may respond in very different ways to the same stressors, the preventive stress management model suggests that there are certain kinds of stressors which are predictable and preventable. This would include chronic workload demands, role ambiguity, role conflict and work–family conflict, which we have discussed in previous chapters. A stress prevention approach would focus on trying to reduce or even remove these stressors, rather than simply alleviating the strain which they create. Changes in job design, work schedules and communication mechanisms are all examples of strategies that may be classified as preventive, especially if they are implemented proactively (before excessive strain has developed).

In sum, while stress management strategies may have some benefits, particularly if the individual can exert some influence and control over the sources of stress, these approaches focus on 'dealing with work-related stress outcomes rather than eliminating its sources, helping individuals to improve their coping skills without attempting to reduce or remove stressors from the work environment' (Giga, Cooper & Faragher 2003, p. 294). Ultimately, this means that the benefits which may arise from such approaches are likely to be short term and unlikely to change the underlying causes of stress. In order to achieve long-term and sustained positive outcomes, such as enhanced worker health and well-being, it is critical to combine SMIs (which are fundamentally reactive) with proactive stress prevention interventions. Furthermore, these efforts should not occur in isolation from other organizational activities; as noted by Murphy and Sauter (2003), stress management (including prevention) initiatives should be integrated with other ongoing human resources activities, and not be viewed as an 'add on'.

Combining individual-level with organization-level interventions

Following on from the above suggestions, it is also important for organizations not to focus solely on interventions which only target individuals' beliefs, attitudes and behaviours, such as stress management training to enhance coping skills, cognitive-behaviour treatment, relaxation and so on. As noted above, while these are valuable when the person can exert control, occupational stress researchers have frequently observed that there is an overwhelming concentration on individual-level interventions, even when such approaches may not be entirely effective in addressing causes of stress (Beehr & O'Driscoll 2002; Giga *et al.* 2003; Murphy & Sauter 2003). Several reasons have been proposed (e.g. Cooper, Dewe & O'Driscoll 2001, p. 188) for this seeming avoidance of more systematic stressor reduction mechanisms at the organizational level, ranging from managers' beliefs about who is responsible for managing individuals' strain through to the (sometimes substantial) costs associated with modifying work environments compared with providing stress management training or health promotion (wellness) programmes. However, accumulated empirical data highlight the necessity of developing organizational-level interventions that, in the longer term, will yield considerable financial and other benefits for organizations (Beehr & O'Driscoll 2002; Noblet & LaMontagne 2006; Semmer 2003). 'Multi-modal' (Semmer 2008) or 'multi-level' (Morrison & Payne 2003) approaches are recommended as viable and ultimately more effective strategies for SMI and more general health promotion.

Worker involvement in intervention design and implementation

A further issue which has been described in some detail earlier is the participation and involvement of affected individuals in both the design and implementation of SMIs. There is compelling evidence that when workers are involved in decision-making processes connected with stress management programmes the likelihood of these initiatives yielding positive benefits is potentiated. In contrast, when interventions are developed and implemented unilaterally by management, with either no or minimal consultation and discussion with employees, research findings suggest that they are unlikely to generate significant and sustained reductions in stress and increased well-being (Nielsen *et al.* 2006; Nielsen, Randall & Albertsen 2007).

There are several important reasons for engaging affected workers (and others) in the design and implementation of interventions. Perhaps the foremost of these is that normally these individuals will have greatest awareness of the factors which contribute to their stress levels, that is the stressors, and often will have constructive suggestions on how best to deal with these stressors. Hence employee participation can enhance the quality and effectiveness of the intervention. On the other hand, if workers' needs and views are not taken into account, management runs a high risk that the nature of the intervention may be unmatched to the problems it is intended to deal with (Hill *et al.* 2007). Second, as is well known from the organizational development and change literature, participation in the design and implementation of interventions typically increases employees' feelings of engagement with these processes as well as reducing any resistance they may harbour towards their implementation (Piderit 2000). The lack of psychological engagement and resistance to an initiative can seriously undermine its successful enactment as well as attenuating any long-term outcomes. Third, involvement and participation can have more widespread benefits for the organization, as it may increase communication between management and employees and generate a more 'open' climate which fosters trust and commitment. The benefits of participation

are therefore not constrained only to the intervention itself, but can perme-
ate to other aspects of management–employee interactions.

It is evident, therefore, that decisions concerning SMIs should not be
made unilaterally by management, even when there are clear indications
that stress levels within the organization are high and that there are significant stressors to be modified or even eliminated. The lack of consultation
and negotiation with affected employees has been illustrated to undermine
the potential benefits of an SMI (Giga, Cooper & Faragher 2003). It is
highly recommended that workers be involved in (a) the identification of
both the levels of strain and the causes of strain (the stressors), (b) decisions about which activities need to be undertaken to alleviate stress, (c)
the manner in which an intervention should be implemented, including
its timing, and (d) ongoing efforts to promote psychological and physical
well-being in the organization.

Diagnosis of stress and well-being

Previously we have discussed the need for systematic exploration to dis-
cover stress levels and to identify the causes of stress. This is a critical
component of any approach to stress management, yet frequently these
assessments can be somewhat haphazard and incomplete. In an earlier
volume (Cooper, Dewe & O'Driscoll 2001) we suggest that questionnaires,
interviews of selected workers and various other means (including observa-
tions of organizational climate) can be utilized to determine levels of strain
for identifying the most important stressors. This is sometimes referred to
as a 'stress audit', and can be accomplished via instruments such as the
ASSET (Johnson & Cooper 2003) or the Occupational Stress Inventory
(Osipow & Spokane 1988), which were developed to explore the types of
stressor which are confronted by workers and the level of strain resulting
from these stressors. Various other techniques have also been constructed
for this type of investigation, including asking individuals to keep a diary
or daily log of events or incidents which they found especially stressful.
This approach has been found to be extremely valuable in identifying
events, situations or people which may be regarded as 'hassles' (e.g. Maybery
et al. 2007). This type of record-keeping may help both individuals and
organizations to identify pervasive sources of strain.

A similar approach is advocated by Quick, Quick and Nelson (1998),
who refer to the importance of identifying 'surveillance indicators' and
comment that these indicators 'are the foundation of an evidence-based

approach to the preventive management of workplace stress' (p. 260). As with a stress audit, surveillance indicators can be obtained through a variety of means (including those mentioned above), which are outlined by Quick and his colleagues. Although the terminology is slightly different, the surveillance-indicator approach overlaps substantially with the notion of stress audit described above.

Finally, we also support the 'risk assessment' paradigm outlined by Cox and his associates (see Leka, Griffiths & Cox 2005). The risk assessment approach entails 'systematic examination of all aspects of the work undertaken to consider what could cause injury or harm, and whether the hazards could be eliminated and, if not, what preventive or protective measures are, or should be, in place to control the risks' (Leka Griffiths & Cox 2005, p. 177). Both psychosocial and physical factors may be classified as hazards and a stepwise process for risk assessment, which is very similar to the stress audit approach mentioned above, is outlined by Leka and colleagues. Together, the stress audit, surveillance indicator and risk assessment paradigms offer considerable advantages for systematic efforts to address stress-related problems in organizations.

Conclusions

In this chapter we have endeavoured to provide an overview of critical issues pertaining to SMIs and health promotion programmes in organizational settings. Our intention was not to describe and evaluate specific types of intervention or programme in detail, but rather to focus on underlying issues and considerations. Ultimately, as we argued in earlier chapters, it is imperative to integrate practice with theoretical models of stressor–strain–coping relationships. We suggest that the transactional model of stress developed and refined by Lazarus and his colleagues (e.g. Lazarus 1966; Lazarus & Folkman 1984) provides a fundamental theoretical platform for the construction of effective SMIs. This theoretical approach offers a valuable framework for consideration of the complexities of the stress coping process and its components, including stressors, strains, appraisal mechanisms and coping behaviours. A corollary of this is that the relationship between the individual person and their environment must be focused upon, and hence that SMIs must be designed to build a constructive rather than counterproductive person–environment match.

The transactional approach suggests that a key element of managing stress is the appraisal process, and that stress arises when individuals perceive incidents occurring in their lives as being threatening to their (psychological or physical) health and well-being. Individuals' interpretations of events and their coping responses are key issues to assess when designing interventions. Based on this precept, many SMIs focus on modifying appraisals so that the impact of the potential stressor is reduced, or that events which may have been appraised as threatening can instead be viewed as 'challenging'. (See our discussion in Chapter 3 of the concept of threat versus challenge appraisals.) However, as we have discussed, initiatives that focus solely on providing people with a wider array of coping skills may have limited impact if they do not also attempt to develop appropriate environmental resources and support for people.

In conclusion, organizational efforts to modify stressors or to reduce their negative impact on health and well-being will be more effective if a stress audit or risk management strategy is systematically adopted and is integrated within the organization's overall human resource management strategy (Murphy & Sauter 2003). Key elements include: (a) identification of factors that may be potential sources of strain or 'harm' to individuals and groups within the organization, (b) comprehensive and systematic assessment of levels of strain, including a range of indicators of reduced well-being (such as psychological well-being, physical health symptoms, job satisfaction, work–life balance, as well as organizationally relevant issues such as task performance, contextual performance, absenteeism and turnover intentions), (c) design and implementation of interventions in a way that incorporates workers' perceptions and needs and that aim to resolve the problem(s) rather than simply addressing the symptoms and, finally, (d) systematic evaluation of both short- and long-term outcomes of these interventions. There are significant challenges for employers and managers, as well as workers themselves, in taking joint responsibility for the prevention and management of excessive stress, but there are also substantial benefits in terms of employee health and well-being and organizational productivity.

Coping with Work Stress: An Agenda for the Future

In Chapter 1 we stated that this book is about coping and, more particularly, coping with work stress. That is still true. But any discussion of coping brings with it a rich history of debate, punctuated at times by passionately expressed views as to what has or hasn't been achieved, what has, if not gone wrong, at least diverted researchers' attention away from what needs to be done and what changes need to occur if we are to advance our understanding of what is the most fundamental aspect of the stress process: coping. The arguments and discussion are, of course, ongoing. Without such debate, coping research would be much poorer and would lose the creative tension that has been so necessary to propel research forward, providing an environment within which change is understood as a necessary and accepted stimulus for innovation, originality and resourcefulness. The rich vein of purpose, vision and inspiration mined by contemporary researchers fashions an agenda which is free from old conventions and established practices, and implies a responsibility to think anew and fulfil our obligation to those whose working lives we study.

As this agenda is drawn from and built on the past, we need to constantly remind ourselves of our past, where we have come from, why different views have assumed a level of importance and why different issues emerged when they did. We need those historical anchors, for without them the present becomes less well understood and limits our ability to unravel contemporary trends, adequately examine our assumptions and consider why new ideas are important and relevant (Cooper & Dewe 2004). Our past is also a constant reminder that change is for all, not to be ignored or left to a few in the hope that the many can continue as before. Change is

Coping with Work Stress: A Review and Critique, Philip J. Dewe, Michael P. O'Driscoll and Cary L. Cooper, © 2010 John Wiley & Sons Ltd.

the yardstick against which we will all be judged, our competence evaluated and our rights and privileges as researchers confirmed. It is for these reasons that setting out any agenda must look both back and forward in order to understand how old, well-trodden paths guide us in identifying new directions that capture the spirit and provide the determination for what needs to be done. In this chapter we outline some of the directions which we believe are critical for future research.

Continuing Debates: Emerging Context

It will come as no surprise if we begin by re-emphasizing the importance of a number of themes that have been sidelined by researchers because for 'valid reasons' there are other more promising avenues to pursue (Schaubroeck 1999). Nevertheless, these themes are no less promising and perhaps more significant as they provide the intellectual framework and empirical context within which work stress and coping research takes place. They include reaching some consensus on the organizing concepts around which theories of work stress should be built, agreeing how best to capture the richness and complexity of the coping process and ensuring that sufficient attention is given to distinguishing between description and meaning. None of these themes is new, and nor are they mutually exclusive, but because much of the debate that surrounds coping has at its core issues of measurement it is important to begin here before moving to new directions that emerge from this debate and suggest broadening our understanding of what constitutes coping thoughts and actions, developing a more explicit understanding of the many roles that meaning plays in coping research, identifying the architecture of what we mean by 'coping effectiveness' and shifting the emphasis from stress to emotions.

Turning first to the issue of whether contemporary approaches to understanding work stress are sufficient to provide researchers with an organizing concept for the future is something of a moot point (Liddle 1994). Researchers (see Dewe & Cooper 2007) would argue that models of work stress are designed to capture the unfolding of a demanding encounter and through the concept of 'fit' or balance point to those components that structurally determine conditions where misfit or imbalance occur. Despite the fact that concepts like appraisal and coping are embedded in the idea of fit or balance, the question facing researchers still remains one of whether such ideas are actually researched in a way that captures the richness and complexity of the stress process (Dewe & Cooper 2007) or remain essentially input–output configurations of how stress occurs (Lazarus 1990), concerned more with the structural characteristic of fit or balance, rather than the dynamic transactional nature of relationships. If, as Lazarus (1990) suggests, stress is transactional in nature, reflecting a dynamic relationship between the person and the environment, understanding the nature of the transaction is essential to increase our knowledge of the stress process.

The authority of the transactional approach to stress lies in its focus on psychological processes that link the individual and the environment. The concept of appraisal becomes the centre of attention, the acceptance that 'where there is stress there is coping' (Lazarus 1990, p. 11), that coping and appraisals – the meanings individuals give to an encounter – are intimately linked and that appraisal acts as the bridge to give the encounter its emotional quality. Developing these understandings becomes the organizing concept of the future, around which our ideas of how stress is experienced should now be built. No doubt the debate as to just how much potential lies in extending our knowledge of appraisals will continue (Schaubroeck 1999), as will concerns about how closely appraisals match reality (Frese & Zapf 1999). Nevertheless, as Lazarus argues, these issues are separate from 'the theoretical and practical importance of appraisals' (1990, p. 8), and until we are better able to understand the significant role that appraisals play in characterizing the stress process, these issues cannot be resolved. Adopting this transactional perspective of stress with its focus on appraisal has, of course, dramatic consequences in terms of measurement and, as 'measurement is always best when it springs from theory' (Lazarus 1990, p. 1), work stress researchers also need to consider the adequacy of contemporary measurement approaches for capturing the transactional nature of stress.

It is clear from earlier chapters that the debate surrounding measurement has attracted the sharpest criticism. An uneasy truce now seems in place around the belief that all researchers should be made aware of the limitations associated with coping checklists and that the circumstances surrounding the application of checklists should now be carefully prescribed (Somerfield 1997a). A consensus seems to be building that stress research has paid a price by failing to better understand how individuals reconstruct a stressful encounter (Lazarus 1990) and that 'the time is now ripe to give alternative approaches a try' (Somerfield 1997b, p. 176). New approaches to researching stress are described in ecological terms, reflect-

ing a style of analysis that is contextual, person-centred, holistic and process-oriented, aimed at capturing the reality of the experience through
techniques like diary studies, in-depth interviews or narratives, how that
experience was constructed and the significance of what is actually happening (Coyne 1997; Coyne & Racioppo 2000; Lazarus 1990, 1997, 2000;
Somerfield 1997a, 1997b; Somerfield & McCrae 2000; Tennen *et al.* 2000).
Using these methods in conjunction with checklists has also received
support not just because it provides an opportunity to compare and evaluate the results from each approach (Lazarus 1990) but also because it aug-
ments checklist findings providing a method for probing the meaning of
endorsed responses (Somerfield 1997a). Yet despite this aura of agreement
there is still, lurking in the minds of many commentators, the view that
the use of such methods and the introduction of innovative and creative
approaches will be left only to those who, when considering traditional
measurement practices, are prepared to question whether these are the best
that we have (Lazarus 1990).

It is clear that 'no particular style of research, by itself, can win out
among researchers', nor can it always answer or solve all questions raised
about coping (Lazarus 1990, p. 48). Nevertheless, researchers still need to
have an organizing concept which enables them to explore a range of
different methods, test their relevance and assess their strengths in terms
of what they can or cannot achieve. The organizing concept around
which coping research needs to develop is one that focuses on the relational nature of stress, those subjective meanings that are captured
through the psychological process of appraisal and which express the
essence of the experience. This may be best explored through a qualitative description of what is happening. This, of course, challenges established measurement practice but offers the opportunity for using new
approaches that need to become part of, and embedded in, our research
repertoire. Setting aside for the moment the need for work stress
researchers to be better acquainted with issues surrounding appraisal and
its measurement, these additional challenges would include the need to
accept that research needs now to draw as much from an emphasis on
synthesis as it has from its more traditional emphasis on analysis (Lazarus
1990), recognize that describing a relationship is different from giving it
meaning (Cooper & Dewe 2004; Dewe & Cooper 2007) and acknowledge
that as *emotions* are at the heart of the transactional approach then it is
through emotions that the stress process is best explored (Lazarus 2001;
Lazarus & Cohen-Charash 2001).

As has been emphasized throughout, these challenges do not call for a wholesale shift from one method to another or abandoning one approach in favour of another. They simply recognize that crucial aspects of the stress process, particularly those transactional issues surrounding appraisal, are more likely to be obscured, surrendered or lost unless explored through alternative methods. Synthesis calls for a more *contextual* person-based holistic approach (Lazarus 1990) that offers a richer description of what is actually going on and how the experience is expressed, providing at the very least an opportunity where this reality can be compared and contrasted with more traditional variable-based measures (Spicer 1997). In a similar fashion there has been a tendency for researchers when describing a relationship to confuse description with meaning. Giving meaning to a relationship requires a substantively different methodological approach from simply describing the relationship (Cooper & Dewe 2004). To confuse the two fails to recognize this distinction and the need for different approaches when exploring the nature of and meaning given to the stressful experience itself.

Finally, there is clearly a need for researchers to put to one side the troublesome and somewhat ambiguous term 'stress'. Since stress is essentially about emotions and since emotions represent 'the coin of the realm' (Lazarus & Cohen-Charash 2001, p. 45), in understanding the nature of the person–environment transaction it is discrete emotions that provide a more discriminating way forward, a causal link that better reflects the transactional nature of the stress process and a level of analysis that overcomes the difficulties associated with the bluntness of the term 'stress'. As is suggested by other theorists (e.g. Beehr & Franz 1987; Cooper, Dewe & O'Driscoll 2001), the term 'stress' should be reserved as a label for the overall stressor–appraisal–strain–coping process, rather than being used to describe a specific component (or construct) in that process.

Building a Future Research Agenda from the Themes of the Past

Set against a context where researchers are urged to explore alternative methods designed to capture the relational transaction in any stressful encounter, what should appear when the agenda for the future is drawn up? As we have already noted, the agenda would include: (a) broadening our understanding of what constitutes coping thoughts and actions,

(b) developing a more explicit understanding of the many roles that meaning plays in coping research, (c) establishing what is meant by 'coping effectiveness', (d) shifting the emphasis from stress to emotions, (e) widening the scope for organizational stress interventions and (f) emphasizing the importance of overall well-being. While these agenda items may be seen as old wine in new bottles, unresolved issues and past debates provide the foundation for future research and, as one cannot easily be completely separated from the other, the whiff of familiarity remains as some issues are rehearsed one more time.

The Characteristics of Coping and Coping Types

We turn first to what constitutes coping thoughts and actions. While the debate surrounding what should or should not be defined as coping raises issues about effort, context and intention, the agenda for the future needs also, when it comes to understanding the nature of coping, to consider the types of coping strategies and the roles they play, the different contexts within which coping may occur, how coping strategies are used, why they are chosen, the relationships between different coping strategies, the role of 'the positive' in coping and, of course, what this means for how these issues are measured and researched. Exploring and identifying the different types of coping should not be seen as a criticism of the classification of coping strategies as either problem-focused or emotion-focused. These issues are simply an acknowledgement that any attempt to understand the nature of coping strategies and their qualities must now pay attention to the social, communal, spiritual and meaning-centred aspects of coping (Folkman & Moskowitz 2004).

Indeed, the efforts of future researchers may best be directed towards understanding the roles that these coping strategies play, their function, characteristics and modes, avoiding at this stage the temptation to immediately classify them within a schema that may well conceal their unique qualities and their explanatory potential. Because coping strategies need to be considered in context, future researchers may wish to abandon the search for a universal schema for classifying coping strategies and focus on the benefits that flow from understanding the roles played by different types of coping strategies and even more importantly how they may relate to one another. Understanding how coping strategies interrelate may eventually offer more in the way of explaining their nature and type than trying to fit them into a schema that was always intended to be a first attempt at classification.

It is not just understanding the relationship between different coping strategies that helps define their nature. Much can be learnt about the nature and characteristics of a type of coping by investigating what can be described as 'within relationships'. This type of analysis involves exploring the relationships between those individual coping strategies that collectively make up a particular style of coping. The way in which individual strategies form patterns and combine together provides further evidence of the role these strategies may play in relation to one another, the different functions they may perform and those qualities that may best help describe the more generic nature of the strategy itself. Exploring the relationships between and within different types of coping will without doubt extend our knowledge about how different strategies work, the complex way in which they are used and the different functions they may perform. Future research needs to ask questions that capture why certain coping strategies are being used, and why they are being used in the way that they are. This approach will move away from imposing a priori labels on strategies and will allow the nature of the strategy to emerge from the way in which it is being used. This, of course, requires a change to current measurement practices, but it also establishes a basis for better understanding the complexity of what we are dealing with and whether when describing coping types we can extend that description beyond the context within which the strategy is being used.

The above suggestions lead to some more specific recommendations about directions for future research on coping with stress. Some of these issues have been raised previously by other commentators, but the seeds would appear to have fallen on stony ground, as coping studies frequently have continued to utilize convenient but not necessarily adequate methods to explore how individuals endeavour to deal with the stressors they confront in their work environment.

Assessment of Coping Behaviours

Several researchers note the numerous difficulties associated with the measurement and assessment of coping behaviours (e.g. Briner, Harris & Daniels 2004; Carver, Scheier & Weintraub 1989; Dewe 2000; Folkman & Moskowitz 2004). Some of these challenges were discussed in Chapter 2, in particular the limitations inherent in coping checklists. As we have argued, although these checklists enable researchers to elicit self-reports of behaviours engaged in during a stressful encounter, such self-reports can provide biased and even inaccurate accounts of what a person has actually done when confronted with a specific stressor. For example, it is well known that there is a social desirability bias in self-reports of coping, whereby individuals are more likely to indicate that they have engaged in problem-focused actions rather than avoidance behaviours in dealing with stressors such as interpersonal conflict with colleagues at work. Reliance solely on a checklist of coping behaviours does not permit an investigation of the accuracy and hence validity of self-reported behaviours.

Above we commented that it would be valuable to utilize mixed methodologies to investigate how people actually respond to specific stressors, and the meanings which they attach to those stressors. A combination of quantitative, questionnaire-based approaches which assess particular behaviours with more qualitative, open-ended methods (e.g. interviews) which explore the individual's appraisal processes are required to develop a more comprehensive assessment of coping. One methodology which has been used, though infrequently, to link stressors to coping behaviours is critical incident analysis (CIA). This technique, first articulated by Flanagan (1954), is often used in structured employment interviews, and has direct application to coping assessment. CIA is a relatively simple procedure which entails asking the respondent to describe a situation where he or she has confronted a particular stressor (e.g. interpersonal conflict). The person is then asked to describe the behaviour(s) which they engaged in to deal with this situation, and the level of effectiveness of these behaviours (i.e. did they resolve the problem). O'Driscoll and Cooper (1996) suggest that CIA enables the researcher to directly link coping actions with specific stressors, which a coping checklist cannot normally do. The CIA approach is also less subject to social desirability and other biases than questionnaire-based measures of coping are, although it still relies on the person providing an accurate account of their actions. A drawback of CIA, however, is that it is difficult (sometimes impossible) to generalize from the specific encounter reported by the person, because the nature of the stressors and their meaning are specific to the person. It may be possible to categorize responses from different people into 'themes', although in practice this can be difficult to achieve (O'Driscoll & Cooper 1996). Finally, compared with questionnaires which can be administered to many respondents with little cost in terms of time and energy, CIA is a time- and energy-consuming methodology for assessing coping strategies and their relative efficacy.

It is evident that no single research strategy can fully capture the complexity of stress-related coping strategies. While questionnaire-based methods have been utilized most often, and have some distinct advantages, we suggest that a combination of methodologies is needed to develop a more comprehensive understanding of the nature of coping behaviours and their meaning for individuals dealing with stressful encounters. Above we have provided two examples of approaches which can shed valuable light on coping processes, including appraisals and the emotions experienced by individuals. Along with other commentators, we recommend that researchers adopt a more holistic view of coping when examining the interaction between stressors, coping and resultant strain.

Coping Styles versus Coping Strategies

Another salient issue, related to the above, is the notion of *styles* versus *strategies* of coping. In simple terms, the question is whether people's coping efforts are highly consistent across situations (irrespective of the nature of the stressor) or vary considerably depending on the nature of the stressor encountered. If an individual displays the same or very similar responses across different types of stressor, this would suggest that a coping 'style' is in operation. Some researchers suggest that such styles are related to personality traits (Jang *et al.* 2007). Conversely, if coping behaviours differ depending on the type of the stressor, it is more appropriate to refer to 'strategies'. Most questionnaire-based coping instruments assess coping styles, as they do not explicitly link the self-reported coping behaviours to specific stressors, but rather tend to elicit more general coping responses.

There has been considerable debate about whether people do in fact display relatively uniform and consistent behaviours across situations or if responses are attuned to specific stressors, and there is evidence to support both arguments. From a theoretical perspective, it is of interest to determine whether generic styles of coping exist, and the relative effectiveness of different styles. From a practical viewpoint, however, it is more beneficial to examine how individuals react to specific types of stressor. For instance, if it is demonstrated that certain behaviours (such as proactive coping) are effective at dealing with particular stressors (e.g. upcoming work demands), stress management interventions could focus explicitly on training individuals to engage in these types of behaviours.

The issue, therefore, is not whether researchers should focus their attention on styles or on strategies, but rather that they need to clearly identify the aims of their investigations. Understanding both coping styles and coping strategies is important for the further development of comprehensive theories of coping, as well as the practical management of stressful encounters.

When considering coping behaviours and coping styles and their assessment it is important to consider that coping is not just confined to the workplace. Future research may also like to consider the issue of context by exploring how other life spheres are used as a means of coping with the stress of work. Different attempts at classifying coping describe strategies that utilize home resources (Dewe & Guest 1990), illustrating the way in which home, family and friends are used when coping with work stress. More recent research exploring issues around work–life balance and work–life conflict has pointed to the crossover between home and work, illustrating the sometimes delicate balance between the two and the complex ways in which one, while at one time providing a source of support, can, at another time, become a source of conflict. While this work is integrated into the stress literature, there is clear evidence that other life spheres also provide a resource for coping with work stress, and future research may wish to explore how these may be better integrated into more mainstream work stress research. The work on leisure as a coping strategy is one example, and religious coping (Folkman & Moskowitz 2004) another.

Finally, when thinking about the nature and characteristics of different ways of coping the 'positive psychology' agenda offers at least three ways forward. The first would be to continue to explore the role and functions of specific positive strategies like proactive coping and to initiate a more focused programme that explores across all coping strategies their positive functions – when, how and why they are used and how this positive quality is determined. In respect of this latter approach it reinforces the view that all coping types have these dual functions (Folkman & Moskowitz 2004), ensuring that positive coping is not simply regarded as a property of those strategies that are distinctly future-oriented. Two further items should be added to the 'positive' agenda. These items simply build on what has already been discussed, but they too require, when thinking about the positive nature of coping, that more focused attention be given to the distinction between coping strategies that accumulate resources as opposed to those that deplete resources (Hobfoll 1998) and those strategies that instil positive meanings giving respite and helping to restore resources (Folkman 1997).

The Role of Meaning in Coping Research

Meanings and the understanding of meanings are fundamental to the relational/transactional view of stress. A future research agenda needs to recognize the importance of meanings in understanding the work stress experience and deliberately focus attention on the role and significance of primary appraisals and on the meaning-centred nature of coping. Turning first to primary appraisal, although work stress researchers acknowledge the importance of appraisals to the stress process, they have hesitated to pursue this line of inquiry owing to a concern that individualizing the stress process makes it difficult to identify interventions that would benefit the well-being of most workers. Nevertheless, they also recognize that this concern can no longer be resolved by debate but needs now to be settled through empirical investigation. So, why focus work stress research on appraisals? Two reasons: the first stems from the fact that individuals can and do make a distinction between the causes of work stress and the meanings they attach to those events. The second is that appraisals act as the conduit, linking the event with the emotional response.

The first step needed in any future agenda where appraisals are the focus is to build an understanding of how individuals appraise and give meanings to work encounters and whether those meanings capture the ideas embodied in the terms 'threat', 'loss' and 'challenge'. Research on work-related stress and other forms of stress needs to develop a more refined understanding of the nature of these meanings and the themes that best express them when they are considered collectively. To do this requires that researchers begin to explore methods that would allow this reality to emerge. Thematic analysis would provide the basic information needed to begin to define meanings and better understand their constituent elements. Using this information, the next step would be to explore whether particular work stressors are associated with particular meanings, how organizational cultures influence the meanings individuals give to demanding encounters, whether meanings vary from context to context and what core meanings are associated with different emotions. The positive psychology movement also provides directions for future research and, in the case of appraisal, these include exploring those meanings associated with challenge and benefit appraisals, identifying their relationship with positive emotions and determining where in the appraisal process positive appraisal plays a part.

While the boundaries between appraisals, reappraisals and coping are not always clear, reviews (Affleck & Tennen 1996; Folkman 1997; Park & Folkman 1997) suggest that attention needs to be directed towards exploring the nature of meaning-centred coping. A number of developments have been identified that signal opportunities for work stress research. These include identifying the benefit-reminding aspect of coping (Tennen & Affleck 2005), coping as a means of finding meaning in, and making sense of, encounters (Park & Folkman 1997) and, under the umbrella of positive psychology, the idea of stress-related growth (Park, Cohen & Murch 1996). The search for meaning-centred activities in coping is aimed at improving our understanding of the functions coping strategies play, the complexity of different types of coping and the different ways in which meanings can be expressed when considered within a relational/transactional context.

In this case investigations would involve, when it comes to benefit-reminding coping, exploring the deliberate way in which benefit-reminding aspects of coping are used, the methodology necessary to understand how and when these strategies unfold during a stressful encounter and how their restorative qualities are best expressed (Tennen & Affleck 2005). Researchers also need to explore coping strategies that are used to search for meaning – meanings that make sense of what is going on, that reduce the dissonance between what has happened and what provides some sense or comprehension of what has happened and what is meaningful – and in so doing take a 'broader conceptual view of the various ways that meaning can be involved in the coping process' (Park & Folkman 1997, p. 132). Finally, in line with the positive emphasis, researchers need now to explore personal growth, that is the ways in which individuals can, through coping with stressful encounters, 'enhance social and personal resources and develop new or improved coping skills' (Park, Cohen & Murch 1996, p. 73).

Coping Effectiveness

Another issue which we have referred to frequently throughout this book is the question of the extent to which personal coping behaviours are efficacious in relieving work-related stress and how coping effectiveness can best be assessed. The most commonly used method for evaluating coping effectiveness has been to correlate the use of particular coping strategies (e.g. problem-focused coping or emotion-focused coping) with stress-related outcomes, such as increased satisfaction and reduced psychological strain. Although this is a useful step in the assessment of coping, by itself it yields incomplete information on whether certain coping strategies are more or less helpful than others are. For a start, a correlational approach is unable to inform us about direction of causality, and even longitudinal correlational research does not provide definitive information about causality, because other (unmeasured) variables may contribute to the outcomes.

Clearly, what is required is more controlled and comprehensive explorations of how coping strategies operate within the context of the transactional framework. As we have outlined above, from the perspective of the transactional model coping behaviours need to be viewed in terms of how individuals perceive and interpret the meaning of stressors for their well-being (i.e. primary appraisal) and their beliefs about options available to them (secondary appraisal). We cannot fully understand why people engage in specific responses to stressors unless we explore both primary and secondary appraisals in particular encounters. Similarly, measuring the efficacy of coping behaviours requires an assessment of these appraisals, which rarely occurs in research on coping effectiveness. As suggested above, research may need to incorporate mixed methodologies in order to obtain a systematic assessment of coping effectiveness.

It is possible, when setting the future research agenda into coping effectiveness, to identify a number of ways forward. All raise questions about how effectiveness should best be understood, defined and measured and each in their own way reflects the debate surrounding established measurement practices versus the need to consider alternative approaches if our understanding of this complex issue is to be advanced. The first deals with the fundamental question of how individuals actually evaluate whether their coping is effective, what criteria they use, whether those criteria change depending on the context and what they are actually describing when they talk about coping as being effective. Understanding how effectiveness is evaluated needs to be considered not only in terms of outcomes and emotional regulation but also in terms of how such evaluations are made, taking into account appraisals, goals and values, the personal and professional costs involved, the compromises made, conflicts between individual and organizational goals, the resources expended and the level of control. Future researchers may also like to assess whether and when mastery or resolution is achieved (Folkman & Moskowitz 2004). Identifying and exploring the nature of the evaluative process reinforces the importance of context (Zeidner & Saklofske 1996), has the potential to provide an understanding of how effectiveness is described and provides a structure for considering how the different themes that emerge from such analysis best express how effectiveness may be defined.

In working through this process at least two other themes emerge. The first concerns what is actually meant by 'outcomes': what would be appropriate outcomes in terms of different types of coping (Aldwin 2000), whether there are some outcomes that cannot be resolved (Zeidner & Saklofske 1996), whether researchers should be more selective in the outcomes measured (Cooper, Dewe & O'Driscoll 2001) and how coping may not simply manage negative outcomes but also support and achieve positive outcomes (Lazarus 2000). The second theme concerns the relationship between coping effectiveness and personality. Here the future research agenda needs to build on the work exploring personality and coping and consider, where individuals have a predisposition towards using certain types of coping, the way in which such predispositions influence coping effectiveness (Suls, David & Harvey 1996), whether and at what stage in the coping process personality has its most significant influence (O'Brien & DeLongis 1996), how personality may influence individuals' competence in using different coping strategies (Suls & David 1996) and whether different personality attributes are expressed more in some contexts than in others, along with the impact this may have on coping effectiveness (O'Brien & DeLongis 1996). In research investigating coping effectiveness, there is no room for prejudging or implying that some coping strategies are inherently more effective than others are. Effectiveness emerges from the complexities of the transactional relationship between the individual and the environment.

Personal Coping versus Organizational Stress Management Interventions

In Chapter 6 we raised questions about the tendency for managers to view work stress as a 'personal issue' and hence the responsibility of the individual employee to sort out for themselves. Despite changes which have occurred over the last decade or so in the legislative view of stress-related problems, and a shift towards conceptualizing work stress as a 'hazard' which management has at least some responsibility for, (Cox *et al.* 2007), there is still a tendency for managers to consider the roots of stress as lying within individuals rather than in the work environment and, mainly owing to concerns over the financial implications of assuming responsibility for stress-related problems, to attempt to downplay the role of work environment factors (including their own management style) as possible work hazards or risk factors for stress.

Consequently, the predominant approach to stress management within organizations remains exactly that: stress 'management' or containment, focusing on helping individuals to cope with the levels of emotional and/ or physical strain they are experiencing rather than making a concerted effort to change environmental factors which may be the major cause of these strains. A salient illustration of this tendency is the manner in which organizations frequently endeavour to deal with a particular stressor which has received considerable attention in recent organizational literature: bullying at work. Research on work-related bullying has often found (Namie 2007) that two prominent strategies adopted by management to deal with this issue are (a) to downplay its extent or significance, a form of acceptance coping, or (b) to attribute the reasons for bullying to characteristics of the perpetrator ('that's just their style') or even the victim ('they brought it upon themselves'), rather than aspects of the organizational culture or climate which may facilitate this form of counterproductive behaviour. By making personal attributions, management may avoid the need to examine and possibly modify characteristics of the environment which promote bullying.

In contrast to the above, as we have suggested throughout this book, a more appropriate and effective perspective is to view stress management as a shared management–worker responsibility. This perspective entails an exploration of not only the individual's perceptions of their environment and their reactions to it (i.e. their personal coping strategies), but also organizational-level issues, and a more solution-oriented approach to organizational stress management. As advocated by other commentators (e.g. Murphy 1995; Murphy & Sauter 2003), the preponderant attention to secondary- and tertiary-level interventions, such as employee assistance programmes (EAPs), needs to be replaced by greater concentration on stressor reduction or removal (primary-level interventions). Researchers too need to couple exploration of personal coping responses with the investigation of organizational strategies.

From Stress to Well-Being

A final recommendation which emerges from new ways of conceptualizing stress and coping is that researchers (and practitioners) need to modify their thinking, away from simply assessing stressors, strains and coping, to research which focuses on factors which promote well-being in the workplace. In keeping with the ascendancy of positive psychology (Seligman & Csikszentmihalyi 2000), which we discussed in Chapter 3, taking a more positive approach to developing healthy workplaces rather than simply trying to ameliorate the negative repercussions of stress will in the long term lead to more constructive and fruitful interventions that are beneficial to both individuals and their organizations. This does not mean ignoring negative elements in work environments, but rather entails endeavouring to further develop the positive features which will enhance individual well-being. Included in this approach is the development of more proactive and preventative approaches to stress management (Folkman & Moskowitz 2003), rather than focusing entirely on reactive coping after strain has occurred, and giving more attention to positive emotional states.

It is also clear from earlier chapters that an agenda for future research must emphasize emotions and their role in the coping process. There are a number of reasons for this, not least of which is the ambiguity that surrounds the word 'stress' and the associated difficulty of understanding what someone is experiencing when they say they are 'under stress'. As stress generates emotional consequences, and as emotions are at the core of the transactional approach to stress and best express what it is that is actually being experienced, then it is emotions that possess the conceptual specificity that has been absent from work stress research (Lazarus 2001; Lazarus & Cohen-Charash 2001). A number of opportunities present themselves when setting an agenda. These would include conceptual issues that would help to develop an understanding of the nature of different emotions, both negative and positive, and more importantly the way they are expressed and used during a demanding encounter, how long they last and the intensity with which they are felt. Operational-level issues would need to explore whether particular appraisals or patterns of appraisals are associated with a specific emotion and whether those appraisals reflect what Lazarus (2001) describes as the emotion's 'core relational meaning' (p. 63). Other operational issues include exploring the causal pathways between different emotions, where in the coping process different emotions occur (Davis, Nolen-Hoeksema & Larson 1998), what this may mean in relation to the expression of positive and negative emotions, whether and in what way organizational culture influences the use and expression of different emotions and the relationship between emotions and different personality constructs.

Conclusions

New wine in old bottles? Maybe, but maybe not. As we have mentioned, the future cannot, of course, be separated from the past and the past therefore becomes the signpost for future action. It is clear that, when all the different signs are brought together and all the different reviews digested, broad themes can be identified which suggest the way in which research should be developed. The coherence of these themes is maintained by an organizing concept that views work stress in relational/transactional terms, focusing on those psychological processes that best express its transactional nature. These themes would include:

- developing our understanding of meaning and the role of meaning as an appraisal, coping strategy and reappraisal, for without this understanding future research would be ignoring perhaps the most powerful of explanatory variables;
- building our knowledge of coping strategies by accepting that coping is best expressed through the context within which it occurs and that it is this context that defines how different strategies are used, reducing the temptation to identify anything but the broadest of classification systems;
- moving the focus of research to consider the role of emotions, their use in a work encounter, their potential for explaining what is actually being experienced and their utility in providing a more specific causal pathway for understanding the stress process;
- developing our understanding of what it is that is being described when coping effectiveness is discussed, how it is being evaluated and the impact it has on the individual, the organization and other life aspects, allowing this knowledge to inform what may or may not be effective, rather than relying on inference or more narrow concepts of what coping effectiveness entails;
- by accepting that stress is transactional and contextual, use these as criteria for exploring interventions recognizing that 'partnership' should

best describe intervention strategies and that this partnership may need to be extended beyond organizational boundaries involving other agencies with appropriate expertise.

All these themes are bound together by three further requirements. These are that the positive be emphasized so that as well as protecting well-being researchers are exploring what allows individuals to flourish and maximize their potential, that progress cannot be maintained without significant changes to the way in which we approach measurement and that this requirement for creative and innovative approaches to measurement becomes accepted as part of our future research repertoire. Finally, we must not forget the moral responsibility we have to those whose working lives we research, using this responsibility to guide the work that we do and the knowledge we create and share.

References

Adams, G. A. & Jex, S. M. (1999) Relationships between time management, control, work–family conflict and strain. *Journal of Occupational Health Psychology* **4**: 72–7.

Affleck, G. & Tennen, H. (1996) Construing benefits from adversity: Adaptational significance and dispositional underpinnings. *Journal of Personality* **64**: 899–922.

Aldwin, C. M. (2000) *Stress, Coping and Development: An integrative perspective.* London: The Guilford Press.

Allen, T. D. (2001) Family-supportive work environments: The role of organizational perceptions. *Journal of Vocational Behavior* **58**(3): 414–35.

Amirkhan, J. H. (1990) A factor analytically derived measure of coping: The coping strategy indicator. *Journal of Personality and Social Psychology* **59**: 1066–74.

Anderson, S. E., Coffey, B. S. & Byerly, R. T. (2002) Formal organizational initiatives and informal workplace practices: Links to work–family conflict and job-related outcomes. *Journal of Management* **28**(6): 787–810.

Aryee, S., Luk, V., Leung, A. & Lo, S. (1999) Role stressors, interrole conflict and wellbeing: The moderating influence of spousal support and coping behaviors among employed parents in Hong Kong. *Journal of Vocational Behavior* **54**(2): 259–78.

Aspinwall, L. G. & Taylor, S. (1997) A stitch in time: Self-regulation and proactive coping. *Psychological Bulletin* **121**: 417–36.

Ayman, R. & Antani, A. (2008) Social support and work–family conflict. In K. Korabik, D. S. Lero & D. L. Whitehead (eds), *Handbook of Work–Family Integration: Research, theory and best practices.* Amsterdam: Elsevier, pp. 287–304.

Bakker, A. B. & Schaufeli, W. B. (2008) Positive organizational behavior: Engaged employees in flourishing organizations. *Journal of Organizational Behavior* **29**: 147–54.

Baltes, B. B. & Heydens-Gahir, H. A. (2003) Reduction of work–family conflict through the use of selection, optimization and compensation behaviors. *Journal of Applied Psychology* **88**(6): 1005–118.

Barling, J. & Carson, J. (2008) Management style and mental well-being at work: State of science review SR-C3. *Foresight Mental Capital and Well-Being Project.* London: The Government Office for Science.

Bar-Tal, Y. & Spitzer, A. (1994) Coping use versus effectiveness as moderating the stress–strain relationship. *Journal of Community and Applied Social Psychology* **4**: 91–100.

Bartlett, D. (1998) *Stress: Perspectives and processes.* Buckingham: Open University Press.

Baumeister, R. F. & Vohs, K. D. (2005) The pursuit of meaningfulness in life. In C. R. Snyder & S. J. Lopez (eds), *Handbook of Positive Psychology.* Oxford: Oxford University Press, pp. 608–18.

Beehr, T. A. & Franz, T. M. (1987) The current debate about the meaning of job stress. In J. M. Ivancevich & D. C. Ganster (eds), *Job Stress: From theory to suggestion.* New York: Haworth Press, pp. 5–18.

Beehr, T. A. & Glazer, S. (2005) Organizational role stress. In J. Barling, E. K. Kelloway & M. R. Frone (eds), *Handbook of Work Stress.* Thousand Oaks, CA: Sage Publications, pp. 7–33.

Beehr, T. A. & McGrath, J. E. (1996) The methodology of research on coping: Conceptual, strategic, and operational-level issues. In M. Zeidner & N. S. Endler (eds), *Handbook of Coping: Theory, research, applications.* New York: John Wiley & Sons, Ltd, pp. 65–82.

Beehr, T. A. & Newman, J. E. (1978) Job stress, employee health, and organizational effectiveness: A facet analysis, model, and literature review. *Personnel Psychology* **31**: 665–99.

Beehr, T. A. & O'Driscoll, M. P. (2002) Organizationally targeted interventions aimed at reducing workplace stress. In J. C. Thomas & M. Hersen (eds), *Handbook of Mental Health in the Workplace.* Thousand Oaks, CA: Sage Publications, pp. 103–19.

Beehr, T. A. & O'Hara, K. (1987) Methodological designs for the evaluation of occupational stress interventions. In S. Kasl & C. L. Cooper (eds), *Stress and Health: Issues in research methodology.* New York: John Wiley & Sons, Ltd, pp. 79–112.

Behfar, K. J., Peterson, R. S., Mannix, E. A. & Trochim, W. M. K. (2008) The critical role of conflict resolution in teams: A close look at the links between conflict type, conflict management strategies, and team outcomes. *Journal of Applied Psychology* **93**(1): 170–88.

Behson, S. J. (2002) Coping with work-to-family conflict: The role of informal work accommodations to family. *Journal of Occupational Health Psychology* **7**(4): 324–41.

Bell, A. & Bryson, C. (2005) Work–life balance: Still a women's issue? In A. Park, J. Curtice, K. Thomson, C. Bromley *et al.* (eds), *British Social Attitudes: Two terms of New Labour: The public's reaction.* The 22nd Report. London: Sage Publications, pp. 33–62.

Berg, C. A. Wiebe, D. J., Butner, J., Bloor, L. *et al.* (2008) Collaborative coping and daily mood in couples dealing with prostate cancer. *Psychology and Aging* 23: 505–16.

Berridge, J. R. & Cooper, C. L. (2000) Coping with the stress of organizational challenges: The role of the employee assistance programme. In P. Dewe, M. Leiter & T. Cox (eds), *Coping, Health and Organizations*. London: Taylor & Francis, pp. 211–36.

Bevan, S. (2003) *Attendance Management*. London: The Work Foundation.

Billings, A. G. & Moos, R. H. (1981) The role of coping responses and social resources in attenuating the stress of life events. *Journal of Behavioral Medicine* 4: 139–57.

Billings, A. G. & Moos, R. H. (1984) Coping, stress and social resources among adults with unipolar depression. *Journal of Personality and Social Psychology* 46: 877–91.

Black, C. (2008) *Working for a healthier tomorrow: Review of the health of Britain's working age population*. Presented to the Secretary of State for Health and the Secretary of State for Works and Pensions. London: The Stationery Office.

Blair-Loy, M. & Wharton, A. S. (2002) Employees' use of work–family policies and the workplace social context. *Social Forces* 80(3): 813–45.

Blair-Loy, M. & Wharton, A. S. (2004) Organizational commitment and constraints on work–family policy use: Corporate flexibility policies in a global firm. *Sociological Perspectives* 47(3): 243.

Brief, A. & Atieh, J. M. (1987) Studying job stress: Are we making mountains out of molehills? *Journal of Occupational Behaviour* 8: 115–26.

Brief, A. P. & George, J. M. (1991) Psychological stress and the workplace: A brief comment on Lazarus' outlook. In P. L. Perrewé (ed.), *Handbook on Job Stress* [special issue]. *Journal of Social Behaviour and Personality* 6: 15–20.

Brightbill, C. K. (1960) *The Challenge of Leisure*. Englewood Cliffs, NJ: Prentice Hall.

Briner, R. B., Harris, C. & Daniels, K. (2004) How do work stress and coping work? Toward a fundamental theoretical reappraisal. *British Journal of Guidance and Counselling* 32(2): 223–34.

Brough, P. & Biggs, A. (2008) *Managing occupational stress experienced by correctional workers*. Proceedings of the Work, Stress, & Health 2008 Conference, March. Washington: American Psychological Association.

Brough, P., O'Driscoll, M. P. & Kalliath, T. J. (2005) The ability of 'family friendly' organizational resources to predict work–family conflict and job and family satisfaction. *Stress & Health* 21(4): 223–34.

Brown, A., Charlwood, C., Forde, C. & Spencer, D. (2006) *Changing job quality in Great Britain 1998–2004*. DTI: Employment Relations Research Series No. 70, London.

Burchell, B. J., Day, D., Hudson, M., Ladipo, D. *et al.* (1999) *Job Insecurity and Work Intensification*. York: Joseph Rowntree Foundation.

Burke, R. J. (1998) Work and non-work stressors and well-being among police officers: The role of coping. *Anxiety, Stress & Coping* **11**: 345–62.

Burke, R. J. (2002) Work stress and coping in organizations; Progress and prospects. In E. Frydenberg (ed.), *Beyond Coping: Meeting goals, visions, and challenges*. Oxford: Oxford University Press, pp. 83–106.

Burke, R. J. & Richardsen, A. M. (2000) Organizational-level interventions designed to reduce occupational stressors. In P. Dewe, M. Leiter & T. Cox (eds), *Coping, Health and Organizations*. London: Taylor & Francis, pp. 191–210.

Carlson, D. S., Kacmar, K. M. & Williams, L. (2000) Construction and initial validation of a multidimensional measure of work/family conflict. *Journal of Vocational Behavior* **56**(2): 249–76.

Cartwright, S. & Cooper, C. L. (1997) *Managing Workplace Stress*. Thousand Oaks, CA: Sage Publications.

Carver, C. S., Scheier, M. F. & Weintraub, J. K. (1989) Assessing coping strategies: A theoretically based approach. *Journal of Personality and Social Psychology* **56**: 267–83.

Cavanaugh, M. A., Boswell, W. R., Roehling, M. V. & Boudreau, J. W. (2000) An empirical examination of self-reported work stress among US managers. *Journal of Applied Psychology* **85**: 65–74.

Chartered Institute of Management (2007) *The Quality of Working Life 2007: Managers' health, motivation and productivity*. London: CIM.

Chartered Institute of Personnel and Development (2003) *Living to Work? Survey Report*. London: CPD.

Chartered Institute of Personnel and Development (2005) *Bullying at Work: Beyond policies to a culture of respect*. London: CPD.

Chartered Institute of Personnel and Development (2007a) *Absence Management*. London: CPD.

Chartered Institute of Personnel and Development (2007b) *Recruitment, Retention and Turnover*. London: CPD.

Chartered Institute of Personnel and Development (2008) *A Barometer of HR Trends and Prospects 2008*. London: CPD.

Coleman, D. & Iso-Ahola, S. E. (1993) Leisure and health: The role of social support and self-determination. *Journal of Leisure Research* **25**: 11–28.

Collins Dictionary & Thesaurus (1993) Glasgow: Harper Collins Publishers.

Confederation of British Industry CBI/AXA (2007) *Attending to Absence: Absence and labour turnover survey 2007*. London: CBI.

Connor-Smith, J. K. & Flachsbart, C. (2007) Relations between personality and coping: A meta-analysis. *Journal of Personality and Social Psychology* **93**: 1080–107.

Cooper, C. L. & Dewe, P. (2004) *Stress: A brief history*. Oxford: Blackwell Publishing.

Cooper, C. L. & Dewe, P. J. (2008) Well-being: Absenteeism, presenteeism, costs and challenges. *Occupational Medicine* **58**: 522–4.

Cooper, C. L., Dewe, P. J. & O'Driscoll, M. P. (2001) *Organizational Stress: A review and critique of theory, research and applications*. Thousand Oaks, CA: Sage Publications.

Cooper, C. L., Dewe, P. J. & O'Driscoll, M. P. (2003) Employee assistance programs. In J. C. Quick & L. E. Tetrick (eds), *Handbook of Occupational Health Psychology*. Washington: American Psychological Association, pp. 289–304.

Cooper, C. L. & Marshall, J. (1976) Occupational sources of stress: A review of the literature relating to coronary heart disease and mental ill-health. *Journal of Occupational Psychology* **49**: 11–28.

Costa, P. T., Somerfield, M. R. & McCrae, R. R. (1996) Personality and coping: A reconceptualization. In M. Zeidner & N.M. Endler (eds), *Handbook of Coping: Theory, research, applications*. New York: John Wiley & Sons, Ltd, pp. 44–61.

Cox, T., Karanika, M., Griffiths, A. & Houdmont, J. (2007) Evaluating organizational-level work stress interventions: Beyond traditional methods. *Work & Stress* **21**(4): 348–62.

Coyle, D. & Quah, D. (2002) *Getting the Measure of the New Economy*. London: The Work Foundation.

Coyne, J. C. (1997) Improving coping research: Raze the slum before any more building! *Journal of Health Psychology* **2**: 153–5.

Coyne, J. C. & Gottlieb, B. H. (1996) The mismeasure of coping by checklist. *Journal of Personality* **64**: 959–91.

Coyne, J. C. & Racioppo, M. W. (2000) Never the twain shall meet? Closing the gap between coping research and clinical intervention research. *American Psychologist* **55**: 655–64.

Creed, P. A. & Bartrum, D. A. (2008) Personal control as a mediator and moderator between life strains and psychological well-being in the unemployed. *Journal of Applied Social Psychology* **38**(2): 460–81.

Crompton, R. & Lyonette, C. (2007) Are we all working too hard? Women, men, and changing attitudes to employment. In A. Park, J. Curtice, K. Thomson, M. Phillips & M. Johnson (eds), *British Social Attitudes: Perspectives on a changing society*. The 23rd Report. London: Sage Publications, pp. 55–70.

Cushman, G. & Laidler, A. (1990) *Recreation, leisure and social policy*. Occasional Paper No. 4, Canterbury, New Zealand: Department of Parks, Recreation & Tourism, Lincoln University.

Daniels, K., Beesley, N., Cheyne, A. & Wimalasiri, V. (2008) Coping processes linking the demands-control-support model, affect and risky decisions at work. *Human Relations* **61**(6): 845–74.

Davis, C. G., Nolen-Hoeksema, S. & Larson, J. (1998) Making sense of loss and benefit from the experience: Two construals of meaning. *Journal of Personality and Social Psychology* **75**: 561–74.

Day, A. L. & Livingstone, H. A. (2001) Chronic and acute stressors among military personnel: Do coping styles buffer their negative impact on health? *Journal of Occupational Health Psychology* **6**: 348–60.

De Dreu, C. K. W., Van Dierendonck, D. & Dijkstra, M. T. M. (2004) Conflict at work and individual well-being. *International Journal of Conflict Management* **15**(1): 6–26.

de Jonge, J. & Dormann, C. (2006) Stressors, resources, and strain at work: A longitudinal test of the triple-match principle. *Journal of Applied Psychology* **91**(6): 1359–74.

Dewe, P. J. (1994) EAPs and stress management: From theory to practice to comprehensiveness. *Personnel Review* **23**: 21–32.

Dewe, P. J. (2000) Measures of coping with stress at work: A review and critique. In P. Dewe, T. Cox and M. Leiter (eds), *Coping and Health in Organisations*. London: Taylor & Francis, pp. 3–28.

Dewe, P. J. (2001) Work stress, coping and well being: Implementing strategies to better understand the relationship. In P. L. Perrewe & D. C. Ganster (eds), *Research in Occupational Stress and Well Being: Vol. 1: Exploring theoretical mechanisms and perspectives*. Amsterdam: Elsevier, pp. 63–96.

Dewe, P. J. (2003) A closer examination of the patterns when coping with work-related stress: Implications for measurement. *Journal of Occupational and Organizational Psychology* **76**: 517–24.

Dewe, P. J. (2008) Positive coping strategies at work. In A. Kinder, R. Hughes & C. L. Cooper (eds), *Employee Well-Being Support: A workplace resource*. Chichester: John Wiley & Sons, Ltd, pp. 91–8.

Dewe, P. J. & Cooper, C. (2007) Coping research and measurement in the context of work related stress. In G. Hodgkinson & K. Ford (eds), *International Review of Industrial and Organizational Psychology* **22**. Chichester: John Wiley & Sons, Ltd, pp. 141–91.

Dewe, P. J., Cox, T. & Ferguson, E. (1993) Individual strategies for coping with stress at work: A review. *Work & Stress* **7**: 5–15.

Dewe, P. J. & Guest, D. (1990) Methods of coping with stress at work: A conceptual analysis and empirical study of measurement issues. *Journal of Organizational Behavior* **11**: 135–50.

Dewe, P. J. & Kompier, M. (2008) *Foresight Mental Capital and Well-Being Project: Well-being and work: Future challenges*. London: The Government Office for Science.

Dijkstra, M. T. M., Van Dierendonck, D. & Evers, A. (2005) Responding to conflict at work and individual well-being: The mediating role of flight behaviour and feelings of helplessness. *European Journal of Work & Organizational Psychology* **14**(2): 119–35.

Drach-Zahavy, A. & Somech, A. (2008) Coping with work–family conflict: Integrating individual and organizational perspectives. In K. Korabik, D. S. Lero

& D. L. Whitehead (eds), *Handbook of Work–Family Integration: Research, theory and best practices.* Amsterdam: Elsevier, pp. 267–86.

Edwards, J. R. (1992) A cybernetic theory of stress, coping and well-being in organizations. *Academy of Management Review* 17(2): 238–74.

Edwards, J. R. & Cooper, C. L. (1990) The person–environment fit approach to stress: Recurring problems and some suggested solutions. *Journal of Organizational Behavior* 11: 293–307.

Einarsen, S. (2000) Harassment and bullying at work: A review of the Scandinavian approach. *Aggression and Violent Behavior* 5(4): 379–401.

Einarsen, S., Hoel, H., Zapf, D. & Cooper, C. (eds) (2003) *Bullying and Emotional Abuse in the Workplace: International perspectives in research and practice.* London: Taylor & Francis.

Elkin, A. & Rosch, P. (1990) Promoting mental health at the workplace: The prevention side of stress management. *Occupational Medicine* 5: 739–54.

Equal Opportunities Commission (2007) *Enter the Timelords: Transforming work to meet the future.* Final report of the EOC's investigation into the Transformation of Work. Manchester: Equal Opportunities Commission.

Erera-Weatherley, P. L. (1996) Coping with stress: Public welfare supervisors doing their best. *Human Relations* 49: 157–70.

Fenlason, K. & Beehr, T. A. (1994) Social support and occupational stress: Effects of talking to others. *Journal of Organizational Behavior* 15(2): 157–75.

Fineman, S. (2006) On being positive: Concerns and counterpoints. *Academy of Management Review* 31: 270–91.

Fisher, C. D. (1998) Effects of internal and external interruptions on boredom at work: Two studies. *Journal of Organizational Behavior* 19: 503–22.

Flanagan, J. (1954) The critical incident technique. *Psychological Bulletin* 51: 327–58.

Folkman, S. (1992) Improving coping assessment: Reply to Stone and Kennedy-Moore. In H. S. Friedman (ed.), *Hostility Coping and Health.* Washington: American Psychological Association, pp. 215–23.

Folkman, S. (1997) Positive psychological states and coping with severe stress. *Social Science & Medicine* 45: 1207–21.

Folkman, S. (2008) The case for positive emotions in the stress process. *Anxiety, Stress & Coping* 21: 3–14.

Folkman, S. & Lazarus, R. (1985) If it changes, it must be a process: Study of emotion and coping during three stages of a college examination. *Journal of Personality and Social Psychology* 48: 150–70.

Folkman, S., Lazarus, R. S., Denkel-Schetter, C., DeLongis, A. & Gruen, R. J. (1986) Dynamics of a stress encounter: Cognitive appraisal, coping and encounter outcomes. *Journal of Personality and Social Psychology* 82: 642–62.

Folkman, S. & Moskowitz, J. T. (2000) The context matters. *Personality and Social Psychology Bulletin* 26: 647–54.

Folkman, S. & Moskowitz, J. T. (2003) Positive psychology from a coping perspective. *Psychological Inquiry* **14**: 121–4.

Folkman, S. & Moskowitz, J. T. (2004) Coping: Pitfalls and promise. *Annual Review of Psychology* **55**: 745–74.

Fox, M., Dwyer, D. & Ganster, D. (1993) Effects of stressful job demands and control on physiological and attitudinal outcomes in a hospital setting. *Academy of Management Journal* **36**: 289–318.

Fredrickson, B. L. (1998) What good are positive emotions? *Review of General Psychology* **2**: 300–319.

Fredrickson, B. L. (2001) The role of positive emotions in positive psychology. *American Psychologist* **56**: 218–26.

Fredrickson, B. L. (2005) Positive emotions. In C. R. Snyder & S. J. Lopez (eds), *Handbook of Positive Psychology*. Oxford: Oxford University Press, pp. 120–38.

Fredrickson, B. L. & Branigan, C. (2005) Positive emotions broaden the scope of attention and thought-action repertoires. *Cognition & Emotion* **19**: 313–32.

Frese, M. & Zapf, D. (1999) On the importance of the objective environment in stress and attribution theory. Counterpoint to Perrewe and Zellars. *Journal of Organizational Behavior* **20**: 761–5.

Frone, M. R. (2003) Work–family balance. In J. C. Quick & L. E. Tetrick (eds), *Handbook of Occupational Health Psychology*. Washington: American Psychological Association, pp. 143–62.

Frye, N. K. & Breaugh, J. A. (2004) Family-friendly policies, supervisor support, work–family conflict, family–work conflict, and satisfaction: A test of a conceptual model. *Journal of Business and Psychology* **19**(2): 197.

Fugate, M., Kinicki, A. J. & Prussia, G. E. (2008) Employee coping with organizational change: An examination of alternative theoretical perspectives and models. *Personnel Psychology* **61**(1): 1–36.

Furnham, A. (1988) *Lay Theories: Everyday understanding of problems in the social sciences*. Oxford: Pergamon Press.

Game, A. M. (2007) Workplace boredom coping: Health, safety, and HR implications. *Personnel Review* **36**(5): 701–21.

Ganster, D. C. (2005) Executive job demands: Suggestions from a stress and decision-making perspective. *Academy of Management Review* **30**(3): 492–502.

Giga, S. I., Cooper, C. L. & Faragher, B. (2003) The development of a framework for a comprehensive approach to stress management interventions at work. *International Journal of Stress Management* **10**(4): 280–96.

Giga, S. I., Noblet, A. J., Faragher, B. & Cooper, C. L. (2003) The UK perspective: A review of research on organisational stress management interventions. *Australian Psychologist* **38**(2): 158–64.

Gilbreath, B. & Benson, P. G. (2004) The contribution of supervisor behaviour to employee psychological well-being. *Work & Stress* **18**(3): 255–66.

Glazer, S. & Beehr, T. A. (2005) Consistency of implications of three role stressors across four countries. *Journal of Organizational Behavior* **26**(5): 467–87.

Glazer, S. & Kruse, B. (2008) The role of organizational commitment in occupational stress models. *International Journal of Stress Management* **15**(4): 329–44.

Glowinkowski, S. P. & Cooper, C. L. (1985). Current issues in organizational stress research. *Bulletin of the British Psychological Society* **38**: 212–16.

Goetzel, R. Z., Long, S. R., Ozminkowski, R. J., Wang, S. & Lynch, W. (2004) Health, absence, disability, and presenteeism cost estimates of certain physical and mental health conditions affecting U.S. employers. *Journal of Occupational and Environmental Medicine* **46**: 398–412.

Goff, S. J., Mount, M. K. & Jamison, R. L. (1990) Employer supported child care, work/family conflict, and absenteeism: A field study. *Personnel Psychology* **43**: 793–809.

Grandey, A. A., Cordeiro, B. L. & Michael, J. H. (2007) Work–family supportiveness organizational perceptions: Important for the well-being of male blue-collar hourly workers? *Journal of Vocational Behavior* **71**(3): 460–78.

Grawitch, M. J., Trares, S. & Kohler, J. M. (2007) Healthy workplace practices and employee outcomes. *International Journal of Stress Management* **14**(3): 275–93.

Gray, D. E. (1974) This alien thing called leisure. In J. F. Murphy (ed.), *Concepts of Leisure*. Englewood Cliffs, NJ: Prentice Hall, p. 42.

Greenglass, E. R. (2002) Proactive coping and quality of life management. In E. Frydenberg (ed.), *Beyond Coping: Meeting goals, visions, and challenges*. Oxford: Oxford University Press, pp. 37–62.

Greenglass, E. R., Burke, R. J. & Moore, K. A. (2003) Reactions to increased workload: Effects on professional efficacy of nurses. *Applied Psychology: An International Review* **52**(4): 580–97.

Greenglass, E. R. & Fiksenbaum, L. (2009) Proactive coping, positive affect, and well-being. *European Psychologist* **14**: 29–39.

Greenhaus, J. H. & Beutell, N. (1985) Sources of conflict between work and family roles. *Academy of Management Review* **10**: 76–88.

Greenhaus, J. H., Collins, K. M. & Shaw, J. D. (2003) The relation between work–family balance and quality of life. *Journal of Vocational Behavior* **63**: 510–31.

Guest, D., Williams, R. & Dewe, P. J. (1978) *Job design and the psychology of boredom*. Paper presented at the Proceedings of the 19th Congress of Applied Psychology, Munich.

Hall, D. T. (1972) A model of coping with role conflict: The role behavior of college educated women. *Administrative Science Quarterly* **17**: 471–89.

Hammer, L. B., Kossek, E. E., Zimmerman, K. & Daniels, R. (2007) Clarifying the construct of family-supportive supervisory behaviors (FSSB): A multilevel perspective. In P. L. Perrewe & D. C. Ganster (eds), *Research in Occupational*

Stress and Well-Being: Exploring the work and non-work interface. Oxford: Elsevier, vol. **6**, pp. 165–2004.

Hammer, L. B., Neal, M. B., Newsom, J. T., Brockwood, K. J. & Colton, C. L. (2005) A longitudinal study of the effects of dual-earner couples' utilization of family-friendly workplace supports on work and family outcomes. *Journal of Applied Psychology* **90**(4): 799–810.

Harden, A., Peersman, G., Oliver, S., Mauthner, M. & Oakley, A. (1999) A systematic review of the effectiveness of health promotion interventions in the workplace. *Occupational Medicine* **49**(8): 540–8.

Harris, J. R. (1991) The utility of the transactional approach for occupational stress research. In P. L. Perrewé (ed.), *Handbook on Job Stress* [special issue]. *Journal of Social Behavior and Personality* **6**: 21–9.

Hart, P. M., Wearing, A. J. & Headey, B. (1995) Police stress and well-being: Integrating personality, coping and daily work experiences. *Journal of Occupational and Organisational Psychology* **68**: 133–56.

Hatinen, M., Kinnunen, U., Pekkonen, M. & Kalimo, R. (2007) Comparing two burnout interventions: Perceived job control mediates decreases in burnout. *International Journal of Stress Management* **14**(3): 227–48.

Hauge, L. J., Skogstad, A. & Einarsen, S. (2007) Relationships between stressful work environments and bullying: Results of a large representative study. *Work & Stress* **21**(3): 220–42.

Haward, L. R. C. (1960) The subjective meaning of stress. *British Journal of Psychology* **33**: 185–94.

Hayman, A. (2008) Major job losses forecast for all of England. Regeneration & Renewal 7th November, http://www.regen.net/news/EmailThisArticle/859991/.

Health & Safety Commission (2000) *Securing Health Together: A long term occupational health strategy for England, Scotland and Wales.* London: Health and Safety Executive.

Health and Safety Executive (2005) *Psychosocial Working Conditions in Great Britain 2005.* London: HSE.

Health and Safety Executive (2006) *Stress-Related and Psychological Disorders.* London: HSE.

Health and Safety Executive (2007a) *Violence at Work.* London: HSE.

Health and Safety Executive (2007b) *Self-Reported Work-Related Illness and Workplace Injuries in 2005/06: Results from the Labour Force Survey.* Caerphilly: HSE Information Services.

Health and Safety Executive (2007c) *Self-Reported Work-Related Illness or Workplace Injury.* London: HSE.

Heintzman, P. & Mannell, R. C. (2003) Spiritual functions of leisure and spiritual well-being: Coping with time pressure. *Leisure Sciences* **25**: 207–30.

Hemp, P. (2004) Presenteeism: At work – but out of it. *Harvard Business Review* 49–58.

Hill, D., Lucy, D., Tyers, C. & James, L. (2007) *What works at work? Review of evidence assessing the effectiveness of workplace interventions to prevent and manage common health problems.* Leeds: Corporate Document Services, pp. 1–87.

Hobfoll, S. E. (1989) Conservation of resources: A new attempt at conceptualizing stress. *American Psychologist* **44**: 513–24.

Hobfoll, S. E. (1998) *Stress, Culture and Community: The psychology and philosophy of stress.* New York: Plenum.

Hobfoll, S. E. (2001) The influence of culture, community, and the nested-self in the stress process: Advancing conservation of resources theory. *Applied Psychology: An International Review* **30**: 337–421.

Hodgson, J. T., Jones, J. R., Clarke, S. D., Blackburn, A. J. *et al.* (2006) *Workplace Health and Safety Survey Programme: 2005 Workers Survey First Findings Report.* Caerphilly: HSE Information Services.

Hogh, A. & Dofradottir, A. (2001) Coping with bullying in the workplace. *European Journal of Work & Organizational Psychology* **10**(4): 485–95.

Holroyd, K. A. & Lazarus, R. S. (1982) Stress, coping and somatic adaptation. In L. Goldberger & S. Breznitz (eds), *Handbook of Stress: Theoretical and clinical aspects.* New York: Free Press, pp. 21–35.

Horowitz, M. J. (1990) Stress, states and person schemas. *Psychological Inquiry* **1**: 25–6.

Hutchinson, S. L., Bland, A. D. & Kleiber, D. A. (2008) Leisure and stress and coping: Implications for therapeutic recreation practice. *Therapeutic Recreation Journal* **42**: 9–23.

Innstrand, S. T., Langballe, E. M., Espnes, G. A., Falkum, E. & Aasland, O. G. (2008) Positive and negative work–family interaction and burnout: A longitudinal study of reciprocal relations. *Work & Stress* **22**(1): 1–15.

Isles, N. (2005) *The Joy of Work?* London: The Work Foundation.

Ivancevich, J. & Matteson, M. (1987) Organizational level stress management interventions: A review and recommendations. *Journal of Organizational Behavior Management* **8**: 229–48.

Iwasaki, Y. (2003) Examining rival models of leisure coping mechanisms. *Leisure Sciences* **25**: 183–206.

Iwasaki, Y., Mackay, K. J., Mactavish, J. B., Ristock, J. & Bartlett, J. (2006) Voices from the margins: Active living and leisure as a contributor to coping with stress. *Leisure Sciences* **28**: 163–80.

Iwasaki, Y., Mactavish, J. & Mackay, K. (2005) Building on strengths and resilience: Leisure as a stress survival strategy. *Journal of Guidance & Counselling* **33**: 81–100.

Iwasaki, Y. & Mannell, R. C. (2000) Hierarchical dimensions of leisure stress coping. *Leisure Sciences* **22**: 163–81.

Iwasaki, Y. & Schneider, I. E. (2003) Leisure, stress, and coping: An evolving area of inquiry. *Leisure Sciences* **25**: 107–13.

Jang, K. L., Thordarson, D. S., Stein, M. B., Cohan, S. L. & Taylor, S. (2007) Coping styles and personality: A biometric analysis. *Anxiety, Stress & Coping* **20**(1): 17–24.

Jennings, J. E. & McDougald, M. S. (2007) Work–family interface experiences and coping strategies: Implications for entrepreneurship research and practice. *Academy of Management Review* **32**(3): 747–60.

Jex, S. M. & Elacqua, T. C. (1999) Time management as a moderator of relations between stressors and employee strain. *Work & Stress* **13**(2): 182–91.

Johnson, R. E., Rosen, C. C. & Levy, P. E. (2008) Getting to the core of core self-evaluation: A review and recommendations. *Journal of Organizational Behavior* **29**(3): 391–413.

Johnson, S. & Cooper, C. L. (2003) The construct validity of the ASSET stress measure. *Stress & Health* **19**(3): 181–5.

Jones, F. & Bright, J. (2001) *Stress: Myth, theory and research.* Harlow: Pearson-Prentice Hall.

Kahn, R. L., Wolfe, D. M., Quinn, R. P., Snoek, J. D. & Rosenthal, R. A. (1964) *Organizational Stress: Studies in role conflict and ambiguity.* New York: John Wiley & Sons Inc.

Kaplan, H. B. (1996) Themes, lacunae and directions in research on psychological stress. In H. B. Kaplan (ed.), *Psychosocial Stress: Perspectives on structure, theory, life courses and methods.* New York: Academic Press, pp. 369–401.

Karasek, R. (1979) Job demands, job decision latitude, and mental strain: Implications for job redesign. *Administrative Science Quarterly* **24**: 285–308.

Kasl, S. V. (1983) Perusing the link between stressful life experiences and disease: A time for reappraisal. In C. L. Cooper (ed.), *Stress Research: Issues for the Eighties.* Chichester: John Wiley & Sons, Ltd, pp. 79–102.

Kelly, E. L., Kossek, E. E., Hammer, L. B., Durham, M. *et al.* (2008) Getting there from here: Research on the effects of work–family initiatives on work–family conflict and business outcomes. *Academy of Management Annals* **2**(1): 305–49.

Kinman, G. & Jones, F. (2005) Lay representations of workplace stress: What do people really mean when they say they are stressed? *Work & Stress* **19**: 101–20.

Kirby, E. L. & Krone, K. J. (2002) 'The policy exists but you can't really use it': Communication and the structuration of work–family policies. *Journal of Applied Communication Research* **30**(1): 50–77.

Kirchmeyer, C. (1995) Managing the work–nonwork boundary: An assessment of organizational responses. *Human Relations* **48**(5): 515–36.

Kirchmeyer, C. & Cohen, A. (1999) Different strategies for managing the work/ nonwork interface: A test of unique pathways to work outcomes. *Work & Stress* **13**: 59–73.

Kirk, A. K. & Brown, D. F. (2003) Employee assistance programs: A review of the management of stress and wellbeing through workplace counselling and consulting. *Australian Psychologist* **38**(2): 138–43.

Kleiber, D. A., Hutchinson, S. L. & Williams, R. (2002) Leisure as a resource in transcending negative life events: Self-protection, self-restoration, and personal transformation. *Leisure Sciences* **24**: 219–35.

Koeske, G. F., Kirk, S. A. & Koeske, R. D. (1993) Coping with job stress: Which strategies work best? *Journal of Occupational and Organizational Psychology* **66**: 319–35.

Kopelman, R. E., Prottas, D. J., Thompson, C. A. & Jahn, E. W. (2006) A multilevel examination of work–life practices: Is more always better? *Journal of Managerial Issues* **18**(2): 232–53.

Lapierre, L. M. & Allen, T. D. (2006) Work-supportive family, family-supportive supervision, use of organizational benefits, and problem-focused coping: Implications for work–family conflict and employee well-being. *Journal of Occupational Health Psychology* **11**(2): 169–81.

Lapierre, L. M., Spector, P. E., Allen, T. D., Poelmans, S. A. *et al.* (2008) Family-supportive organization perceptions, multiple dimensions of work–family conflict, and employee satisfaction: A test of model across five samples. *Journal of Vocational Behavior* **73**(1): 92–106.

Latack, J. C. & Havlovic, S. J. (1992) Coping with job stress: A conceptual evaluation framework for coping measures. *Journal of Organizational Behavior* **13**: 479–508.

Latack, J., Kinicki, A. & Prussia, G. (1995) An integrative process model of coping with job loss. *Academy of Management Review* **20**: 311–42.

Lazarus, R. L. (1966) *Psychological Stress and the Coping Process*. New York: McGraw-Hill.

Lazarus, R. S. (1990) Theory-based stress measurement. *Psychological Inquiry* **1**: 3–13.

Lazarus, R. S. (1991) Psychological stress in the workplace. In P. L. Perrewé (ed.), *Handbook on Job Stress* [special issue]. *Journal of Social Behavior and Personality* **6**: 1–13.

Lazarus, R. S. (1995) Vexing research problems inherent in cognitive-mediational theories of emotion – and some solutions. *Psychological Inquiry* **6**: 183–96.

Lazarus, R. S. (1997) Hurrah for a systems approach. *Journal of Health Psychology* **2**: 158–60.

Lazarus, R. S. (1999) *Stress and Emotion: A new synthesis*. London: Free Association Books.

Lazarus, R. S. (2000) Toward better research on stress and coping. *American Psychologist* **55**: 665–73.

Lazarus, R. S. (2001) Relational meaning and discrete emotions. In K. R. Scherer, A. Schorr & T. Johnstone (eds), *Appraisal Processes in Emotion*. Oxford: Oxford University Press, pp. 37– 67.

Lazarus, R. S. (2003a) Does the positive psychology movement have legs? *Psychological Inquiry* **14**: 93–109.

Lazarus, R. S. (2003b) The Lazarus manifesto for positive psychology and psychology in general. *Psychological Inquiry* **14**: 173–89.

Lazarus, R. S. & Cohen-Charash, Y. (2001) Discrete emotions in organizational life. In R. L. Payne & C. L. Cooper (eds), *Emotions at Work: Theory, research and applications for management*. Chichester: John Wiley & Sons, Ltd, pp. 45–81.

Lazarus, R. S. & Folkman, S. (1984) *Stress, Appraisal and Coping*. New York: Springer.

Leka, S., Griffiths, A. & Cox, T. (2005) Work-related stress: The risk management paradigm. In A.-S. G. Antoniou & C. L. Cooper (eds), *Research Companion to Organizational Health Psychology*. Chichester: Edward Elgar, pp. 174–87.

Lepine, J. A., Podsakoff, N. P. & Lepine M. A. (2006) A meta-analytic test of the challenge stressor-hindrance stressor framework: An explanation for inconsistent relationships among stressors and performance. *Academy of Management Journal* **48**: 764–75.

Liddle, H. A. (1994) Contextualizing resiliency. In M. C. Wong & E.W. Gordon (eds), *Educational Resilience in Inner-City America*. Hillsdale, NY: Erlbaum, pp. 167–77.

Liu, C., Spector, P. E. & Shi, L. (2007) Cross-national job stress: A quantitative and qualitative study. *Journal of Organizational Behavior* **28**(2): 209.

Lofland, J. H., Pizzi, L. & Frick, K. D. (2004) A review of health-related workplace productivity loss instruments. *Pharmacoeconomics* **22**: 166–84.

Luthans, F. (2002) The need for and meaning of positive organizational behavior. *Journal of Organizational Behavior* **23**: 695–706.

Luthans, F. & Avolio, B. J. (2009) The 'point' of positive organizational behavior. *Journal of Organizational Behavior* **30**: 291–308.

Luthans, F., Avolio, B. J., Avey, J. B. & Norman, S. M. (2007) Positive psychological capital: Measurement and relationship with performance and satisfaction. *Personnel Psychology* **60**: 541–72.

Mackenzie, M. J., Carlson, L. E., Munoz, M. & Speca, M. (2007) A qualitative study of self-perceived effects of mindfulness-based stress reduction (MBSR) in a psychosocial oncology setting. *Stress & Health* **23**(1): 59–69.

Madouros, V. (2006) *Labour Force Projections 2006–2020*. London: Office for National Statistics.

Mantler, J., Matejicek, A., Matheson, K. & Anisman, H. (2005) Coping with employment uncertainty: A comparison of employed and unemployed workers. *Journal of Occupational Health Psychology* **10**(3): 200–209.

Matsui, T., Ohsawa, T. & Onglatco, M.-L. (1995) Work–family conflict and the stress-buffering effects of husband support and coping behavior among Japanese married working women. *Journal of Vocational Behavior* **47**: 178–92.

Maybery, D. J., Neale, J., Arentz, A. & Jones-Ellis, J. (2007) The Negative Event Scale: Measuring frequency and intensity of adult hassles. *Anxiety, Stress & Coping* **20**(2): 163–76.

Medibank (2007) Sick at work: The cost of presenteeism to your business, employees and the economy. Medibank Private Ltd, http://www.medibank.com.au/Client/Documents/Pdfs/sick_at_work.pdf.

Morrell, K., Loan-Clarke, J. & Wilkinson, A. (2001) *Unweaving Leaving: The use of models in the management of employee turnover.* Research Series Paper 2001. Business School: Loughborough University: January.

Morrison, D. L. & Payne, R. L. (2003) Multilevel approaches to stress management. *Australian Psychologist* **38**(2): 128–37.

Murphy, L. R. (1995) *Job Stress Interventions.* Washington: American Psychological Association.

Murphy, L. R. & Sauter, S. L. (2003) The USA perspective: Current issues and trends in the management of work stress. *Australian Psychologist* **38**(2): 151–7.

Namie, G. (2007) The challenge of workplace bullying. *Employment Relations Today* **34**(2): 43–51.

Newman, J. & Beehr, T. A. (1979) Personal and organizational strategies for handling job stress: A review of research and opinion. *Personnel Psychology* **32**: 1–43.

Newton, T. (1995) *'Managing' Stress: Emotion and power at work.* London: Sage Publications.

Nielsen, K., Fredslund, H., Christensen, K. B. & Albertsen, K. (2006) Success or failure? Interpreting and understanding the impact of interventions in four similar worksites. *Work & Stress* **20**(3): 272–87.

Nielsen, K., Randall, R. & Albertsen, K. (2007) Participants' appraisals of process issues and the effects of stress management interventions. *Journal of Organizational Behavior* **28**(6): 793–810.

Niiyama, E., Okamura, H., Kohama, A., Taniguchi, T. *et al.* (2009) A survey of nurses who experienced trauma in the workplace: Influence of coping strategies on traumatic stress. *Stress & Health* **25**(1): 3–9.

Noblet, A. J. & LaMontagne, A. D. (2006) The role of workplace health promotion in addressing job stress. *Health Promotion International* **21**(4): 346–53.

Noblet, A. J. & LaMontagne, A. D. (2008) The challenges of developing, implementing and evaluating interventions. In S. Cartwright & C. L. Cooper (eds),

Oxford Handbook of Organisational Well-Being. Oxford: Oxford University Press, pp. 466–96.

Norlander, T., Von Schedvin, H. & Archer, T. (2005) Thriving as a function of affective personality: Relation to personality factors, coping strategies and stress. *Anxiety, Stress & Coping* **18**(2): 105–16.

Nytro, K., Saksvik, P. O., Mikkelsen, A., Bohle, P. & Quinlan, M. (2000) An appraisal of key factors in the implementation of occupational stress interventions. *Work & Stress* **14**(3): 213–25.

O'Brien, T. B. & DeLongis, A. (1996) The interactional context of problem-, emotion-, and relationship-focused coping: The role of the big-five personality factors. *Journal of Personality* **64**: 775–813.

O'Driscoll, M. P. & Beehr, T. A. (1994) Supervisor behaviors, role stressors and uncertainty as predictors of personal outcomes for subordinates. *Journal of Organizational Behavior* **15**(2): 141–55.

O'Driscoll, M. P. & Beehr, T. A. (2000) Moderating effects of perceived control and need for clarity on the relationship between role stressors and employee affective reactions. *Journal of Social Psychology* **140**(2): 151–9.

O'Driscoll, M. P., Brough, P. & Kalliath, T. (2006) Work–family conflict and facilitation. In F. Jones, R. Burke & M. Westman (eds), *Managing the Work–Home Interface*. Hove: Psychology Press, pp. 117–42.

O'Driscoll, M. P., Brough, P. & Kalliath, T. J. (2009) Stress and coping. In S. Cartwright & C. L. Cooper (eds), *The Oxford Handbook of Organizational Well-Being*. Oxford: Oxford University Press, pp. 236–66.

O'Driscoll, M. P. & Cooper, C. L. (1994) Coping with work related stress: A critique of existing measures and proposal for an alternative methodology. *Journal of Occupational and Organizational Psychology* **67**: 343–54.

O'Driscoll, M. P. & Cooper, C. L. (1996) A critical incident analysis of stress-coping behaviours at work. *Stress Medicine* **12**: 123–8.

O'Driscoll, M. & O'Driscoll, E. (2008) New technology and well-being at work. State of science review: SR-C5. *Foresight Mental Capital and Well-Being Project*. London: The Government Office for Science.

O'Driscoll, M. P., Poelmans, S. A., Spector, P. E., Kalliath, T. *et al.* (2003) Family-responsive interventions, perceived organizational and supervisor support, work–family conflict and psychological strain. *International Journal of Stress Management* **10**(4): 326–44.

Olafsson, R. F. & Johannsdottir, H. L. (2004) Coping with bullying in the workplace: The effect of gender, age and type of bullying. *British Journal of Guidance & Counselling* **32**(3): 319–33.

Ortgvist, D. & Wincent, J. (2006) Prominent consequences of role stress: A meta-analytic review. *International Journal of Stress Management* **13**: 399–422.

Osipow, S. & Spokane, A. (1988) *Occupational Stress Inventory*. Odessa, FL: PAR Inc.

Oxford Economics (2007) *Mental Health and the UK Economy*. Oxford: Oxford Economics.

Ozminkowski, R. J., Goetzel, R. Z., Chang, S. & Long, S. (2004) The application of two health and productivity instruments at a large employer. *Journal of Occupational and Environmental Medicine* **46**: 635–48.

Park, C. L., Cohen, L. H. & Murch, R. L. (1996) Assessment and prediction of stress-related growth. *Journal of Personality* **64**: 71–105.

Park, C. L. & Folkman, S. (1997) Meaning in the context of stress and coping. *Review of General Psychology* **1**: 115–44.

Parker, D. F. & De Cotiis, T. A. (1983) Organizational determinants of job stress. *Organizational Behavior and Human Performance* **32**: 160–77.

Parker, J. D. A. & Endler, N. S. (1996) Coping and defence: A historical overview. In M. Zeidner & N. S. Endler (eds), *Handbook of Coping: Theory, research applications*. New York: John Wiley & Sons, Inc, pp. 3–23.

Parks, K. M. & Steelman, L. A. (2008) Organizational wellness programs: A meta-analysis. *Journal of Occupational Health Psychology* **13**(1): 58–68.

Parr, M. G. & Lashua, B. D. (2004) What is leisure? The perceptions of recreation practitioners and others. *Leisure Sciences* **26**: 1–17.

Patton, W. & Donohue, R. (1998) Coping and long-term unemployment. *Journal of Community and Applied Social Psychology* **8**(5): 331–43.

Payne, J. (2006) Emotional labour and skill: A re-appraisal. SKOPE: Issues paper no. 10, May, http://www.skope.ox.ac.uk.

Peeters, M. A. G. & Rutte, C. G. (2005) Time management behavior as a moderator for the job demand–control interaction. *Journal of Occupational Health Psychology* **10**(1): 64–75.

Pekrun, R. & Frese, M. (1992) Emotions in work and achievement. *International Review of Industrial and Organizational Psychology* **7**: 153–200.

Perrewé, P. L. & Zellars, K. L. (1999) An examination of attributions and emotions in the transactional approach to the organizational stress process. *Journal of Organizational Behavior* **20**: 739–52.

Perry-Smith, J. E. & Blum, T. C. (2000) Work–family human resource bundles and perceived organizational performance. *Academy of Management Journal* **43**(6): 1107–17.

Piderit, S. (2000) Rethinking resistance and recognizing ambivalence: A multidimensional view of attitudes toward an organizational change. *Academy of Management Review* **25**(4): 783–95.

Pinquart, M. & Silbereisen, R. K. (2008) Coping with increased uncertainty in the field of work and family life. *International Journal of Stress Management* **15**(3): 209–21.

Pomaki, G., Supeli, A. & Verhoeven, C. (2007) Role conflict and health behaviors: Moderating effects on psychological distress and somatic complaints. *Psychology & Health* **22**(3): 317–35.

Porath, C. & Pearson, C. (2009) How toxic colleagues corrode performance. *Harvard Business Review* **87**(4): 24.

Portello, J. Y. & Long, B. C. (2001) Appraisals and coping with workplace interpersonal stress: A model for women managers. *Journal of Counseling Psychology* **48**(2): 144–56.

Probst, T. M. (2009) Job insecurity, unemployment and organizational well-being: Oxymoron or possibility? In S. Cartwright & C. L. Cooper (eds), *The Oxford Handbook of Organizational Well-Being*. Oxford: Oxford University Press, pp. 387–410.

Quick, J. D., Quick, J. C. & Nelson, D. L. (1998) The theory of preventive stress management in organizations. In C. L. Cooper (ed.), *Theories of Organizational Stress*. Oxford: Oxford University Press, pp. 246–68.

Rafferty, A. E. & Griffin, M. A. (2006) Perceptions of organizational change: A stress and coping perspective. *Journal of Applied Psychology* **91**(5): 1154–62.

Rahim, M. A. & Bonoma, T. V. (1979) Managing organizational conflict: A model for diagnosis and intervention. *Psychological Reports* **44**: 1323–44.

Randall, R., Griffiths, A. & Cox, T. (2005) Evaluating organizational stress-management interventions using adapted study designs. *European Journal of Work & Organizational Psychology* **14**(1): 23–41.

Reichers, A. E. & Schneider, B. (1990) Climate and culture: An evolution of constructs. In B. Schneider (ed.), *Organizational Climate and Culture*. San Francisco: Jossey-Bass.

Richardson, K. M. & Rothstein, H. R. (2008) Effects of occupational stress management intervention programs: A meta-analysis. *Journal of Occupational Health Psychology* **13**(1): 69–93.

Roberts, L. M. (2006) Response: Shifting the lens on organizational life: The added value of positive scholarship. *Academy of Management Review* **31**: 292–305.

Roesch, S. C., Aldridge, A. A. Huff, T. L. P., Langner, K. *et al.* (2009) On the dimensionality of the proactive coping inventory: 7, 5, 3 factors? *Anxiety, Stress & Coping* **22**: 327–40.

Rolfe, H., Foreman J. & Tylee, A. (2006) *Welfare or farewell? Mental health and stress in the workplace*. National Institute of Economic and Social Research Discussion Paper 28. London: Nuffield Foundation/NIESR http://www.niesr. ac.uk/pdf/270306_133707.pdf.

Rothbard, N. P., Philips, K. W. & Dumas, T. L. (2005) Managing multiple roles: Work–family policies and individuals' desire for segmentation. *Organization Science* **16**: 243–58.

Rotondo, D. M., Carlson, D. S. & Kincaid, J. F. (2003) Coping with multiple dimensions of work–family conflict. *Personnel Review* **32**(3): 275–96.

Rotondo, D. M. & Kincaid, J. F. (2008) Conflict, facilitation, and individual coping styles across the work and family domains. *Journal of Managerial Psychology* **23**(5): 484–506.

Sainsbury Centre for Mental Health (2007a) *Mental Health at Work: Developing the business case.* Policy Paper 8. London: Sainsbury Centre for Mental Health, http://www.scmh.org.uk/pdfs/mental_health_at_work.pdf.

Sainsbury Centre for Mental Health (2007b) *Briefing 34: Work and Wellbeing: Developing primary mental health care services.* London: Sainsbury Centre for Mental Health.

Schaubroeck, J. (1999) Should the subjective be the objective? On studying mental processes, coping behavior, and actual exposures in organizational stress research. *Journal of Organizational Behavior* **20**: 753–60.

Schaufeli, W. B. (2002) Coping with job stress. In N. J. Smelser & P. B. Baltes (eds), *International Encyclopedia of the Social & Behavioral Sciences.* Oxford: Elsevier, pp. 7984–7.

Schneider, I. E. & Wilhelm Stanis, S. A. (2007) An alternative conceptualization for constraint and accommodation. *Leisure Sciences* **29**: 391–401.

Schwarzer, R. (2001) Stress, resources, and proactive coping. *Applied Psychology: An International Review* **50**: 400–407.

Schwarzer, R. (2004) Manage stress at work through preventive and proactive coping. In E. A. Locke (ed.), *The Blackwell Handbook of Principles of Organizational Behavior.* Oxford: Blackwell Publishing, pp. 342–55.

Schwarzer, R. & Schwarzer, C. (1996) A critical survey of coping instruments. In M. Zeidner & N. S. Endler. (eds), *Handbook of Coping: Theory, research, applications.* New York: John Wiley & Sons, Ltd, pp. 107–32.

Schwarzer, R. & Taubert, S. (2002) Tenacious goal pursuits and strivings: Toward personal growth. In E. Frydenberg (ed.), *Beyond Coping: Meeting goals, visions, and challenges.* Oxford: Oxford University Press, pp. 19–35.

Seligman, M. E. P. & Csikszentmihalyi, M. (2000) Positive psychology: An introduction. *American Psychologist* **55**: 5–14.

Semmer, N. K. (2003) Job stress interventions and organization of work. In J. C. Quick & L. E. Tetrick (eds), *Handbook of Occupational Health Psychology.* Washington: American Psychological Association, pp. 325–54.

Semmer, N. K. (2008) Stress management and wellbeing interventions in the workplace. State of science review SR-C6. *Foresight Mental Capital and Well-Being Project.* London: The Government Office for Science.

Shaw Trust (2006a) Mental Health: The last workplace taboo. Independent research into what British business thinks. Commissioned by Shaw Trust and conducted by the Future Foundation.

Shaw Trust (2006b) Mental Health: The last workplace taboo: Key findings from independent research into what British business thinks. Commissioned by Shaw Trust and conducted by the Future Foundation.

Sheldon, K. M. & King, L. (2001) Why positive psychology is necessary. *American Psychologist* **56**: 216–17.

Shockley, K. M. & Allen, T. D. (2007) When flexibility helps: Another look at the availability of flexible work arrangements and work–family conflict. *Journal of Vocational Behavior* 71(3): 479–93.

Singleton, N., Bumstead, R., O'Brien, M., Lee, A. & Meltzer, H. (2001) *Psychiatric Morbidity Among Adults Living in Private Households, 2000: Summary Report.* London: Office for National Statistics.

Siu, O.-L., Spector, P. E., Cooper, C. L., Lu, L. & Yu, S. (2002) Managerial stress in China: The direct and moderator effects of coping strategies and work locus of control. *Applied Psychology: An International Review* 51(4): 608–32.

Skinner, E. A., Edge, K., Altman, J. & Sherwood, H. (2003) Searching for the structure of coping: A review and critique of category systems for classifying ways of coping. *Psychological Bulletin* 129: 216–69.

Snow, D. L., Swan, S. C., Raghavan, C., Connell, C. M. & Klein, I. (2003) The relationship of work stressors, coping and social support to psychological symptoms among female secretarial employees. *Work & Stress* 17(3): 241–63.

Snyder, C. R. (1999) *Coping: The psychology of what works.* New York: Oxford University Press.

Snyder, C. R. (ed.) (2001) *Coping with Stress: Effective people and processes.* Oxford: Oxford University Press.

Somech, A. & Drach-Zahavy, A. (2007) Strategies for coping with work–family conflict: The distinctive relationships of gender role ideology. *Journal of Occupational Health Psychology* 12(1): 1–19.

Somerfield, M. R. (1997a) The utility of systems models of stress and coping for applied research. *Journal of Health Psychology* 2: 133–51.

Somerfield, M. R. (1997b) The future of coping research as we know it. *Journal of Health Psychology* 2: 173–83.

Somerfield, M. R. & McCrae, R. R. (2000) Stress and coping research: Methodological challenges, theoretical advances. *American Psychologist* 55: 620–625.

Spector, P. E. (1994) Using self-report questionnaires in OB research: A comment on the use of a controversial method. *Journal of Organizational Behavior* 15: 385–92.

Spell, C. S. & Arnold, T. (2007) An appraisal perspective of justice, structure, and job control as antecedents of psychological distress. *Journal of Organizational Behavior* 28(6): 729–51.

Spicer, J. (1997) Systems analysis of stress and coping: A testing proposition. *Journal of Health Psychology* 2: 167–70.

Stanton, A. L., Danoff-Burg, S., Cameron, C. L. & Ellis, A. P. (1994) Coping through emotional approach: Problems of conceptualization and confounding. *Journal of Personality and Social Psychology* 66: 350–62.

Stanton, A. L., Kirk, S. B., Cameron, C. L. & Danoff-Berg, S. (2000) Coping through emotional approach: Scale construction and validation. *Journal of Personality and Social Psychology* 78: 1150–69.

Stanton, A. L., Parsa, A. & Austenfeld, J. L. (2005) The adaptive potential of coping through emotion approach. In C. R. Snyder & S. J. Lopez (eds), *Handbook of Positive Psychology*. Oxford: Oxford University Press, pp. 148–158.

Stewart, W. F., Ricci, J. A., Chee, E., Hahn, S. R. & Morganstein, D. (2003) Cost of lost productive work time among US workers with depression. *Journal of the American Medical Association* **259**: 3135–44.

Stone, A. A., Greenberg, M. A., Kennedy-Moore, E. & Newman, M. G. (1991) Self-report, situation specific coping questionnaires: What are they measuring? *Journal of Personality and Social Psychology* **61**: 648–58.

Stone, A. A., Helder, L. & Schneider, M. S. (1988) Coping dimensions and issues. In L. H. Cohen (ed.), *Life Events and Psychological Functioning: Theoretical and methodological issues*. London: Sage Publications, pp. 182–210.

Stone, A. A. & Kennedy-Moore, E. (1992) Assessing situational coping: Conceptual and methodological considerations. In H. S. Friedman (ed.), *Hostility Coping and Health*. Washington: American Psychological Association, pp. 203–14.

Stone, A. A. & Neale, J. M. (1984) New measure of daily coping: Development and preliminary results. *Journal of Personality and Social Psychology* **46**: 892–906.

Stone, A. A. & Shiffman, S. (1994) Ecological momentary assessment (EMA) in behavioral medicine. *Annals of Behavioral Medicine* **16**: 199–202.

Suls, J. & David, P. D. (1996) Coping and personality: Third time's the charm? *Journal of Personality* **64**: 993–1005.

Suls, J., David, J. P. & Harvey, J. H. (1996) Personality and coping: Three generations of research. *Journal of Personality* **64**: 711–35.

Sulsky, L. & Smith, C. (2005) *Work Stress*. Belmont, CA: Thomson Wadsworth.

Tabak, N. & Koprak, O. (2007) Relationship between how nurses resolve their conflicts with doctors, their stress and job satisfaction. *Journal of Nursing Management* **15**(3): 321–31.

Tamres, L. K., Janicki, D. & Hegelson, V. S. (2002) Sex differences in coping behavior: A meta-analytic review and an examination of relative coping. *Personality and Social Psychology Review* **6**(1): 2–30.

Tennen, H. & Affleck, G. (1999) Finding benefit in adversity. In C. R. Snyder (ed.), *Coping: The psychology of what works*. New York: Oxford University Press, pp. 279–304.

Tennen, H. & Affleck, G. (2005) Benefit-finding and benefit-reminding. In C. R. Snyder & S. J. Lopez (eds), *Handbook of Positive Psychology*. Oxford: Oxford University Press, pp. 564–97.

Tennen, H., Affleck, G., Armeli, S. & Carney, M. A. (2000) A daily process approach to coping: Linking theory, research, and practice. *American Psychologist* **5**: 626–36.

Terry, D. J. & Jimmieson, N. L. (2003) A stress and coping approach to organisational change: Evidence from three field studies. *Australian Psychologist* **38**(2): 92–101.

Tetrick, L. E. (2002) Individual and organizational health. In P. L. Perrewé & D. C. Ganster (eds), *Historical and Current Perspectives on Stress and Health*. Amsterdam: JAI: Elsevier Science, pp. 117–42.

Tetrick, L. E., Quick, J. C. & Quick, J. D. (2005) Prevention perspectives in occupational health psychology. In A.-S. G. Antoniou & C. L. Cooper (eds), *Research Companion to Organizational Health Psychology*. Cheltenham: Edward Elgar, pp. 209–17.

Thomas, L. T. & Ganster, D. C. (1995) Impact of family-supportive work variables on work–family conflicts and strain. *Journal of Applied Psychology* **80**(1): 6–15.

Thompson, C. A., Beauvais, L. & Lyness, K. (1999) When work–family benefits are not enough: The influence of work–family culture on benefit utilization, organizational attachment and work–family conflict. *Journal of Vocational Behavior* **54**(3): 392–415.

Thompson, C. A., Jahn, E. W., Kopelman, R. E. & Prottas, D. J. (2004) Perceived organizational family support: A longitudinal and multilevel analysis. *Journal of Managerial Issues* **16**(4): 545–65.

Thompson, C. A., Poelmans, S. A., Allen, T. D. & Andreassi, J. K. (2007) On the importance of coping: A model and new directions for research on work and family. In P. L. Perrewé & D. C. Ganster (eds), *Research in Occupational Stress and Well-Being: Exploring the work and non-work interface*. Oxford: Elsevier, vol. **6**, pp. 73–114.

Tidd, S. T. & Friedman, R. A. (2002) Conflict style and coping with role conflict: An extension of the uncertainty model of work stress. *International Journal of Conflict Management* **13**(3): 236–57.

Towers Perrin (2006) *Winning strategies for a global workforce: Attracting, retaining and engaging employees for competitive advantage*. HR Services Executive Report. London: Towers Perrin.

Trenberth, L. & Dewe, P. (2002) An exploration of the importance of leisure as a means of coping with work related stress. *Counselling Psychology Quarterly* **15**: 39–72.

Trenberth, L. & Dewe, P. (2005) An exploration of the role of leisure in coping with work related stress using sequential tree analysis. *British Journal of Guidance and Counselling* **33**: 101–16.

Tucker, J. S., Sinclair, R. R., Mohr, C. D., Adler, A. B. *et al.* (2008) A temporal investigation of the direct, interactive, and reverse relations between demand and control and affective strain. *Work & Stress* **22**(2): 81–95.

Turner, N., Barling, J. & Zacharatos, A. (2005) Positive psychology at work. In C. R. Snyder & S. J. Lopez (eds), *Handbook of Positive Psychology*. Oxford: Oxford University Press, pp. 715–28.

Union of Shop, Distributive and Allied Workers (2007) *Freedom from Fear Campaign*, http://www.usdaw.org.uk/campaigns/freedom_from_fear.

UNISON (2005) Report of the National Housing Seminar: Violence at work workshop (summary), November, Birmingham.

Van Dierendonck, D. & Mevissen, N. (2002) Aggressive behavior of passengers, conflict management behavior and burnout among trolley car drivers. *International Journal of Stress Management* 9: 345–56.

Van Maanen, J. (1979) Reclaiming qualitative methods for organizational research: A preface. *Administrative Science Quarterly* 24: 520–26.

Waddell, G. & Burton, A. K. (2006) *Is Work Good for your Health and Well-Being?* London: The Stationery Office.

Wainwright, D. & Calnan, M. (2002) *Work stress: The making of an epidemic.* Buckingham: Open University Press.

Walach, H., Nord, E., Zier, C., Dietz-Waschkowski, B. *et al.* (2007) Mindfulness-based stress reduction as a method for personnel development: A pilot evaluation. *International Journal of Stress Management* 14(2): 188–98.

Warr, P. B. (2005) Work, well-being and mental health. In J. Barling, E. K. Kelloway & M. R. Frone (eds), *Handbook of Work Stress.* Thousand Oaks, CA: Sage Publications, pp. 547–74.

Watkins, M. (2000) Ways of learning about leisure meanings. *Leisure Sciences* 23: 93–107.

Watkins, M. & Bond, C. (2007) Ways of experiencing leisure. *Leisure Sciences* 29: 287–307.

Watson, D. & Hubbard, B. (1996) Adaptational style and dispositional structure: Coping in the context of the five-factor model. *Journal of Personality* 64: 737–74.

Weber, H. & Laux, L. (1990) Bringing the person back into stress and coping measurement. *Psychological Inquiry* 1: 37–40.

Welbourne, J. L., Eggerth, D., Hartley, T. A., Andrew, M. E. & Sanchez, F. (2007) Coping strategies in the workplace: Relationships with attributional style and job satisfaction. *Journal of Vocational Behavior* 70(2): 312–25.

Wiersma, U. J. (1994) A taxonomy of behavioral strategies for coping with work–home role conflict. *Human Relations* 47(2): 211–21.

Williams, K. & Alliger, G. (1994) Role stressors, mood spillover, and perceptions of work–family conflict in employed parents. *Academy of Management Journal* 37: 837–68.

Wright T. A. (2003) Positive organizational behavior: An idea whose time has truly come. *Journal of Organizational Behavior* 24: 437–42.

Wright, T. A. & Quick, J. C. (2009) The role of positive based research in building the science of organizational behavior. *Journal of Organizational Behavior* 30: 329–36.

Wu, A., Folkman, S., McPhee, S. & Lo, B. (1993) Do house officers learn from their mistakes? *Journal of the American Medical Association* 265: 2089–94.

Zapf, D. & Gross, C. (2001) Conflict escalation and coping with workplace bully-
    ing: A replication and extension. *European Journal of Work & Organizational
    Psychology* **10**(4): 497–522.
Zeidner, M. & Saklofske, D. (1996) Adaptive and maladaptive coping. In M.
    Zeidner & N. S. Endler (eds), *Handbook of Coping: Theory, research, applica-
    tions.* New York: John Wiley & Sons, Ltd, pp. 505–31.

Index